INEFFABILITY AND ITS METAPHYSICS

INEFFABILITY AND ITS METAPHYSICS

THE UNSPEAKABLE IN ART, RELIGION, AND PHILOSOPHY

Silvia Jonas

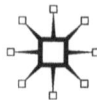

INEFFABILITY AND ITS METAPHYSICS
Copyright © Silvia Jonas 2016
Softcover reprint of the 1st edition 2016

All rights reserved. No reproduction, copy or transmission of this publication may be made without written permission. No portion of this publication may be reproduced, copied or transmitted save with written permission. In accordance with the provisions of the Copyright, Designs and Patents Act 1988, or under the terms of any licence permitting limited copying issued by the Copyright Licensing Agency, Saffron House, 6-10 Kirby Street, London EC1N 8TS.

Any person who does any unauthorized act in relation to this publication may be liable to criminal prosecution and civil claims for damages.

First published 2016 by
PALGRAVE MACMILLAN

The author has asserted their right to be identified as the author of this work in accordance with the Copyright, Designs and Patents Act 1988.

Palgrave Macmillan in the UK is an imprint of Macmillan Publishers Limited, registered in England, company number 785998, of Houndmills, Basingstoke, Hampshire RG21 6XS.

Palgrave Macmillan in the US is a division of Nature America, Inc., One New York Plaza, Suite 4500, New York, NY 10004-1562.

Palgrave Macmillan is the global academic imprint of the above companies and has companies and representatives throughout the world.

ISBN: 978–1–349–95424–7   ISBN: 978–1–137–57955–3 (eBook)
DOI: 10.1057/978-1-137-57955-3

Distribution in the UK, Europe and the rest of the world is by Palgrave Macmillan®, a division of Macmillan Publishers Limited, registered in England, company number 785998, of Houndmills, Basingstoke, Hampshire RG21 6XS.

Library of Congress Cataloging-in-Publication Data

Jonas, Silvia L. Y. N. (Silvia Luise Yael Nili), 1983–
   Ineffability and its metaphysics : the unspeakable in art, religion, and philosophy / Silvia Jonas.
     pages cm
   Includes bibliographical references and index.
   ISBN 978–1–137–57954–6—
     1. Ineffable, The. 2. Art–Philosophy. 3. Religion–Philosophy.
   I. Title.
B105.I533J66 2016
110–dc23   2015029068

A catalogue record for the book is available from the British Library.

*For my extraordinary grandmother
Inge Leopoldine (1944–2014)*

CONTENTS

List of Figures   ix

Acknowledgements   xi

1. Introduction   1
   1.1. Philosophy and Ineffability   1
   1.2. Getting a Grip on the Topic   2
   1.3. The Relevant Cases   4
   1.4. A Brief History of Ineffability   10
   1.5. Four Ways of Predicate Application   22
   1.6. Structure of the Book   24

2. Terminology   27
   2.1. Content   27
   2.2. Representations   29
   2.3. Experience   32
   2.4. Truth and Truth-Bearers   34
   2.5. Expressibility and Ineffability   38

3. Ineffable Properties and Objects   51
   3.1. Why Ineffable Properties and Objects?   51
   3.2. Absoluteness   52
   3.3. Haecceities   60
   3.4. Bare Particulars   67

4. Ineffable Propositions   73
   4.1. Why Ineffable Propositions?   73
   4.2. Inaccessibility   75
   4.3. Semantic Paradoxes   77
   4.4. Unformulable Mathematical Propositions   79
   4.5. Excess Propositions   82
   4.6. Perspectival Propositions   87

5. Ineffable Content — 101
  5.1. Why Ineffable Content? — 101
  5.2. Nonconceptual Content in Perception — 103
  5.3. The Contents of Aesthetic Experience — 111
  5.4. The Contents of Religious Experience — 120

6. Ineffable Knowledge I — 129
  6.1. Why Ineffable Knowledge? — 129
  6.2. Objective Ineffable knowledge — 129
  6.3. Knowledge-How — 130
  6.4. Basic Logical Knowledge — 135
  6.5. Nonrepresentational Knowledge — 142

7. Ineffable Knowledge II — 157
  7.1. Subjective Ineffable Knowledge — 157
  7.2. Indexical Knowledge — 158
  7.3. Phenomenal Knowledge — 161
  7.4. Self-Acquaintance — 166

8. Conclusion — 183

Notes — 185

Bibliography — 205

Index — 215

FIGURES

3.1 Possible reasons for the ineffability of an object   71
4.1 Varieties of ineffable propositions   99
5.1 Varieties of ineffable content   127
6.1 Varieties of ineffable knowledge   155
7.1 Varieties of ineffable knowledge   182

ACKNOWLEDGMENTS

This book has come a long way.

I am deeply grateful to my three philosophical mentors Michael Inwood, Edward Kanterian, and R.A.H. King for their continuous, invaluable guidance and encouragement.

Heartfelt thanks are also due to my esteemed professional seniors who supervised, taught, or otherwise advised me: Anita Avramides, Peter Clark, Antony Eagle, Fiona Ellis, David Enoch, John Hawthorne, Ofra Magidor, A.W. Moore, Gabriel Motzkin, Carl Posy, Tobias Rosefeldt, Stewart Shapiro, and Eleonore Vickers.

Without the friendship and help of my academic colleagues I could not have written this book. Warmest thanks to Ana Bajzelj, Claire Benn, Sharon Berry, Giulia Bistagnino, Neta Bodner, Katherine Dormandy, Peter Gerdes, George Grech, Lisa Herzog, Angela Matthies, Lior Nitzan, Sebastian Petzolt, Dani Rabinowitz, Julian Sempill, Olla Solomyak, Michaela Soyer, Levi Spectre, Barbara Vetter, Sharon Weisser, and Thomas Wyrwich.

I am also most grateful for the enthusiasm and professional guidance of my editor at Palgrave Macmillan, Phil Getz, and editorial assistant, Alexis Nelson.

Finally, I would like to express my gratitude for the doctoral funding I received from the Konrad-Adenauer-Foundation, the German Academic Exchange Service (DAAD), and the Humboldt University Women's Fund, and to Leonard Polonsky, who created the Polonsky Academy at the Van Leer Jerusalem Institute, where this book came into completion.

It goes without saying (but I'm saying it anyway) that I would have achieved nothing without the loving support of my family: Mami, Papi, Omi, Lydia, Jürgen, Catrin, Oma, Opa, Gitti, Hermann, Hanna, and Benjamin; and even less without the constant support of my wonderful Yeshaia.

CHAPTER 1

INTRODUCTION

1.1 Philosophy and Ineffability

Can art, religion, or philosophy afford ineffable insights—and if so, what are they? The idea of ineffability has puzzled philosophers from Laozi to Wittgenstein. In this book, I examine different ways of thinking about what ineffable insights might involve metaphysically, and show which of these ways are in fact incoherent. Ultimately I defend the idea that ineffable insights are best understood in terms of a particular kind of non-propositional knowledge and provide a framework for so understanding them.

Ineffability is a nonissue in contemporary philosophy, but why this is so is unclear. To be sure, there are many reasons that make it an obnoxious topic to deal with, starting with the fact that the concept often appears in rather mawkish contexts involving rather personal experiences—a horror for the coolly detached mind of the analytical philosopher. However, the history of philosophy abounds with references to ineffability. It is a topic that has baffled philosophical minds for over two thousand years. Is it likely that philosophers should have lost interest all of a sudden? I don't think so. Rather, the rise of new standards aimed at rendering philosophical discourse analytically rigorous, logically stringent, and scientifically minded has made it much more difficult to tackle a topic that is, by definition, beyond the grasp of language. This book is written for philosophers with an unsatisfied interest in the notoriously elusive topic of ineffability. It develops a theory that makes the concept tangible and ready for use in various philosophical contexts.

The issue of ineffability still hovers silently over many areas of discourse in metaphysics, epistemology, aesthetics, and philosophy of religion. Numerous contemporary philosophers have declared certain objects, properties, states of affairs, experiences, mental states, sensations, etc. to be beyond the limits of language. While historical examples of ineffability usually appear in the context of questions regarding the ultimate nature of the world, reality, absoluteness, oneness, God, or one's experience thereof, today the topic typically appears in the context of other hotly debated issues such as the metaphysical status and accessibility of qualia; the identity or nonidentity of indiscernibles; inexpressible truths and propositions; irreducible metaphors; nonconceptual content; knowledge-how, etc. For each of those debates, there exists a vast body of literature. However, there is virtually no systematic, context-independent examination of the metaphysics of ineffability itself. This book fills this gap in the philosophical literature. Methodologically, it combines "analytical" rigour with the "continental" ambition of providing a comprehensive explanation of ineffability applicable across various philosophical contexts. It offers an examination of the metaphysical structure underlying instances of ineffability and develops a comprehensive, systematic, and original theory thereof.

The central question is: what does ineffability consist in metaphysically? This book provides an answer in four steps. It delivers an *analysis* of the concept ineffability and its related key terms; a *categorization* of ineffability examples; *refutations* of unsuccessful explanatory accounts; and the *construction* of a unified theory of the metaphysics of ineffability. The goal is to understand which entities and/or states are involved when ineffability occurs.

Four such candidate accounts are considered: ineffable properties and objects; ineffable propositions; ineffable content; and ineffable knowledge. In each of the respective chapters, the study traces a possible explanatory account of ineffability in terms of the particular candidate entity/state, and then shows where those accounts fail to explain the metaphysics of ineffability. By considering each one of these accounts in turn, the concept of ineffability is brought to bear on a wide range of influential debates in metaphysics, epistemology, philosophy of perception, aesthetics, and philosophy of religion. The developed account of the metaphysics of ineffability sheds new light both on the role of ineffability in current debates and on its various occurrences throughout the history of philosophy.

Let's now move on and try to get a grip on this notoriously elusive topic.

1.2   Getting a Grip on the Topic

Everyone experiences moments of speechlessness. Only sometimes, though, does such ineffability feel significant. This raises two questions:

in which cases do we attach importance to what we are unable to put into words? And what distinguishes those cases from mundane moments of speechlessness? The first question can be answered rather quickly: ineffability captures our attention in those cases where it feels meaningful, that is, where it raises questions about its source:

> What cannot be told of, we want to know, knowing also that we cannot say: the ineffable is that about which all that is to be said is that nothing more is sayable. Still, one persists in wanting to know, there must be some explanation of that which at once stimulates and frustrates our descriptive impulses: at least we want to know if the difficulties are due to the ineffable itself, or to speech.[1]

Someone might say: "I don't associate ineffability with importance at all—the state of being speechless is nothing more than a temporary failure of one's cognitive apparatus!" However, statements of this kind are inaccurate in at least some cases. One can experience ineffability of two kinds: a trivial kind and a meaningful kind. Trivial cases of ineffability such as temporarily forgetting someone's name are hardly worth remembering. There are other cases of ineffability, however, that stick with us. This brings us to the second question, that is, the question of what distinguishes "ordinary" moments of ineffability from the rare and meaningful ones. We remember those occasions time and again, and continue to feel puzzled by our inability to express what we experienced. For example, when we feel that a piece of music "tells" us something, or that we "understand" something in a moment of prayer. Yet we cannot say what it was that we were "told" or what it was that we "understood," and most explanatory attempts fail to account for the deep sense of understanding attached to these experiences. Slightly less common, but perhaps even more fascinating are certain cases of philosophical insights we seem to be unable express. I will say a lot more about the different ways in which the concept of meaningful ineffability has been invoked throughout the history of philosophy shortly.

What makes a case of ineffability interesting is if there seems to be something meaningful and important lurking behind the linguistic barrier. This book is an attempt to develop an understanding of this barrier and of what could possibly lie behind it by developing a comprehensive and systematic theory of the metaphysical constitution of ineffability. More precisely, this book

1. provides a number of exemplary cases of ineffability,
2. separates the philosophically relevant from the philosophically irrelevant cases,

3. provides a brief overview over the philosophical history of ineffability,
4. clarifies the terminology by offering a number of core definitions,
5. structures the discussion along four ways in which the predicate 'ineffable' can be applied,
6. provides a critical examination of four corresponding kinds of ineffability theories, and finally,
7. develops a unified account that explains and ties together the philosophically relevant cases of ineffability.

It is not an easy task to explore a phenomenon that is, by definition, inexpressible. As Donald Davidson put it, "so often in philosophy, it is hard to improve intelligibility while retaining the excitement."[2] My goal is to show that the metaphysics of ineffability can be made intelligible while retaining the associated sense of excitement.

1.3 The Relevant Cases

Before I start my brief romp through the history of the concept of ineffability, one important distinction must be made. The distinction is between those kinds of ineffability this book is concerned with (the "meaningful," "mysterious," "nontrivial" cases of ineffability), and those that will be ignored (the trivial cases of ineffability).

Put generally, I am interested in what is *in principle* ineffable, and by this I mean what William Kennick has described so appropriately:

> That is ineffable in principle which no one can put into words, that for which there are and can be no suitable words, that for the expression of which all possible worlds are unsuitable. Only the ineffable in principle is of philosophical interest.[3]

The following three classes of examples illustrate three trivial kinds of ineffability this book is not about. Since these cases don't fall under the working definition of ineffability I provide in Chapter 2, I will refer to them as cases of ineffability,* the asterisk marking the fact that they do not constitute cases of ineffability in the sense discussed in this book, even though they involve an incapability of verbalizing something at a given time.

The first kind of ineffability* I will not tackle in this book is due to nescience. If one cannot express a person's name because one doesn't know it, someone might say that the person's name is, in a trivial way, ineffable. There are also terms that cannot be expressed at a specific place and are therefore ineffable at a certain place. For example, certain people living on some tiny Polynesian island in the Pacific ocean might not be able to express the term 'jack-hammer', simply because they don't even know that jack-hammers exist. With relation to temporal location, there are terms that cannot be expressed at this very moment in time: names for animals or diseases that haven't been discovered yet, names of historical events lying in the future, names of people from the distant past, etc. The common source of these cases of trivial ineffability* is nescience, that is, a lack of knowledge that could, in principle, be removed by gaining additional information, by learning processes, or by the future becoming the present. In cases of ineffability* caused by nescience, the concept 'ineffable' is applied to names and terms that are not *in principle* ineffable, but only for specific subjects with specific epistemic constraints (I explain which epistemic constraints are relevant to my definition of ineffability in Chapter 2). Put differently, the alleged ineffability in these cases is not a consequence of an intrinsic property of the respective names or propositions. Rather, it is a consequence of their extrinsic properties, that is, of the way in which the subjects in question are related to the respective entities. As a result, there is nothing particularly mysterious about ineffability* caused by a removable lack of knowledge, and thus, my discussion won't be concerned with it.

The second kind of ineffability* that will not be considered in this book is due to various forms of physical constraints. If Peter cannot express Paula's name because Peter is gagged, Paula's name is trivially ineffable for Peter. This kind of ineffability* is uninteresting because its sole cause is evidently a physical obstacle (the gag) and could, as a matter of both nomological and logical possibility, be removed. In a similar vein, it is arguably impossible to express one's knowledge that this is Lew's rather than Keith's face—we might lack the ability to consciously discriminate all of the details in their faces that make up for their specific looks. This does not mean, however, that any single one of those details is not, in principle, expressible. It is the abundance of detail that overcharges our conceptual resources, not an intrinsic resistance to expression of a face's features.

Analogously, if Jane cannot express a proposition p because p is infinite and expressing p would require forming an infinite sentence, p is trivially ineffable* for Jane—after all, being a finite being, Jane can only express what can be expressed using finite resources in a finite amount of time. The conjunction of all mathematical truths, for example, is an infinite proposition and could thus, as a matter of both nomological and logical possibility, never be expressed by a finite being with merely finite conceptual resources. This kind of ineffability* is uninteresting because its sole cause is the "physical obstacle" (Russell calls it a "merely medical" constraint[4]) of being a finite being. Again, the alleged ineffability* in these cases is not a consequence of an intrinsic property of the respective names or propositions. Rather, it is a consequence of their extrinsic properties, that is, of the way in which the subjects in question happen to be spatiotemporally related to them. The way I see it, there is nothing particularly mysterious about being gagged, nor about not being able to express an abundance of perceptual details, and not even about being finite. Hence, cases of these kinds of ineffability* will be ignored in my examination.

Finally, and perhaps most trivially, the third kind of ineffability* I shall neglect is due to category mistakes. Consider the following example: it is trivially impossible to express a stone because a stone is not the kind of entity that could ever be expressed. We arguably express abstract objects like thoughts, propositions, or sentences, but we don't ever express concrete objects like stones. Hence, in a very odd sense of the word, someone might say that stones are ineffable*.

The same holds for what some people call 'sense perceptions', others 'qualia', and yet others 'raw feels'. I will stick to the term 'sense perceptions'. Given that it is impossible to express the sense perception of tasting saffron *in such a way that another person will come to know how saffron tastes*, sense perceptions are ineffable. Sense perceptions, just like stones, are just not the kinds of things that can be expressed; they can at best be described, but in order to fully understand what saffron tastes like, no description will ever be enough; I have to taste saffron myself.[5] The application of the predicate 'ineffable' cannot be meaningfully applied to entities whose expression is *logically* impossible—attempting it constitutes a category mistake. The alleged ineffability* of concrete objects and sense perceptions results from an inappropriate application of the predicate 'ineffable'. Put differently, concrete objects and sense perceptions are *ineffable by definition* and therefore, not particularly mysterious.[6]

The three examples provided suffice to give the reader an idea of the trivial kinds of ineffability* I consider irrelevant for my project. Neither one of these cases is particularly puzzling, much less in need of philosophical clarification. By contrast, here are three exemplary cases in which the predicate 'ineffable' is applied in what I consider the nontrivial, interesting way.

The first class of truly puzzling ineffability examples can be found in aesthetic contexts. I assume that many people will intuitively agree to the claim that there is an ineffable aspect to (some) works of art, that is, an aspect of its meaning that goes beyond matter, form, and context. I further assume that many would agree that it is impossible to express the meaning of a painting, a melody, or a poem in literal language without remainder. One might argue even more radically that, if there were no substantial difference between meaning that can be transported through literal language and meaning that can be conveyed through works of art, art would be pointless. In order to contemplate a work of art adequately, that is, in order to grasp its meaning, both that which can be captured by means of art theory, and that which points *beyond* the purely aesthetic aspects have to be taken into account. This has led some philosophers to conclude that there is no linguistic category capable of capturing the essence of a work of art. This is because, so it is argued, the essence of works of art is essentially ineffable. I consider such aesthetic ineffability to be of great philosophical interest. It is experienced by almost everyone at some point in their lives. Sooner or later, everybody is confronted with a piece of art, or an aesthetically gripping natural scene, which seizes them and reveals something to them that they cannot express. Thus, the ineffability experienced in the presence of those works of art is a phenomenon the exploration of which is not only of interest for philosophers, but for every person with an affinity to art.

In an analogous way, the ineffability found in religious contexts deserves to be examined in depth, both because of the large number of people who experience it at some point or other in their lives, and because of the enormous meaningfulness commonly attached to religious experiences. It is almost tautological to say that it is impossible to express one's knowledge of God in such a way that somebody else comes to know that God exists. Likewise, it is impossible to express other religious experiences, for example the oneness of everything there is, in a way that enables another person to have the same experience.

Now someone might wonder whether expecting a religious experience to be expressible in a way that enables another person to have the same experience constitutes a category mistake. Couldn't we argue that religious experiences are *trivially* ineffable in the same way the taste of saffron is? That is to say, isn't it simply a category mistake to expect religious experiences to be expressible? I don't think it is. Religious experiences are *experiences*. This means that they share certain features with other experiences.[7] For example, all experiences require there to be a subject having the experience; all experiences can arguably be said to be streams of dynamic mental occurrences; and, most importantly for this context, all experiences have a phenomenology, which is to say that there is *something it is like* to have that experience. It is this last feature of experiences that is trivially ineffable.

If Peter asks Paula what vanilla ice cream tastes like, he is not asking her to express the phenomenology of *her* eating vanilla ice cream. That would constitute a category mistake because it is by definition that Peter cannot experience what vanilla ice cream tastes like to *Paula*. This is due to the simple fact that Peter is not identical to Paula, and there is nothing mysterious about this fact. In short, all experiences, religious and nonreligious, have an ineffable aspect, namely, their phenomenology, the expression of which is trivially impossible. Religious experiences, however, seem to have an additional ineffable aspect which is a result of an essential difference between religious and nonreligious experiences. The difference consists in the fact that ordinary experiences like tasting ice cream or feeling pain can be intentionally invoked, whereas religious experiences cannot. Take Peter and Paula for example. If Paula wants Peter to understand what vanilla ice cream tastes like, she can pass over her cone and let him taste the ice cream.

The same would not work with a religious experience. If Charlie experiences God and Lucy wants to understand what experiencing God is like, there is no obvious way in which Charlie could invoke the experience of God in Lucy. Besides their special content, it seems to be an additional common feature of religious experiences that not everyone can have them. Moreover, those who have reported having had a religious experience tend to suggest that some kind of significant insight was imparted through this religious experiences. It is this insight that makes experiences of this kind so impressive and explains the long-lasting impact they usually have on their subjects. In short, the nontrivial ineffability of religious experiences is certainly both widespread and mysterious enough to deserve proper examination.

Besides the ineffability involved in aesthetic and religious experiences, there is a third class of purely philosophical ineffability examples. Very often, the topic of ineffability appears in philosophical debates revolving around the question of how to (and if to) accommodate subjectivity, mind, or individuality in our metaphysics. For example, it appears to be impossible to express certain versions of the philosophical intuition known as 'idealism'[8] without saying something incoherent.[9] Despite the fact that it is an assumption of many contemporary analytical philosophers that idealism as a philosophical doctrine is plainly false (Kant's transcendental idealism is either considered incoherent,[10] or is not even considered a metaphysical doctrine at all[11]), the intuition that mind, individuality, and subjectivity must be accommodated in the metaphysics of our world *somehow* is remarkably persistent.

Today, instead of debating whether "the world as a whole" is somehow mind-dependent, for example, we prefer to focus on more local issues: we discuss the ontological status of moral facts, aesthetic properties, numbers, causation, possible worlds, etc. and ask to what extent these things are subject-dependent. Contemporary philosophers who believe in the mind-dependence of some class of objects usually refrain from calling themselves "idealists"; rather, they prefer labels like 'antirealists', 'constructivists', 'expressivists', etc. Yet insofar as those doctrines make the truth of true propositions a function of our cognitive capacities, they arguably try to provide a distinct place for the subjective in their metaphysics. Thus, in a way, the spirit of idealism is still hovering over contemporary philosophy, and the task of integrating subjectivity into our metaphysics is as difficult nowadays as it used to be at Kant's lifetime. As Gideon Rosen puts it,

> We sense that there is a heady metaphysical thesis at stake in these debates about realism—a question on a par in point of depth with the issues Kant first raised about the status of nature. But after a point, when every attempt to say just what the issue is has come up empty, we have no real choice but to conclude that despite all the wonderful, suggestive imagery, there is ultimately nothing in the neighbourhood to discuss.[12]

Rosen thus resigns into quietism about the realism-idealism debate because he can't even see a cogent way of formulating it:

> Some philosophers will be tempted to conclude that to say that there is no clear statement of the fugitive question is to say, in effect, that the realist wins on the grounds that his opponent has failed to stake out a genuine thesis. My own view, by contrast, is that it would be more accurate to say that in that case, neither side wins. If it makes no good sense to deny the realist's characteristic claims, then it makes no good sense to affirm them either.[13]

Rosen thus rejects the very question to which realism or idealism were supposed to be the answer, as a result of failing to even formulate the question appropriately.

This supports my point: something about our idealist intuitions resists linguistic formulation. The question is: what exactly is it? Is it the doctrine itself? Or is it the objects involved in it that are ineffable, that is, certain entities or mental states by means of which we try to accommodate the realm of the subjective into our metaphysics? This question is certainly highly relevant for philosophers and thus deserves closer attention.

What remains to be said now is that nontrivial, meaningful ineffability is of course not an exclusive phenomenon of aesthetic, religious, or philosophical contexts. It can be experienced in mundane contexts as well, that is, in contexts where it is not evident that there is any aesthetic, religious, or philosophical source to be associated with the occurrence of ineffability. However, in order to give the reader some way of structuring the material that will be discussed, it is helpful to have this initial taxonomy of ineffability at hand. In addition to this, the following extracts from the history of philosophy will be useful to flesh out the sort of ineffability that forms the subject matter of this book a little further.

1.4 A Brief History of Ineffability

The history of philosophy provides a motivation for this project that goes far beyond personal interest: it abounds with allusions and references to the ineffable. We can find arguments for the inadequacy of language to capture the ultimate nature of reality in Gorgias, Lao Tse, Plotinus, Aquinas, Kant, Kierkegaard, Schopenhauer, Schelling, Nietzsche, Heidegger, Wittgenstein, Adorno, and many others, as well as in the works of some of the most important literary figures: Dostoyevsky, Kafka, Huxley, Beckett, and Celan, just to mention a few.

Here is a very brief overview of the philosophical history of ineffability. As Henry Sheffer put it, "the spirit of ineffability in philosophy is subtly pervasive."[14] I will now provide a few select examples from different periods of the history of philosophy, but these examples do by no means constitute an exhaustive list.

A very ancient, Eastern work of philosophy that makes use of the concept of ineffability is the *Daodejing* by Laozi. Together with the book *Zhuangzi* by the author of the same name, the *Daodejing* is considered the central work of philosophical Daoism. Presented in the form of a collection of aphorisms, it constitutes a critique of Confucianism as practiced both by common people and by political leaders. Contrary to Confucianism, which was the predominant philosophy in China at the time and which stood for a life governed by normative rules, Daoism promotes leading a life in accordance with the Dao, which could perhaps be described as the world's fundamental principle. The following passage helps to understand this concept:

> The Dao that can be trodden is not the enduring and unchanging Dao. The name that can be named is not the enduring and unchanging name. (Conceived of as) having no name, it is the Originator of heaven and earth; (conceived of as) having a name, it is the Mother of all things.[15]

Laozi provides a description of different kinds of reaction to the Dao—reactions that can still be found today with regard to the ineffable:

> Scholars of the highest class, when they hear about the Dao, earnestly carry it into practice. Scholars of the middle class, when they have heard about it, seem now to keep it and now to lose it. Scholars of the lowest class, when they have heard about it, laugh greatly at it. If it were not (thus) laughed at, it would not be fit to be the Dao.[16]

The quintessential claim the *Daodejing* defends is that the Dao, considered as that which is "unchanging",[17] is ineffable:

No characterization can fully capture Dao; the Dao would immediately transcend any characterization, so that it would not be identified with any thing or any aspect of things in the world. In this sense Dao is simply no-thing, beyond our conceptualization or delimitation.[18]

Moreover, even though it is possible for the virtuous to gain knowledge about the Dao, that knowledge cannot be put into words: "One who knows does not speak; one who speaks does not know."[19] Consequently, Laozi argues that the Dao cannot be "studied" systematically. We can accumulate knowledge about some aspects of it, but the only way to comprehend the Dao as a whole is "Learning that doesn't use words."[20] The *Daodejing* thus argues that the unchanging aspect, or principle, of the world, though knowable, is ineffable.

One of the first times the concept of ineffability appears in Western philosophical thought is in Gorgias' *On Nature or the Non-Existent*. Though the book itself is lost, the argument he proposes in it can be reconstructed from what is reported in Sextus Empiricus' *Against Professors*.[21] In that work, he argues for the following three claims:

1. Nothing exists.
2. Even if something existed, we could not know anything about it.
3. Even if we could know something about it, that knowledge would be incommunicable.

The purpose of Gorgias' argument is to refute Parmenides, who holds that thought and being are the same, and that what exists is an unchanging, uniform, eternal One. I will not go into the details of his argument, much less defend it. Rather, what I want to highlight is that Gorgias' argument contains a substantial thesis about ineffability. In (3), he seems to propose that if something existed, and if we could have knowledge about it, we would still be unable to communicate that knowledge. Now, assuming that something exists, and assuming that we have at least some knowledge of it, Gorgias would still hold that that knowledge is ineffable.

A related argument can be found in Plotinus' *Enneads*. Plotinus describes three fundamental metaphysical principles: the Soul, the Intellect and The One (he also calls it The Unity or The Supreme). Regarding their existence, these three principles form a metaphysical hierarchy. The Soul depends for its existence on the Intellect, which, in turn, depends for its existence on the One. Being at the top of this hierarchy, the One does not depend for its existence on anything else: it exists necessarily. According to Plotinus, the One as a universal is metaphysically prior to anything else because a world in which Oneness is not fundamental is inconceivable. Without Oneness, it would be impossible to conceive of the unity and identity of the things that make up the world; it would be impossible to conceive of numbers, etc. Plotinus considers the One ineffable because

> The One is in truth beyond all statement: any affirmation is of a thing; but the all-transcending, resting above even the most august divine Mind, possesses alone of all true being, and is not a thing among things; we can give it no name because that would imply predication: we can but try to indicate, in our own feeble way, something concerning it.[22]

It is not incoherent for Plotinus to consider the One ineffable and, at the same time, to say a great deal about it. As he understands the matter, the One is ineffable in the sense that one cannot predicate anything of it; however, we can talk about its relation to other metaphysical entities and about its general ontological status by approximation, that is, through similes and metaphors. The phenomenal qualities of coming to know the One are described as follows:

> The man is changed, no longer himself nor self-belonging; he is merged with the Supreme, sunken into it, one with it: center coincides with center, for on this higher plane things that touch at all are one; only in separation is there duality; by our holding away, the Supreme is set outside. This is why the vision baffles telling; we cannot detach the Supreme to state it; if we have seen something thus detached we have failed of the Supreme which is to be known only as one with ourselves.[23]

We can thus see that Plotinus argues both for the ineffability of the highest, or perhaps most fundamental, metaphysical principle, and for the ineffability of experiencing it.

A similar claim, yet with a more explicit connotation, can be found in Maimonides (also known as Moses Ben Maimon or Rambam). He is probably the most famous Jewish philosopher who subscribes to the view that God is ineffable because his attributes are. In *The Guide of the Perplexed*, he states the following:

> We cannot describe the Creator by any means except by negative attributes. An attribute does not exclusively belong to the one object to which it is related; while qualifying one thing, it can also be employed to qualify other things, and is in that case not peculiar to that one thing.... The negative attributes have this in common with the positive, that they necessarily circumscribe the object to some extent, although such circumscription consists only in the exclusion of what otherwise would not be excluded. In the following point, however, the negative attributes are distinguished from the positive. The positive attributes, although not peculiar to one thing, describe a portion of what we desire to know, either some part of its essence or some of its accidents: the negative attributes, on the other hand, do not,

as regards the essence of the thing which we desire to know, in any way tell us what it is, except it be indirectly.[24]

The central assumption of this apophatic approach is that God, being entirely unique and different from all other beings, could never be appropriately described by means of ordinary, human concepts. The only way human beings can approximate God's nature is indirectly, by way of negation. His true nature can thus never be described appropriately: it is and always will be ineffable.

Immanuel Kant also admits a realm of ineffability in his philosophical system. Besides the "thing in itself," whose ineffability is a matter of exegetical controversy that cannot be discussed adequately here, Kant also mentions ineffability in the context of experiences of the sublime in nature:

> When I see numerous animal species in a single drop of water, predatory kinds equipped with instruments of destruction, intent upon the pursuit of their prey, but in their turn annihilated by the still more powerful tyrants of this aquatic world; when I contemplate the intrigues, the violence, the scenes of commotion in a single particle of matter, and when from thence I direct my gaze upwards to the immeasurable spaces of the heavens teeming with worlds as with specks of dust—when I contemplate all this, no human language can express the feelings aroused by such a thought; and all subtle metaphysical analysis falls far short of the sublimity and dignity characteristic of such an intuition.[25]

For Kant, the sublimity of nature is a source of ineffable experiences that cannot be captured by human language. Scientific language is completely unequipped for the task of capturing the ineffable, but even poetic language fails to do justice to ineffable experiences as he describes them. However, not being able to express something does not entail not being able to know it:

> In the universal stillness of nature and the tranquility of the mind, the immortal soul's hidden capacity to know speaks an unnameable language and provides inchoate ideas which are certainly felt but are incapable of being described.[26]

He expresses this thought most impressively in the *Critique of Pure Reason*, where he describes the inability to grasp the world in all its variation, causal relationships, and beauty, as follows:

> The present world discloses to us such an immeasurable showplace of manifoldness, order, purposiveness, and beauty, whether one pursues these in the infinity of space or in the unlimited division of it, that in accordance

with even the knowledge about it that our weak understanding can acquire, all speech concerning so many and such unfathomable wonders must lose its power to express, all numbers their power to measure, and even our thoughts lack boundaries, so that our judgement upon the whole must resolve itself into a speechless, but nonetheless eloquent, astonishment.[27]

Without elaborating on this "eloquent astonishment" any further, Kant thus seems to suggest that there are things we can come to experience and perhaps also to know without being able to express them.

In a slightly more mysterious vein, Sören Kierkegaard confronts the reader in many of his works with the claim that language both reveals and destroys truth. He argues that language is ultimately paradoxical and therefore a suspicious means to acquire truth. This fact, however, should not prevent us from engaging with language and everything that can be created from it:

> One should not think ill of the paradox, for the paradox is the passion of thought, and the thinker without the paradox is like the lover without passion: a mediocre fellow. But the ultimate potentiation of every passion is always to will its own downfall, and so it is also the ultimate passion of the understanding to will the collision, although in one way or another the collision must become its downfall. This, then, is the ultimate paradox of thought: to want to discover something that thought itself cannot think.[28]

Language thus brings us closer to truth, but at the same time, it is language that precludes any success in knowing truth. It is both the ultimate tool and the ultimate obstacle to our quest for truth. For Kierkegaard, this becomes especially pertinent in matters of faith, the ineffability of which he considers to be a precondition for having it.[29]

Also in F. W. J. Schelling's works we can find allusions to the ineffable. As so many of his philosophical predecessors, the early Schelling too considers the absolute ground of reality to be ineffable, and human language and concepts incapable of grasping it. This absolute ground he identifies with the "absolute I," which he explains as "that which can never become an object at all."[30] As Schelling understands this notion, its existence can only be posited, never proved:

> As soon as we turn that which can never become an object into a *logical* object to be investigated, such investigations would labor under a peculiar incomprehensibility. We cannot at all confine it as an object, and we could not even talk about it nor understand each other with regard to it.[31]

Schelling's idea of an ineffable absolute identical with an absolute I was fiercely criticized, most notably by his contemporaries J. B. Erhard and Friedrich Hölderlin, which led him to eventually give it up. However, the idea that there is some absolute aspect of reality that cannot be rendered verbally is still prevalent in his writings on art:

> If aesthetic intuition is merely intellectual intuition become objective, it is self-evident that art is at once the only true and eternal organ and document of philosophy, which ever and again continues to speak to us of what philosophy cannot depict in external form, namely the unconscious element in acting and producing, and its original identity. Art is paramount to the philosopher, precisely because it opens up to him, as it were, the holy of holies, where burns in eternal and original unity, as if in a single flame, that which in nature and history is rent asunder, and in life and action, no less than in thought, must forever fly apart.[32]

For Schelling, art thus provides a means of objective expression fundamentally different than other forms of expression such as philosophy. Art can show what cannot be said and as such, is a means of understanding that which can never be an object of our knowledge.

Arthur Schopenhauer is another philosopher who has argued extensively for the importance of ineffable insights through art. His central claim in this respect is that even though words are useful, they don't reveal reality itself. His main work, *The World as Will and Representation*, is divided into four books. Book I develops his epistemological views, which are very similar to Kant's. The subject of knowledge can never know itself; the subjectivity of the knowing subject is the "blind spot" of her knowledge. Schopenhauer attempts to close the epistemic gap between knowing a subject as subject and knowing a subject as object by postulating the "Will" as ultimate concept. Book II deals with ontology, that is, with reality as existing independently of the subject, and with our interest in this very independent reality. Book IV contains ethical considerations. In Book III, he introduces a kind of intuitive insight or understanding that, unlike ordinary, scientific understanding, is not subject to the "Principle of Sufficient Reason": aesthetic experience. In an aesthetic experience, the essence of the world (the Will) appears to the subject in a way unmediated through concepts, so that the subject of the experience perceives the world in the most direct, immediate way:

> Time, space, and causality are that arrangement of our intellect by virtue of which the *one* being of each kind that alone really exists, manifests itself to us as a plurality of homogenous beings, always being originated anew and passing away in endless succession. The apprehension of things by means of

and in accordance with this arrangement is *immanent*; on the other hand, that which is conscious of the true state of things is *transcendental*. We obtain this *in abstracto* through the *Critique of Pure Reason*, but in exceptional cases it can also appear intuitively.[33]

According to Schopenhauer, these exceptional cases occur mainly in aesthetic contexts, and it is the experiences had in such cases that are ineffable. It is important to note that for Schopenhauer, an aesthetic experience does not consist in experiencing a work of art; rather, it consists in receiving reality from a specific perspective, namely, from a perspective detached from the Will.

One of the most notorious dispraisers of language and defenders of the ineffability of reality is Friedrich Nietzsche. In the posthumously published paper *On Truth and Lies in a Non-Moral Sense*,[34] for example, he claims that words obscure the real differences in the world, and that all logical axioms depend on the false assumption that things can be identical. Starting from the question why humans strive to know the truth, he develops an entirely subjectivist account of truth:

> Truth is a mobile army of metaphors, metonyms, anthropomorphisms, in short a sum of human relations which have been subjected to poetic and rhetorical intensification, translation and decoration…; truths are illusions of which we have forgotten that they are illusions, metaphors which have become worn by frequent use and have lost all sensuous vigour. Yet we still do not know where the drive to truth comes from, for so far we have only heard about the obligation to be truthful which society imposes in order to exist.[35]

Nietzsche attacks both the concept of objective truth and the possibility of genuine linguistic expression. For him, language determines truth. The essence of reality, however, is ineffable. He draws the rather gloomy conclusion that, in order to escape the self-inflicted metaphorical imprisonment, one must deny every form of linguistic abstraction and devote oneself to speechless intuition.

In Martin Heidegger's work too we find allusions to the ineffable. He famously considers Being the "transcendens pure and simple."[36] Perhaps best described as "the factor that makes beings intelligible as beings,"[37] our ordinary language today cannot reveal the true nature of Being anymore because, so Heidegger argues, its true meanings have been forgotten. Language has thereby been reduced to a mere means of abstraction. Only what he calls "primordial speech," as spoken, for example, by the ancient Greeks, manages to convey the true nature of Being. This is because words still had their original meaning then.[38] For this reason, language today is most genuine when it is not spoken:

> When does language speak itself as language? Curiously enough, when we cannot find the right word for anything that concerns us, carries us away, oppresses us or encourages us. Then we leave unspoken what we have in mind and, without rightly giving it thought, undergo moments in which language itself has distantly and fleetingly touched us with its essential being.[39]

Interestingly, though, Heidegger also holds that what language cannot achieve anymore can still be achieved by art. The way he sees it, "art is: the creative preserving of truth in the work. Art then is the becoming and happening of truth."[40] The essentially concealed nature of Being becomes unconcealed through art: "Unconcealedness sets itself into work, a setting which is accomplished by art."[41] In fact, as Guy Bennett-Hunter argues, Heidegger's *The Origin of the Work of Art*[42] can be seen as marking a shift in his philosophical emphasis from the human world to questions of its source,[43] and this source is essentially ineffable.

Ludwig Wittgenstein may be the philosopher who engages most extensively with the concept of ineffability, and he is certainly the figure most commonly associated with the concept of ineffability in philosophy. While some have argued that also the later Wittgenstein is relevant to discussions of ineffability,[44] the main reference in this regard is usually to his early work. In the *Tractatus*, he argues that words reveal only the abstractions of logical interrelations but cannot provide access to ethical, aesthetic, and religious values. The way Wittgenstein sees it, the nature of language is such that there are things that cannot be expressed by it, but are in some sense shown by language.

A notorious difficulty with Wittgenstein is that, as a result of the ambiguity of his writings, it is almost impossible to know what exactly he is arguing for metaphysically (if he is to be read as making metaphysical claims at all). There are two main competing directions of interpretation. Adherents to a metaphysical reading of Wittgenstein's work[45] understand him to be saying that the logic of language is ontologically grounded, so that the intrinsic features of reality—reality being independent of language and thought—determine the structure of language. On this reading, these intrinsic features and their structures are ineffable. A central problem of this view is the tension between the fact that, on the one hand, Wittgenstein seems to be making metaphysical assertions, while on the other hand, he claims that assertions of this kind are nonsensical. Wittgenstein's proposed solution of making a distinction between "saying" and "showing" is widely considered unsatisfactory.

Adherents to a non-metaphysical reading of Wittgenstein,[46] on the other hand, hold that "talk of the world, facts, objects, and so on, is shown to be empty, and we now abandon it: we cannot approach the ontological constitution of the world in the way this talk assumes."[47] According to this view, which is sometimes referred to as the 'therapeutical reading', there are no ineffable truths lurking "behind" the text of the *Tractatus*. Rather, it is a collection of nonsensical sentences and a few proper assertions.[48] An obvious problem with views of this kind is that those sentences in the *Tractatus* that are considered nonsensical nevertheless seem meaningful. Put differently, it is unclear what constitutes the difference between a nonsensical Tractarian sentence and a nonsensical sentence like "Colorless green ideas sleep furiously."[49] Marie McGinn summarizes these two opposed readings as follows:

> According to the metaphysical reading, the most important of these insights is that the logic of our language is grounded in the intrinsic features of an independent reality; it is these features which cannot be described, but which our language shows.... The therapeutic reading, by contrast, entirely rejects the idea that there are any ineffable truths lying behind Wittgenstein's nonsensical remarks.... On this reading, the idea of an objective realm of necessity underlying our capacity to make sense, which cannot be described in language but which language necessarily mirrors, is Wittgenstein's principal target.[50]

Thus, the overarching disagreement with regard to the *Tractatus* is whether it does or does not contain, reveal, or show ineffable truths. Unfortunately, the scope of this book does not allow me to engage in much Wittgenstein exegesis here. Suffice it to enumerate the things that, according to the *Tractatus*, lie beyond the reach of language:

The first one of these is the harmony between thought, language, and reality, consisting in a shared form, or pictorial agreement, between both true and false propositions with the reality they depict. According to Wittgenstein, propositions show or display the logical form of reality but can never express their own pictorial form.[51]

Second, fundamental logical relations between propositions are ineffable because it is impossible to say that one proposition follows from the other. However, Wittgenstein claims that a tautology consisting of two logically equivalent propositions *shows* the internal relations between its constituent propositions.[52]

Third, the limits of thought are beyond the reach of language. This is because in order to describe what can be thought by means of describing what cannot be thought, one would have to think what cannot be thought, which is impossible. We also cannot express the limits of reality and of the logical structure of the world. However, the limits *manifest* themselves in the totality of elementary propositions.

Finally, the metaphysics of experience are ineffable. When a solipsist declares that his mind and his world are all there is, according to Wittgenstein, he is right but what he has said is wrong. That this is the case cannot be said but manifests itself in the limits of my language being the limits of my world.[53]

Depending on one's interpretative angle, we can see that Wittgenstein's work can be interpreted as providing arguments for the existence of ineffable truths, for ineffable content, and for ineffable knowledge.

Just like Wittgenstein and Nietzsche, Theodor W. Adorno also has strong reservations about what language can achieve. However, whereas the former two simply declare that some things are beyond the limits of language and thus, we should not try to talk about them, Adorno insists that language itself draws our attention toward the limits of its expressive capacity. He points out that the only thing that might qualify as the central aim of philosophy is such that it can never be attained:

> If philosophy can be defined at all, it is an effort to express things one cannot speak about, to help express the Nonidentical despite the fact that expressing it identifies it at the same time.[54]

Adorno's entire philosophical work revolves, in one way or another, around the dilemma that philosophy ought to be concerned with what matters, yet what matters is essentially ineffable. In Adorno's eyes, the philosopher who found the most appropriate way of dealing with this dilemma is Hegel:

> Hegel attempts to [express the Ineffable]. Because it can never be said directly, because everything direct and unmediated is false—and therefore necessarily unclear in its expression—he tirelessly says it in mediated form. This is one reason why Hegel invokes totality, however problematic that concept may be. A philosophy that relinquishes this effort in the name of a temptingly mathematicized formal logic denies its own concept a priori—its intention—and a constitutive part of that intention is the impossibility that Wittgenstein and his followers have turned into a taboo of reason on philosophy, a taboo that virtually abolishes reason itself.[55]

Adorno thus credits Hegel with having understood what Wittgenstein and his followers—the founders of analytical philosophy—failed to understand: the importance of the ineffable for every philosophical endeavor.[56] He argues that it cannot be the mere application of *a priori* concepts to *a priori* intuitions through the imagination that enables genuine experience. Rather, it is that which exceeds the grasp of thought that enables experience. This excess is what he calls the "Nonidentical." The only cognitive access we can gain to the Nonidentical is through determinate negations, which shed light on the contradictions between certain thought claims and what thought actually delivers. Thus, contrary to Hegel's insistence that truth is essentially contradictory, with opposites being unified in one big Absolute, Adorno holds that truth is essentially ineffable.

Ineffability is, of course, not only a topic of philosophy; it plays a central role in numerous works of literature and other forms of art as well. To mention just one example, take Dostoyevsky's *The Idiot*. Prince Myshkin, who suffers from epilepsy, describes what he experiences during his seizures as follows:

> The sensation of life and self-awareness increased almost tenfold at those moments, which had a duration like that of lightning. The mind, the heart were flooded with an extraordinary light; all his unrest, all his doubts, all his anxieties were as if pacified at once, were resolved into a kind of higher calm, full of a serene, harmonious joy and hope, full of reason and the final cause. But these moments, these flashes were still merely the presentiment of that final second (never more than a second), with which the fit itself began. That second was, of course, unendurable. These nebulous expressions seemed to him very clear, though too weak. But that it was really "beauty and prayer," that it really was "the highest synthesis of life," of that he could be in no doubt. These moments were simply an extraordinary intensification of self-awareness and at the same time of a self-perception in the highest degree direct.[57]

Prince Myshkin further describes those moments as a feeling of "extreme consciousness" of himself; a "sudden rupture of normal conditions"; "harmony and beauty in the highest degree—an instant of deepest sensation, overflowing with unbounded joy and rapture, ecstatic devotion, and completest life." Not only is Myshkin fascinated with the "beauty and harmony in those abnormal moments," he is also convinced "that they really contained the highest synthesis of life." Even though Prince Myshkin is aware of the inexpressibility of his experience, he tries to give voice to its phenomenal quality, the result of which is a language made up almost exclusively from metaphors.[58]

There are countless further literary figures who engage with the ineffable: Elias Canetti, Franz Kafka, Samuel Beckett, Paul Celan, etc. Unfortunately, mentioning all those thinkers who ought to be mentioned with regard to ineffability goes beyond the scope of this book. It is, after all, the philosophical exploration of ineffability that constitutes the core of this study.

A few remarks on methodology. Attempts to examine the ineffable philosophically are notoriously difficult. Nevertheless, given that so many major philosophers have invoked, in one form or another, the concept of ineffability by declaring certain entities ineffable, it still is astonishing that nobody has ever attempted a comprehensive examination of the metaphysical constitution of ineffability.[59] Typically, discussions of ineffability are mere corollaries of other discussions: Is God ineffable? Are there ineffable religious or mystical experiences? Does Wittgenstein's *Tractatus* convey ineffable truths? Do artworks contain unparaphrasable aesthetic content? For each of these questions, there is a vast body of literature; however, there is virtually no systematic, context-independent examination of the possible metaphysics underlying the concept of ineffability itself. The goal of my book is to fill this gap. More precisely, my goal is to identify the common *object* of ineffable experiences (if there is one). This endeavor is guided by a deep conviction of the importance of the ineffable. I fully agree with Roger Scruton's observation that

> There are many who dismiss [the ineffable] as an unscientific fiction. And people of this scientistic cast of mind are disagreeable to me. Their nerdish conviction that facts alone can signify, and that the "transcendental" and the eternal are nothing but words, mark them out as incomplete. There is an aspect of the human condition that is denied to them.[60]

I take it for granted that a majority of people have experienced the kind of philosophically interesting ineffability that this book seeks to examine. Quoting Scruton again, I believe that

> Anybody who goes through life with open mind and open heart will encounter these moments of revelation, moments that are saturated with meaning, but whose meaning cannot be put into words. These moments are precious to us. When they occur it is as though, on the winding ill-lit stairway of our life, we suddenly come across a window, through which we catch sight of another and brighter world—a world to which we belong but which we cannot enter.[61]

William James uses a very similar image:

> It must always remain an open question whether [ineffable] states may not possibly be such superior points of view, windows through which the mind looks out upon a more extensive and inclusive world. The difference of the views seen from the different mystical windows need not prevent us from entertaining this supposition. The wider world would in that case prove to have a mixed constitution like that of this world, that is all. It would have its celestial and its infernal regions, its tempting and its saving moments, its

valid experiences and its counterfeit ones, just as our world has them; but it would be a wider world all the same. We should have to use its experiences by selecting and subordinating and substituting just as is our custom in this ordinary naturalistic world; we should be liable to error just as we are now; yet the counting in of that wider world of meanings, and the serious dealing with it, might, in spite of all the perplexity, be indispensable stages in our approach to the final fullness of the truth.[62]

Someone might wonder: isn't the alleged ineffability of religious experiences quite different from the ineffability of an artwork? What does Wittgensteinian ineffability have in common with ineffability in Adorno's sense? Do they have something in common at all? These worries are perfectly legitimate, and I will address them in due course. Therefore, without much further ado, let us proceed to the exploration of the metaphysical constitution of ineffability.

1.5 Four Ways of Predicate Application

It should be clear by now that the interest in the concept and the metaphysics of ineffability is as old as the history of philosophy itself, and that it is expedient to provide a thorough examination of it. The next step is to identify an adequate way of structuring the discussion. One obvious way would be to engage with the different appearances of the concept throughout the history of philosophy, thereby adopting a historical perspective on the subject matter. However, given that my goal is to provide a *systematic* analysis of the concept and the metaphysics of ineffability, it is preferable to structure the discussion according to the specific contexts in which concept of ineffability is used, and the respective theories of ineffability designed to accommodate the features of those contexts. The different contexts are characterized by the *application* of the predicate 'ineffable', that is, the kind of entity the predicate is applied to. As the historical examples outlined earlier show, there are four general ways in which the predicate can be applied.

Objects The predicate 'ineffable' can be applied to one of the following: some aspects of reality, its essence, its entirety ('the Absolute', 'the One', 'the Whole'), its origin, or its first principle (God, 'the Will'). In other words, the predicate is applied to *objects*.[63] An example for a philosopher who explains ineffability in this way is Plotinus, who argues for the ineffability of the supreme One, or Maimonides, who argues for the ineffability of God, or more precisely, His attributes. Demonstrating the parallels between these historical ideas and contemporary discussions in analytical metaphysics, Chapter 3 examines the notion of ineffable objects and their properties within the framework of current debates about haecceities and bare particulars. I will show why the notion of ineffable objects does not withstand scrutiny and is therefore unsuitable to explain the metaphysics of ineffability.

Propositions The predicate 'ineffable' can be applied to truths, that is, true propositions, the primary kind of *truth-bearer*.[64] The best-known example for a philosopher who can be interpreted as arguing for the existence of ineffable truths in this way is, of course, Wittgenstein. In Chapter 4, I will discuss the notion of ineffable propositions in the context of current debates about semantic paradoxes, unformulable mathematical truths, Lewisian excess propositions, and perspectival propositions. I will show why the notion of ineffable propositions is incoherent and therefore unsuitable to explain the metaphysics of ineffability.

Contents The predicate 'ineffable' can be applied to the content of a subject's experience of reality, particularly in perceptual, aesthetic, and religious contexts. The predicate is thus applied to *mental contents*. Philosophers who evoke ineffability with regard to specific experiences are, for example, Kierkegaard and Schopenhauer. Chapter 5 examines contemporary accounts that try to make sense of ineffable contents. I show where these accounts fail and demonstrate why the notion of ineffable contents is unsuitable to explain the metaphysics of ineffability.

Knowledge The predicate 'ineffable' can be applied to (some parts of) our knowledge of reality and of ourself. The predicate is thus applied to *epistemic states*. Philosophers who invoke ineffability in this way are, for example, Gorgias, Nietzsche, and Adorno.

These four general ways in which the predicate 'ineffable' can be applied analogously suggest four ways in which one can attempt to explain the phenomenon of ineffability: one can try to explain ineffability in terms of ineffable objects ("Ineffability occurs when we are confronted with ineffable objects"); one can try to explain it in terms of ineffable truths ("Ineffability occurs when we are trying to express ineffable propositions"); one can try to explain it in terms of ineffable mental contents ("Ineffability occurs when we try to render ineffable contents in propositional form"); and one can try to explain it in terms of ineffable knowledge ("Ineffability occurs when we try to express ineffable insights"). Some of the accounts I consider may seem quite remote from the contexts in which ineffability is typically encountered. What, for example, does a theory of haecceities have to do with an ineffable religious experience? On the face of it, nothing.

However, there is a strategy behind this. My idea is that we first of all need to find at least one cogent way of arguing for a metaphysical structure that explains ineffability. Once we find such a way of giving ineffability a coherent metaphysical frame, we can then, in a second step, try to apply this account to cases of ineffability from all kinds of contexts. As we shall see, the theory which survives these thorough examinations in the end can be applied most naturally to the philosophically interesting cases of ineffability. The critical examination of these four possible ways of explaining the metaphysics of ineffability constitutes the main focus of this book.

1.6 Structure of the Book

Chapter 2, "Terminology", specifies the scope of the research question and provides the conceptual tools for the arguments to follow by setting up the terminological framework for the subsequent examination. It provides short discussions, each concluding with a working definition, of six concepts that will be used frequently: 'content', 'representations', 'experience', 'truth' and 'truth-bearers', 'expression' and 'expressibility', and of course, 'ineffability'. The definitions are intended to provide the terminological equipment needed to get the discussion started. It goes without saying, however, that the discussions are not exhaustive treatments of every possible account and argument out there, and the resulting definitions are not proper analyses framed in terms of necessary and sufficient conditions of the terms defined—providing such analyses for each term would require writing six additional books. Rather, the purpose of the definitions is to give the reader a rough idea of the terms in use. It will also be necessary to explicitly rule out certain definitions that would prevent my discussion from getting off the ground. For example, it would be impossible to even raise the question whether there are genuinely ineffable truths if we assumed a deflationary theory according to which truth is nothing but a trivially transparent property of all instances of the equivalence schema "$\langle p \rangle$ is true iff p." On such a deflationist picture, the impossibility of ineffable truths is a direct consequence of the way in which truth is defined. Thus, a deflationist could not even meaningfully ask whether ineffability is to be explained in terms of ineffable truths. The purpose of Chapter 2 is to clarify such terminological issues.

Chapter 3, "Ineffable Objects and Properties", discusses the concept of ineffable properties and objects. Drawing on some of the most well-known historical references to the ineffable, I raise the question whether the metaphysics of ineffability as experienced in aesthetic, religious, and philosophical contexts can be explained in terms of ineffable properties or objects. Starting with a discussion of the concept of an 'Absolute' object, I examine what the ineffability of such an object could consist in. I argue that for an object to be coherently called ineffable, it must either instantiate a property that is causally responsible for its ineffability, or instantiate no property at all. I first examine the concept of an ineffable property in the context of contemporary haecceity theories and debates about the identity of indiscernibles. The argument then proceeds to discuss the notion of objects without properties within the framework of recent debates revolving around the notion of bare particulars. I outline some of the main worries about haecceities and bare particulars and suggest that it is questionable whether such things actually exist. I then argue that, even if they could be shown to exist, they would be insufficient to account for a metaphysics of ineffability as experienced in aesthetic, religious, and philosophical contexts.

Chapter 4, "Ineffable Propositions", examines the concept of ineffable propositions. I raise the question whether the metaphysics of ineffability as experienced in aesthetic, religious, and philosophical contexts can be explained in terms of ineffable propositions, and I answer it negatively. I argue that for a proposition to be ineffable without being trivially empty, it must be strictly inaccessible. First, two cases of contingently inaccessible propositions are considered—self-referential semantic paradoxes and inaccessible mathematical truths—and their metaphysical relevance is dismissed. I then outline two ways of arguing for strict propositional inaccessibility: via functionalist access conditions, and via perspectival access conditions. On the former account, the accessibility of a proposition depends on the functional role the proposition plays for its subject. On the latter account, the accessibility of a proposition depends on the perspective from which it can be accessed, that is, the spatiotemporal location and/or the psycho-physical constitution of the subject. I show why neither functional nor perspectival access conditions provide a model of ineffable propositions suitable for explaining the metaphysics of ineffability.

In Chapter 5, "Ineffable Content", I raise the question whether the metaphysics of ineffability can be explained in terms of ineffable content. Three classes of potentially ineffable content are examined: nonconceptual content in perceptual experience; aesthetic content; and the content of religious experience. Each category is considered separately yet a common reason for the failure of those accounts is identified. I argue that ineffable content is possible only if there is a kind of content which cannot be analyzed without remainder into a combination of phenomenal qualities and conceptual content. I then proceed to show that every token of perceptual, aesthetic, and religious content can be analyzed in this way, rendering the existence of ineffable content questionable.

In Chapter 6, "Ineffable Knowledge", I raise the question whether the metaphysics of ineffability can be explained in terms of ineffable knowledge and give a first positive indication that it can. Three kinds of ineffable knowledge are discussed: knowledge-how, logical knowledge, and nonrepresentational knowledge. The existence of ineffable knowledge as an independent epistemological category is thus demonstrated. I show how the concept of ineffable knowledge avoids the metaphysical inconsistencies faced by the concepts of ineffable objects, ineffable propositions, and ineffable content, and highlight some general metaphysical features of ineffable knowledge.

Based on the conclusions drawn in the preceding chapter, Chapter 7, "Self-Acquaintance," provides an expansion of the category of ineffable knowledge by introducing three kinds of subjective ineffable knowledge. While indexical knowledge enables a subject to recognize her unique spatiotemporal location, knowledge-how enables her to perform certain actions, and logical knowledge enables her to systematize her propositional knowledge into a unified logical structure, *Self-acquaintance* acquaints a subject with her own subjectivity, that is, her Self. In ordinary perceptual contexts, it is argued, a subject gains phenomenal knowledge by being acquainted with the phenomenal features of her environment. In extraordinary perceptual contexts such as aesthetic and religious contexts, a subject gains phenomenal knowledge of her Self by being acquainted with her Self. The concept of Self-acquaintance is then used to explain the paradigmatic cases of ineffability.

Chapter 8, the conclusion, summarizes the results of the preceding chapters: the metaphysics of ineffability cannot be explained in terms of ineffable entities such as objects, propositions, or pieces of content. Rather, ineffability is to be explained in terms of four kinds of ineffable knowledge: knowledge-how, logical knowledge, indexical knowledge and knowledge by acquaintance. The latter manages to explain the ineffability typically experienced in aesthetic, religious, and certain philosophical contexts. Furthermore, the conclusion provides a prospect of the possible philosophical applications of this theory of ineffability.

A clear understanding of what ineffability could and could not be helps to understand the historical examples in which the concepts occurs, and the contemporary debates in which the concept plays a central (if only implicit) role. In both historical and contemporary systematic contexts, this understanding of the metaphysics of ineffability opens up the possibility of new insights and alternative interpretations. The theory of ineffability developed in this book thus makes an allegedly elusive concept tangible and ready for use in numerous philosophical contexts.

CHAPTER 2

TERMINOLOGY

Every philosophical discussion requires a proper definitional framework for three reasons. First, in order to set up a terminological frame of reference that allows raising the intended research question coherently. Second, in order to clarify the research question and its scope. And third, in order to provide the linguistic tools needed for the inquiry. The core terms that will occur frequently in my discussion are: 'content,' 'representations,' 'experience,' 'truth'/'truth-bearers,' 'expression'/'expressibility,' and 'ineffability.' It goes without saying that it is impossible to give proper analyses, that is, necessary and sufficient conditions of all these terms here. Rather, my explanations are meant to provide a rough idea of which candidate theories are in play and which ones are explicitly ruled out.

2.1 Content

'Content' is a term with countless interpretations. We can distinguish between the content of a bucket, the content of a book, the content of a proposition, the content of an experience, etc. In all cases, the term refers to that which either constitutes, or is contained in, the respective item or entity. If I fill a bucket with a gallon of wine, the wine becomes the content of the bucket. This is because it is contained in the bucket. If the bucket contains not only wine but also a bathing duck, then the wine is part of the content of the bucket, and the duck is another part. Analogously, we say that the story of Mowgli and his animal friends in the jungle constitutes the content of *The Jungle Book* because that story is contained in the book. Given that the story is made up of different characters and their actions, the characters and their actions arguably form part of the content of the story. That there is a difference between a content like a story, and a content like a gallon of wine is trivial. What the difference is seems obvious, too. Wine is metaphysically concrete. It is a liquid with certain characteristic properties, we can drink, smell, touch it, etc. A story, on the other hand, is metaphysically abstract. While we can surely take a book into our hands, feel it, smell the pages, etc., we cannot take the story into our hands. In my discussion, when employing the term 'content,' I will henceforth be referring to the abstract kind of content if not otherwise stated.

I take the characteristic features of content to be that it *informs* and *characterizes* a subject's mental state. If a subject S receives a piece of content c by reading a story, for example, c informs and characterizes S's mental state m. A piece of content c informs S's mental state m because it provides the informational data the mental state is about.[1] A piece of content c characterizes S's mental state m because it invokes a cognitive classification, that is, it forms the basis on which S relates to c in a certain way, for example, by forming a propositional attitude toward c, by displaying an emotional reaction to c, by embedding c in a network of beliefs, memories, etc. For example, imagine that Wendy sees Peter Pan crying over his lost shadow. This scenario provides certain informational data: Wendy sees Peter searching frantically, she hears him crying about his lost shadow, etc. Let's assume that part[2] of the content she receives in this scenario is that Peter Pan is upset about having lost his shadow. Let's further assume that she commiserates. Then we can say that the piece of content—that Peter Pan is upset about having lost his shadow—both informs and characterizes her mental state in that scenario. It informs her mental state because it provides the information that Peter Pan is upset about having lost his shadow. It characterizes her mental state because it forms the basis on which Wendy cognitively classifies the information, that is, the basis on which she has the emotional reaction of commiseration, and the basis on which she may form a propositional attitude toward the proposition "Peter Pan is upset about having lost his shadow."

Following these explications, the definition of content I shall employ in my inquiry is the following:

> **Content** Content is either a concrete or an abstract entity. Only content as an abstract entity can become mental content. A piece of mental content c is what informs and characterizes the mental state of a subject S at a given time t. It consists in the informational data contained in a subject's mental state at time t and on the basis of which S cognitively classifies the informational data.[3]

Note that this definition does not preclude the existence of non-propositional (nonconceptual) content. This is especially important for my argument in Chapter 5. If my definition *did* rule out nonconceptual content, it would not be necessary to argue against the concept: we would have "defined it out of existence." However, given that content can be defined perfectly well without adding the clause that it must be propositional in form, arguing against nonconceptual content is certainly the more interesting way of rejecting it than simply defining it away.

Note further that according to my definition, content consists of informational data. While informational data is not necessarily propositional (sense perceptions, for example, provide visual, auditory, olfactory, gustatory, and haptic contents that are clearly nonpropositional in form), it must nevertheless be distinguished from mere sensations like pain or itching. Sensations of this kind arguably do not provide informational data except the one that they are "had" by a respective subject at the respective time.

2.2 Representations

I take 'representations' to be a term of art invoked to denote information-bearing mental entities. To be perfectly accurate, one should actually speak of '*mental* representations.' After all, there arguably are representations that are not mental: one might call a photograph of a frog a representation of that frog, for example. For brevity's sake, however, I will simply speak of 'representations' throughout this book, and if not stated otherwise, I will mean mental representations by that.

A subject represents aspects of the world by entertaining a representation. Representations are geared toward accuracy. The information a representation carries is its content. If the content of a representation is propositional in form, the representation arguably has semantic properties like reference, truth-conditions, truth-value, etc. If the content of a representation is not propositional in form, whether or not it has (all of) the above mentioned semantic properties depends on whether one holds that semantic properties are instantiated only by linguistic entities such as propositions and sentences, or whether one allows that also nonlinguistic signs can have semantic properties. This, in turn, depends on what one considers a sign.

'Semantics' (from the Greek term '$\sigma\eta\mu\alpha\iota\nu\epsilon\iota\nu$' = 'to mean,' 'to denote') refers to the theory of the meaning of signs. Depending on what exactly is considered a sign and what isn't, semantics either fall under the class of linguistics, or under the class of semiotics. Those who consider semantics to fall under the class of linguistics ascribe semantic properties to linguistic representations only. Those who consider semantics to have a broader application, that is, those who think that also nonlinguistic symbols such as gestures or other haptic, pictorial, or acoustic symbols can be signs, would ascribe semantic properties both to linguistic and to nonlinguistic representations. My discussion is neutral with regard to this point.

Even though the first association with the term 'representation' is usually a visual one (suggesting something like "an image in front of one's inner eye"), representations can, of course, be auditory, olfactory, gustatory, and haptic. If I recall the sound of a groundhog I heard on my recent hiking trip, the representation is auditory; if I remember how soft its fur felt, the representation is haptic, if I remember both at the same time, the representation is both acoustic and haptic, etc.

Different relations can hold between a subject and a representation (or, to be precise, between a subject's mental state and the respective representation). Let's say that a subject, call him Martin, entertains a representation of a cup filled with Jasmine tea. Call this representation JT. If Martin *desires* Jasmine tea, he relates to JT in a different way than if he *believed* that his cup was filled with Jasmine tea. In the former case, he relates to JT in a way that informs the wish he expresses by saying 'I want Jasmine tea!.' In order to evaluate this expression, one would apply the standard of *appropriateness*: is it appropriate for Martin to desire Jasmine tea? In the latter case, Martin relates to JT in a way that informs the belief he expresses by saying 'There is Jasmine tea in my cup.' In order to evaluate this expression, one would apply the standard of *truth*: is it true that there is Jasmine tea in Martin's cup?

I consciously refrain from calling the different relations that can hold between a subject and a representation 'propositional attitudes.' Propositional attitudes on the one hand, and relations between subjects and representations on the other, are not identical. As the term indicates, a propositional attitude is an attitude a subject holds toward a *proposition*. Whenever we form a propositional attitude by holding a belief, thinking a thought, uttering a sentence, we produce a propositional representation. Note, however, that only propositional attitudes aimed at truth, such as beliefs, convictions, assertions, etc. are *representations*. Other propositional attitudes, such as desires, fears, etc. which are not aimed at truth, are not representations of the world because they do not attempt to represent a fact about the world. Rather, they constitute a way in which a subject *relates* to a fact about the world. Conversely, not all representations are propositional in form. In fact, most representations we entertain are probably of a nonpropositional, perceptual kind. Just think about all the visual representations we constantly form of the world surrounding us. It is plausible to assume that a subject can be related to such a visual representation without holding a propositional attitude, simply because there is no proposition to be related to.

A representation is truth-apt if it has content in virtue of which it is either true or false. Roughly, the content of a true representation is how the world must be if the representation is to be true of the world.[4] A central question in this context is whether *all* representations, that is, both propositional and non-propositional representations, are truth-apt. It is not at all obvious what the answer to this question should be. It is uncontroversial that representations represent their objects, that is, aspects of the world, either accurately or inaccurately. If I remember the elephant I saw at the zoo yesterday as looking sad, the representation is accurate. If I remember the elephant as being pink all over, the representation is inaccurate. What is a matter of controversy, however, is whether nonpropositional representations are also truth-apt. An entity is truth-apt if it has a truth-value (either 'true' or 'false'). As explained earlier, propositional representations clearly have the semantic property of having truth-values. Whether nonpropositional representations also have truth-values is a matter of debate. Some philosophers argue, for instance, that pictorial representations such as photographs, or emotional representations such as anger, are truth-apt.[5] Others prefer reserving the predicate 'true' for propositions and linguistic tokens expressing propositions, such as sentences, utterances etc., while calling nonpropositional representations 'accurate' or 'appropriate.'[6] Space restrictions do not allow me to get into the details of this debate here. However, this is also not necessary, and here is why.

In my examination, I will simply *assume* the view that all representations, both propositional and nonpropositional, are truth-apt. This is a strong assumption, yet I have a very good reason for making it. The reason is that ineffable truths, that is, true, non-propositional representations, ought not to be defined "out of existence." If ineffable truths turn out to be impossible, their impossibility ought to be a result of my argument, and not the result of a stipulative definition. If there is an independent argument that establishes that nonpropositional representations are not truth-apt, that is, if it turned out (which is doubtful) that a definition of representations must indeed include a clause to the effect that they are necessarily propositional, so much the worse for the defender of ineffable truths.

Finally, it needs to be clarified what I take to be the distinguishing mark between representations and content. Every characteristic of representations I have established so far could be argued to be a characteristic of content as well: both contents and representations are information-bearing mental entities; both contents and representations can arguably be propositional as well as nonpropositional in form; one can stand in different relations to both contents and representations; and I consider both contents and representations to be truth-apt. Now, what is the difference between the two concepts?

The difference is that a particular representation cannot be entertained by two different individuals. Imagine two subjects, Peter and Paula, looking at their baby, Mary, thereby each forming a representation of Mary that involves the way she looks (cute), the way she smells (good), the way she babbles (incomprehensible), and so forth. The content of Peter's and Paula's representation is clearly identical (I leave aside here unnecessary complications such as the different spatiotemporal locations occupied by Peter and Paula). However, the difference between their representations is precisely that Peter's representation is entertained by Peter, and Paula's representation is entertained by Paula. I will not try to spell out what this difference comes down to metaphysically by introducing the concept of a 'point of view' or a 'mode of presentation.' That would clearly go beyond the scope of this inquiry. Moreover, in order to give the reader an idea of what I mean by a representation, it is not necessary to come up with an all-the-way-down analysis of the concept. Suffice it to say that a particular representation cannot be shared by two individuals in the way a given piece of content can. Thus, following these explications, the definition of representations I shall employ in my inquiry is the following:

Representations Representations are content-bearing mental entities entertained by individuals. They can be propositional as well as nonpropositional in form and are, by assumption, always truth-apt. A subject entertaining a particular representation R can stand in different relations to R. A particular representation R can be entertained by one individual only; it can't be shared by two individuals.

2.3 Experience

I take experiences to be mental events,[7] or streams of mental events, in the consciousness of sentient beings, which are characterized by their phenomenal qualities. The phenomenal quality of an experience e is *what it is like* for a sentient being to have experience e.[8] Experiences feature both perceptual and propositional components. For instance, experiencing a hefty argument between two people involves perceptual components (sounds, movements, colors) and propositional components (what Jimmy yells at Johnny, etc.).

Bodily sensations[9] like itches, pain, or heat are often considered to be relevantly different from sense perceptions like seeing or hearing something. What is considered the crucial difference is that sense perceptions like seeing or hearing somehow 'resemble' their causal sources (e.g., the sense perception of seeing a rainbow arguably somehow 'resembles' the rainbow), whereas bodily sensations such as pains or itches don't resemble their sources in any straightforward way (e.g., an itch does not resemble the mosquito responsible for it). Given this difference, it has been a matter of discussion whether bodily sensations, contrary to sense perceptions, lack content altogether, that is, whether bodily sensations contain any informational data except the one that they are "had" by the respective subject at the respective time.

The alleged distinction between bodily sensations and sense perceptions is also relevant to questions concerning the truth-aptitude of experiences. There are two general classes of views: the first one of them considers all of the contents of experience to have accuracy conditions and therefore, to be truth-evaluable; the second one considers none or only some of the contents of experience to be truth-evaluable. The former notion—that experiences have accuracy conditions—is often spelled out by arguing that experiences somehow derive from the contents of belief: some hold that experiences are acquisitions of belief, others argue that experiences are dispositions to form beliefs; and yet others claim that experiences are grounds of dispositions to form beliefs.[10] There are also different ways in which the opposite view—that experiences don't have accuracy conditions—can be spelled out: experiences can be considered 'raw feels'[11], 'qualia'[12] or 'sense data'[13], or one can embrace some form of adverbialism[14] or naïve realism[15] about experiences.

Due to space restrictions, I cannot provide a comprehensive discussion of the issues regarding the alleged distinction between bodily sensations and the truth-aptitude of experiences here. Moreover, the fact that it is unclear whether the adversaries in those discussions even employ the same definition of content, for example, whether they agree or disagree on questions regarding the existence of nonconceptual content, adds another dimension of complexity. Fortunately, however, the question whether sense perceptions such as tasting vanilla ice-cream ought to be distinguished from bodily sensations such as being in pain does not affect my argument. This becomes evident once we spell out the two available options: if bodily sensations are indeed different from sense perceptions in that they don't contain any informational data except the one that they are "had" by a subject, then bodily sensations are ineffable by definition and fall under the category of trivial ineffability* I have already ruled out as irrelevant for this project. If, on the other hand, both bodily sensations and sense perceptions do contain content (and are thus truth-apt), then my argument in Chapter 5 will apply to both of them. In either case, both bodily sensations and sense perceptions are covered by my argument, which uses the following definition:

Experience Experiences are (streams of) mental events in the consciousness of sentient beings and are characterized by their phenomenal qualities. Experiences either exhibit perceptual content, or propositional content, or both (whether bodily sensations like pains and itches exhibit content is a matter of debate). The phenomenology of experiences is essentially personal, that is, what it is like to have a given experience e cannot be shared by two subjects; the content of a given experience e can, under suitable circumstances, be shared by two subjects.

2.4 Truth and Truth-Bearers

It is important to say a few words about what kind of truth theory forms the background of this study. By this formulation I don't mean to suggest that the validity of my argument depends on the assumption of a specific theory of truth. Rather, I want to show that the question about the metaphysical constitution of ineffability can only be meaningfully formulated if one particular theory of truth is ruled out. To be specific, my research question, specifically the question of ineffable truths, would *not* get off the ground if we assumed a deflationary theory of truth. Here is why.

Most contemporary theories of truth assume that the truth-predicate can only be ascribed to truth-bearers of propositional form. However, the fact that most truth theorists assume that the truth-predicate can only be ascribed to propositions does not imply that they assume that all propositions are in fact formulable. David Lewis, who argues for inexpressible propositions, is an example for such a view.[16] This means that someone who insists that the truth-predicate is only applicable to propositional truth-bearers does not necessarily exclude the possibility of ineffable propositions. The fact is that most truth theorists remain silent on the topic. Deflationists, however, rely *explicitly* on the in-principle formulability of all truths.

Deflationary theories of truth are called 'deflationary' because their goal is to metaphysically *deflate* the notion of truth, that is, to show that truth is not a metaphysically substantial concept.[17] Take Paul Horwich's minimalism, a very well-developed deflationary theory of truth, for example. Its central claim is that everything there is to know about the concept 'truth' is contained in the Equivalence Schema "⟨p⟩ is true iff p," where ⟨p⟩ stands for any proposition.[18] Given that equivalence relations are reflexive, symmetrical, and transitive, every instance of the schema has the following general form:

> For any object x: x is an axiom of the minimal theory if and only if, for some y, when the function E* is applied to y, its value is x.[19] [where (E*) stands for propositions with the structure ⟨⟨p⟩ is true iff p ⟩].[20]

By arguing that everything there is to know about the concept 'truth' is contained in the Equivalence Schema '⟨p⟩ is true iff p', deflationists like Horwich reject five central aspects of traditional, that is, nondeflationary accounts of truth: (1) the idea that truth is compositional, that is, that the truth-value of, say, a sentence depends on the semantic properties of its parts;[21] (2) the view that understanding truth requires being able to conceptually analyze every true sentence into philosophically unproblematic terms; (3) the idea that truth is a naturalistic property;[22] (4) the possibility of an explicit theory of truth that is both nontrivial and finite (deflationary theories of truth necessarily comprise infinitely many axioms); and (5), the idea that truth stands in necessary relations with other concepts such as assertion, verification, reference, meaning, success, or logical entailment. In short, a deflationary theory of truth like Horwich's Minimalism

> involves nothing more than the equivalence schema; it is non-compositional; it denies that truth and reference are complex or naturalistic properties; and it does not insist on an eliminative account of truth attributions. In this way minimalism aims for a maximally deflationary theory of truth, which, though complete, has no extraneous content—a theory about truth, the whole of truth, and nothing but the truth.[23]

No matter whether one agrees with deflationism about truth (as many contemporary analytical philosophers do), or whether one thinks that it fails to accommodate everything there is to say about truth (as I am inclined to think), what is important to note is that deflationism is no suitable theory of truth if one wants to examine the nature of ineffability. This is because it is too restrictive. Deflationist theories of truth are based on the assumption that the truth predicate is a linguistic device and thus, talk about truth is only appropriate in linguistic contexts. This does not hold of other truth theories, even if they assume that the truth-predicate can only be applied to truth-bearers whose form is propositional.

Moreover, it is a presupposition of deflationism that all truths either have, or can be reduced to, a common form. Without this assumption the deflationist could not hold that all truths fit into the Equivalence Schema. Thus, deflationists are forced to reject the possibility of nonpropositional truths because only propositionally shaped truths fit the schema. As will become clear in Chapter 4, attempts to argue for the existence of ineffable truths often involve the idea of truths that are nonpropositional in form. And it is clear that a theory of truth that deprives a defender of ineffable truths of its central argument is not suitable for an examination of ineffability.

For the sake of completeness, it must be mentioned that deflationists are not entirely mute with regard to ineffable truths. In fact, Horwich even concedes that his theory of truth itself cannot be formulated explicitly.[24] The Equivalence Schema '$\langle p \rangle$ is true iff p' is supposed to contain everything that can be said about truth *implicitly*.

> In the first place the number of axioms that we have the terminology to formulate is too great; there are infinitely many and though each one of them can be expressed it is not possible to write down the whole collection. In the second place there are many propositions we cannot express in current terminology. And for those the corresponding equivalence axioms are themselves inexpressible—although, as we have seen, it is none the less possible to say what they are.[25]

According to Horwich, the inability to formulate his deflationary theory of truth explicitly ought not to worry us because it suffices for a theory of truth to state which *general* form its axioms would have, namely '$\langle p \rangle$ is true iff p', even if not all of the instances can be formulated.[26] In fact, he seems to think that the only reason why the concept of truth is so interesting to philosophers is its ability to deal with unformulable instances of the Equivalence Schema. He claims that propositions involving the truth-predicate have an inferential property allowing us to infer a general schema where a specific one is not within our reach, that is, when we hit the limits of linguistic expressibility. For example, while it is impossible for us to spell out the conjunction of all instances of the law of the excluded middle, we can easily formulate the general schema "Every proposition of the form 〈 everything is F or not F 〉 is true."[27] According to Horwich, it is due to this feature—and not as the name of some baffling ingredient of nature—that the concept of truth is interesting to philosophers at all.[28] Unfortunately, however, Horwich does not explain how he arrives at the conclusion that all truths can, in principle, be fitted into the Equivalence Schema. Without further elaboration, he takes propositions to be the primary truth-bearers[29] and states:

> For the sake of simplicity and conformity with natural language I begin by developing the account of truth for propositions. However, I shall go on to argue that the minimalist conception applies equally well to the 'truth' of utterances, mental attitudes, and other types of entity.[30]

The argument he provides for this claim can be summarized as follows: if somebody does not want to accept propositions as truth-bearers, an analogous minimalist theory can be constructed, which works for utterances and for all kinds of propositional attitudes, for example, beliefs. This analogous theory consist of an interpretation schema, (DT) (Int (u) ∈ *p*) → (u is true iff p),[31] which is supposed to enable us

> to 'project' attributions of truth from our own current utterances onto other, 'equivalent' ones—where u and our 'p' are 'equivalent' when 'p' is the correct interpretation of u (i.e., Int(u) ∈ 'p'), and where interpretation is a matter of translation plus context adjustment.[32]

Furthermore, we need to add two "auxiliary assumptions," the first of which must specify the conditions for an utterance (belief, claim, insinuation) to express a proposition, and the second of which must specify the relationship between truth for propositions and truth for utterances (beliefs, claims, insinuations).[33] However, Horwich leaves the crucial point open, that is, how we are supposed to perform this translation. He provides no explicit rules for the translation of utterances plus context into equivalent propositions; he does not even argue for the *theoretical* possibility of developing such a translation rule. Instead, he claims that

> Ordinary language suggests that truth is a property of propositions, and that utterances, beliefs, assertions, etc., inherit their truth-like character from their relationship to propositions. However, the above derivations show that this way of seeing things has no particular explanatory merit. The truth-like conception for each type of entity is equally minimalistic. And by assuming any one of them we can easily derive the others.[34]

Hence, his assumption is that even if, instead of propositions, we take beliefs (or sentences, utterances, etc.) to be the primary bearers of truth, an Equivalence Schema structurally analogous to the one for propositions will hold, for example, something like "(EB) The belief (etc.) that p is true iff p."[35] Thus, he seems to believe that no matter what class of entities we take truth to be a property of, its instances are assumed to have a common form, so that we can derive a generalized equivalence axiom like 'The belief that p is true iff p' or '⟨p⟩ is true iff p'. Yet can we really assume that all truths have a common form? Horwich seems to think that we can:

> We can characterize the 'equivalence axioms' for unformulatable propositions by considering what would result if we could formulate them and could instantiate those formulations in our equivalence schema. Thus we may specify the axioms of the theory of truth as what are expressed when the schema (E) '⟨p⟩ is true iff p' is instantiated by sentences in any possible extension of English. Alternatively, instead of identifying the axioms

indirectly in terms of how they would be expressed, we can solve the problem by directly specifying the propositional structure which all and only the axioms have in common.[36]

This is a far-ranging assumption, and I am not going to argue against it.[37] Rather, I want to point out that, if one's goal is to find out what ineffability is, one cannot leave out the concept of ineffable truths. And in order to examine the concept of ineffable truths, one's underlying theory of truth must in principle be open to the possibility of their existence, to the possibility of their form being nonpropositional, and thus, to the possibility that the structure of their respective equivalence axioms might be completely opaque. For these reasons, I explicitly rule out deflationism as underlying theory of truth for this project. Other than that, my expositions in this book are neutral with regard to truth-theories.[38]

Truth With the exception of deflationism, my examination of ineffability is neutral with regard to its underlying theory of truth.

Truth-Bearers In line with this restriction, my book is based on the minimal assumption that there must be some kind of necessary relation between true entities on the one hand, and facts on the other.[39] Propositions are truth-bearers of a form that is in principle, that is, absent physical constraints of any sort, suitable for linguistic expression. I refrain from claiming that propositions are the only kind of truth-bearers there are; there may be truth-bearers which are not propositional in form.[40]

2.5 Expressibility and Ineffability

Before I say anything about expressibility and its antonym, ineffability, it is important to emphasize that there is a crucial difference between something being ineffable and something being indescribable. Intuitively, the difference is simply that something ineffable may very well be describable. This can be illustrated by replacing 'to express' with 'to describe' in some of the examples I have mentioned earlier: clearly, one can describe a stone; equally clearly, one can't express a stone. The same holds for sense perceptions, aesthetic experiences, religious knowledge, etc. Once our working definitions of 'expression' and 'expressibility' are in place, we will be able to distinguish ineffability from indescribability in a more formal, and less intuitive way.

It is furthermore worth mentioning that the ineffable is not identical with the unknowable:

One may assert that some things [like Kant's things-in-themselves] are both ineffable and unknowable; nevertheless, the concept of the ineffable is usually so construed that it makes sense to say, 'I know something somehow, but I cannot put it into words; I cannot say what I know.'[41]

When we ask ourselves which things are expressible and which aren't, we have to be careful to distinguish between three ways in which this question can be interpreted. The first interpretation is: out of all things, which are the ones that can be expressed? The second interpretation is: out of all things that can be expressed *somehow*, which are the ones that can be expressed *linguistically*? The third interpretation is: out of all things that can be expressed linguistically, which are the ones that can be expressed *literally*? In short, we have to ask ourselves how wide we would like to have our quantifiers open. Let me briefly elaborate on those three interpretations, in reverse order.

2.5.1 Literal Expressibility

When we think about different ways in which we can express something in language, several things come to mind. Besides literal expressions like "Yogurt is made of milk" or "Tigers live in India," we can express states of affairs metaphorically ("Life is a journey," "Frege does not begrudge a pinch of salt"), where a metaphor can be defined—roughly—as a figure of speech whereby one subject is described in terms suggestive of another, otherwise unrelated, subject. Moreover, we can also employ contradictory terms in order to express something. For instance, if I want to reveal some sort of inner conflict, I can say that I both am and am not happy, or that Arthur is both a kind and a cruel person. Or, if I want to illustrate a semantic paradox like the Liar, I can say that the Liar both does and does not say the truth. Some defenders of paraconsistent logical systems such as dialetheism even argue that some such contradictions are true.[42] A central question arising in this context is whether *all* linguistic expressions are reducible to noncontradictory, literal expressions.

There are countless arguments meant to show, either, that some expressions are irreducibly metaphorical, or, that all metaphorical expressions can ultimately be translated into literal expression. For example, William Alston argues that "a statement cannot possess a propositional content unless it is, in principle, possible that a language should contain words that have the meanings required for the literal expression of that content."[43] Janet Soskice, on the other hand, argues that metaphors "should be treated as fully cognitive and capable of saying that which may be said in no other way."[44] Likewise, Mary Hesse's seminal argument for the unsubstitutability of metaphorical language aims to establish the view that literal language as used (and sought for) in science ought to be conceived of as distillations from the more metaphorical, less committal way in which we use ordinary language.[45]

I will discuss the issue of metaphorical expression more elaborately in Chapter 5, but I would like to note two things at this point. The first one is that I am inclined to think that one cannot be "right" or "wrong" about the question whether all figurative (metaphorical, contradictory) language is translatable into literal expressions. Rather, it seems to me that one's conclusion about this issue depends on what one considers a successful translation, which in turn depends on whether one expects a translation to transport nothing but the bare information of an expression, or also its emotive qualities. The second—and more important—point is that my examination of ineffability is targeted at ineffability understood strictly. I am not interested in the question whether some things are ineffable in literal language and what their ineffability comes down to—I am interested in the question whether some things resist *all* linguistic expression, literal and nonliteral, and how the nature of this absolute ineffability can be explained.

2.5.2 *Linguistic versus Nonlinguistic Expressibility*

Naturally, language is not the only medium of expression available to us. Human beings use their entire body to express themselves: their current emotions, desires, moods, opinions, etc. A gesture can express insecurity, happiness, perplexity; a person's posture can express his sadness, despair, enthusiasm; facial expressions indicate the emotional state of its bearer, etc. Furthermore, a person's actions can also be interpreted as expressing that person's convictions, mood, desires, dreams, etc.[46]

In this book, however, when I speak about "expression" and "expressibility," I will be referring to *linguistic* expression. I do this in order to narrow down the cases of ineffability relevant for this project. Arguably, linguistic expression is more fine-grained than bodily expression, that is, the class of concepts, judgments, attitudes, etc. that can be expressed by linguistic means is much bigger than the class of concepts, judgments, and attitudes that can be expressed in a bodily or facial manner.[47] For example, we can imagine Silvia sitting at a table, a bowl of lentils in front of her. Judging from the expression on her face, we can tell that she very much dislikes lentils. Her facial expression might even be able to reveal different degrees of disgust, ranging from mild dislike to severe repulsion. However, any expression that goes beyond different degrees of that particular emotion are too complicated to be expressed mimically. The concepts available for linguistic expression, on the other hand, are more fine-grained: Silvia can explain to us what exactly she doesn't like about lentils (their floury texture, their color), why exactly she doesn't like those features (they remind her of sand), what exactly she feels when she is forced to eat lentils (you don't want to know), etc. As a consequence of the fact that linguistic expression is more fine-grained than nonlinguistic expression, the class of things that cannot be expressed linguistically is much narrower than the class of things that cannot be expressed by means of bodily expressions, and those concepts, judgments, attitudes, etc. that can be expressed in a bodily manner can arguably be expressed linguistically as well (as in the lentil case).[48]

2.5.3 Categorical Expressibility

The third way in which one can interpret the question of which things are expressible is as a question about categorical classification. As already mentioned in the introduction, there are some things that are by definition, that is, as a consequence of the metaphysical category they belong to, impossible to express, and I have ruled out those cases that constitute category *mistakes*, such as expecting a stone to be expressible (rather than merely describable). However, this leaves open the possibility of a metaphysical category of entities (e.g., objects, truths, contents, or knowledge) that resist expression, not as a consequence of some sort of categorical misclassification, but due to their nature. Put differently, it is possible that there exists a class of entities *intrinsically* characterized by the fact that they resist linguistic expression. For instance, if ineffable truths or ineffable contents existed, they would have to be part of this class of entities: ineffability would be an intrinsic property of those entities. It is this class of entities, that is, the class of entities that are *intrinsically* ineffable, that constitutes the subject matter of this book. The goal of my project is to find out whether any such entities can be coherently argued for, and if so, whether they succeed in providing a unified account of the metaphysics of ineffability, that is, an account that covers *both* purely philosophical cases *and* daily life cases of ineffability as experienced, for example, in aesthetic and religious contexts.

Before we can venture to define 'ineffability,' we need a proper grasp of its opposite, expressibility. And in order to understand the *modal* term 'expressibility,' we first need to define what constitutes an *actual* instance of expression. This is because, arguably, an entity y is expressible if and only if there exists an x such that x expresses y. The best place to start looking for a definition is, of course, the dictionary. Unfortunately, this does not get us very far. The Oxford English Dictionary defines the verb 'to express'[49] in terms of the verb 'to convey'; the verb 'to convey'[50] is explained in terms of the verb 'to communicate'; the verb 'to communicate'[51] is explained in terms of the verb 'to convey,' and so forth. It seems to be exceedingly difficult to *define*—and not merely *paraphrase*—what expression is; and it seems to be even more difficult to do this in a noncircular way.

The lack of definitions of 'expression' and 'to express' in philosophical literature—a lack that is all the more stunning in light of the ever increasing interest in the philosophy of language—suggests that this is also very difficult for philosophers. One of the few definitions has been provided by A. W. Moore, who suggests the following definition of 'x expresses y':

> "x expresses y if and only if (i) x is a linguistic item with content that makes it either true or false, (ii) y is a non-linguistic item with content that makes it either true or false, and (iii) the content of x entails the content of y."[52]

Note that clause (ii) implies the possibility of nonlinguistic truth-bearers, which is crucial for the reasons discussed in the earlier section about truth.

Despite its general plausibility, Moore's definition is problematic in two ways. The first problem is that, if y is either a tautology or a necessary truth, then y is entailed by every possible x, and if x is a contradiction, then x entails every possible y. I call this the Entailment Problem. The second problem is that Moore's definition is unsuitable for a proper examination of ineffability because it extends to truth-apt entities only, and because its employed concept of content is unclear. I call this the Extension Problem. Let me briefly address those two issues.

The Entailment Problem is, of course, a general consequence of logical entailment. Had Moore formulated clause (iii) of his definition in terms of equivalence rather than entailment ("the content of x is *equivalent* to the content of y"), tautologies, necessary truths, and contradictions would be unproblematic. However, Moore's choice of entailment over equivalence is a conscious one. First, because he wants a sentence like 'Grass is green and coal is black' to count as an expression of the belief that grass is green,[53] that is, he does not want his definition of expression to be unreasonably narrow. Second, because he aims to refute David Lewis's argument for ineffable truths, and his refutation only works on the background of a definition of expression in terms of entailment.[54] This latter reason alone would not be enough to justify his choice of entailment over equivalence; however, I agree with Moore that a definition of expression in terms of equivalence is too narrow, and that a sentence like 'Grass is green and coal is black' ought to count as an expression of the belief that grass is green. Hence, I don't think that the difficulties arising from a definition of expression in terms of entailment ought to be solved by replacing the formulation in terms of entailment with a formulation in terms of equivalence. Yet of course, they ought to be solved somehow, and this is something Moore fails to do.

How can the Entailment Problem be solved? One possibility would be to restrict x to noncontradictory assertions, and to restrict y to non-tautologous, contingent truths. I think it is obvious that this is not the right way to go. Restricting x to noncontradictory assertions would rule out a large number of false assertions that ought not to be ruled out. For example, if x was not allowed to contain contradictions, then it would be impossible for me to express my (false) belief that some bachelors are married. Restricting y to non-tautologous, contingent truths in order to avoid rampant entailment would make it impossible to express tautologies and necessary truths, so that the sentence "All bachelors are unmarried men" would neither express a tautology, nor a necessary truth—an absurd consequence. Reformulating the definition of expression in terms of some kind of relevance logic seems to me an undesirable way to go as well, partly for the simple reason that nonclassical logic systems are always accompanied by an entire new set of difficulties, and partly because the relevant logician's strategy of simply avoiding the claim that a contradictory proposition entails any proposition at all would arguably rule out many expressions of false beliefs, which is a rather undesirable consequence.

What I would like to suggest instead is to add a qualification that simply rules out cases of trivial entailment:

> x expresses y if and only if (i) x is a linguistic item with content that makes it either true or false, (ii) y is a nonlinguistic item with content that makes it either true or false, and (iii) the content of x nontrivially entails the content of y, *so that x cannot entail both A and not-A, and so that y cannot be entailed by any given x whatsoever.*

According to this definition, 'x expresses y' pertains to the state of affairs in which, for a given nonlinguistic item y, there is a corresponding linguistic item x whose content entails the content of y without it being the case that x entails both the content of y and its opposite, and without it being the case that y is entailed by any possible x.

The Extension Problem Moore's definition faces arises as follows. Looking closely at it reveals that it is unclear how the term 'content,' which features in all three clauses of his definition of 'x expresses y,' is supposed to be understood. Clause (i) reads: "x is a linguistic item with content that makes it either true or false." Prime examples of linguistic items are sentences, so let's assume that x is a sentence. According to Moore's definition, x has content that makes it either true or false. Usually, we take the content of a linguistic item like a sentence to be a proposition,[55] so it is plausible to assume that 'content' in clause (i) refers to propositions. So far, so good. Now clause (ii) reads: "y is a nonlinguistic item with content that makes it either true or false." Here, it is already much less obvious what 'content' is supposed to refer to. This is partly due to the fact that it is difficult to say what a prime example of a nonlinguistic item is. Chairs, smells, gestures, numbers are all nonlinguistic items, and even if we could say of all of them that they have content, they certainly don't have the same *kind* of content. But let's not try to be overly accurate. Given that Moore continuously refers to the example of the sentence 'Grass is green and coal is black,' which he takes to be an expression of the belief that grass is green, it is safe to assume that what Moore has in mind when he speaks about 'nonlinguistic items' are propositional attitudes such as beliefs, and that he takes propositions to be the contents of both linguistic items such as sentences, and of nonlinguistic items such as beliefs.

However, his definition is still not entirely clear. Given that he emphasizes that y is a nonlinguistic item with content *that makes it either true or false*, it seems that y stands for propositional attitudes aimed at truth (such as beliefs), and not for propositional attitudes not aimed at truth (such as desires, fears, and hopes).[56] Besides the fact that this is a very unusual way of interpreting the verb 'to express,' what adds to the confusion is that Moore insists that it is the *content* of x that makes x true or false, and that it is the content of y that makes y true or false. This sounds very much like a confusion of truth-bearers with truth-makers. Contents such as propositions are *bearers* of truth that are made true by *facts*. Perhaps one could argue that contents are *inter alia* truth-makers, but surely the primary truth-makers are facts.

The fact that Moore does not elaborate on how he understands the notion of a 'linguistic item with content' is also problematic because, as Moore's definition stands, all kinds of odd scenarios qualify as cases of expression. A dialogue in Lewis Carroll's *Through the Looking Glass* illustrates my point:

> 'When I use a word,' Humpty Dumpty said in rather a scornful tone, 'it means just what I choose it to mean——neither more nor less.'
>
> 'The question is,' said Alice, 'whether you CAN make words mean so many different things.'
>
> 'The question is,' said Humpty Dumpty, 'which is to be master—that's all.'[57]

The question is: what is a linguistic item? Should a word that was invented by Humpty Dumpty and that can only be understood by Humpty Dumpty qualify as an expression? Or should it be at least possible that other people come to understand it? An answer to the question what qualifies as a genuine expression depends on how we understand language, and, in a derivative sense, who or what we take to be capable of producing genuine expressions. Moore indicates a range of possible answers:

can a truth be expressed linguistically only if there is a sentence in some existing language that has precisely that truth as its content? Or does it suffice that there be some (true) sentence in an existing language that has that truth as *part* of its content? If the latter, in what sense of 'part'? Does it perhaps suffice that there be some sentence in an *extension* of an existing language that has that truth as its content? If so, then what counts as an extension of an existing language? Or is the appeal to existing languages too restrictive? Does it suffice that there be some (true) sentence in some *possible* language that has that truth as (part of) its content? Then what counts as a possible language?[58]

The standards I will adopt are quite low.[59] On my view, a genuine expression is a piece of a possible language (it doesn't have to be a piece of an actual language). However, a genuine expression must, in principle, be capable of being formed and understood by more than one finite being. I am consciously restricting attention to finite beings, so when I talk about expression, I mean what can be expressed, in the sense of the above definition, by a finite being. I deliberately rule out infinite beings, and this is purely stipulative. One might ask: why the stipulation? Why make expression a matter of temporality? First of all, if expressions had to be capable of being understood by infinite beings only, it would expand the notion of expressibility in such a way that it wouldn't cover the intuitive cases I think it should cover. Put differently, if infinite linguistic items were granted the status of expressions, the notions of 'expression,' and 'communication' would drift apart to such an extent that the resulting notion of ineffability would be very remote from the kind of ineffability human beings experience. Moreover, given that we are finite beings, the distinction to be drawn between what can be expressively achieved using finite resources, and what would be possible for an infinite being, marks an essential, highly relevant difference for us. It also seems to me that this is a much more relevant distinction to be drawn than any of the distinctions that might be drawn between all sorts of different finite beings.[60]

When I say that an expression must be 'in principle capable of being understood,' I mean that an expression must be communicable, that is, sharable[61] through some process of learning. This allows for Humpty-Dumpty-style word inventions as long as the meaning of such an invented expression is learnable by other finite beings. The qualification rules out private languages because they cannot, by definition, be learned by someone else.

Someone might worry that different groups of individuals might possess conceptual schemes so different from one another that they resist inter-translation, such that a linguistic item that qualifies as an expression of y in one (linguistic) community has no counterpart in another (linguistic) community, and as a result, y would be effable in one community but ineffable in another. However, this worry can be alleviated with an argument by Davidson. He refutes the doctrine according to which there are or could be conceptual schemes so different from one another that they resist inter-translation. Conceptual schemes are described as "ways of organizing experience;... systems of categories that give form to the data of sensation;... points of view from which individuals, cultures, or periods survey the passing scene."[62]

If, as conceptual relativists argue, there are conceptual schemes so different from one another that an intelligible concept in one scheme cannot be translated into an intelligible concept in another scheme, then it seems that "the beliefs, desires, hopes and bits of knowledge that characterize one person have no true counterparts for the subscriber to another scheme."[63]

Davidson argues that neither the notion of a complete failure of translatability nor of a partial failure of translatability of conceptual schemes is intelligible. To see why, he asks the reader to consider how we decide whether a conceptual scheme is an adequate one. A conceptual scheme qualifies as adequate if it 'fits the facts' or 'fits the totality of possible sensory evidence.' These two expressions are nothing else but a circumlocution for 'being true.' Davidson notes:

> Our attempt to characterize languages or conceptual schemes in terms of the notion of fitting some entity has come down, then, to the simple thought that something is an acceptable conceptual scheme or theory if it is true. ... And the criterion of a conceptual scheme different from our own now becomes: largely true but not translatable. The question whether this is a useful criterion is just the question how well we understand the notion of truth, as applied to language, independent of the notion of translation. The answer is, I think, that we do not understand it independently at all.[64]

Applying Davidson's argument to our concerns, we can conclude that, if there is a linguistic item that qualifies as a suitable expression of a given content y in one conceptual scheme, it is in principle possible to transport that expression into another conceptual scheme by translation.

Having defined an *actual* instance of expression by defining 'x expresses y,' we can now extend our definition to *possible* instances of expression: 'y is expressible if it can be expressed by some x.' However, there is a problem with the word 'can' that makes the content of this definition less clear than it at first appears. The problem is that we tacitly give a context-defining interpretation to the word 'can.' In an article on the foundations of mathematics, Friedrich Waismann touches on the problem of reading the word 'can' adequately. He raises the problem of how to establish that two sets *can* be paired-up in a one-to-one relation.[65] A possible answer would be that a set of cups and a set of spoons are equal in number if we can place exactly one spoon into each cup. Waismann then asks: what if the cups and the spoons are in different drawers and it is therefore impossible to place the spoons in the cups?, and provides the answer himself:

> One will reply that this was not the intention of the explanation; it does not depend on whether I actually place the spoons in the cups but whether I *can* place them in the cups. Very well! But what does the expression 'I can' mean here? Is it that I have to be physically able to distribute the spoons among the cups? This would be entirely uninteresting. Obviously, what we wish to say is that I can distribute the spoons among the cups because there are just as many samples of both sorts. That is, in order to recognize whether the correspondence is possible, I must already know that the sets are numerically equivalent.... The statement: 'The two sets *can* be associated to one another,' is being reinterpreted into the statement which is entirely distinct from it: 'The two sets *are* associated to one another,' which means, 'There is actually a relation which permits such a correspondence.'[66]

Waismann makes a crucial point in this section: the word 'can' (more precisely: the words 'can be') is tacitly reinterpreted as 'are'; a modal claim is read as an actual fact. Waismann's worry applies to all occurrences of 'can' where it is not clear from the context how 'can' should be interpreted.[67] When we say that 'y is expressible iff it can be expressed by some x,' it is not clear from the context how 'can' should be interpreted; so it requires clarification.

There are several different kinds of possibilities that the word 'can' can express: logical, metaphysical, nomological possibility come to mind.[68] Something, say P, is logically possible if and only if no contradiction can be derived from P (perhaps in conjunction with certain definitions) using the standard rules of deductive inference. Something is nomologically possible for a relevant body of (e.g., physical or biological) laws, if and only if P is consistent with the body of truths entailed by those laws. Metaphysical possibility is usually taken as a primitive, although it can be described in terms of 'how things might have been.'[69] These different kinds of possibilities are usually taken to differ in strength. Metaphysical possibility is a stronger notion of possibility than logical possibility because metaphysical possibility *implies* logical possibility. The reverse does not hold, that is, logical possibility does not imply metaphysical possibility. Likewise, nomological possibility implies metaphysical possibility (and thus also logical possibility), but metaphysical possibility does not imply nomological possibility. Why is this relevant to our discussion of ineffability?

It is relevant because our definition of 'expressibility' depends on the kind of possibility we take the word 'can' to signify. Thus, our definition of expressibility 'y is expressible iff it can be expressed by some x' can be read as (a) 'y is expressible iff it is logically possible that there be some x which expresses y'; or it can be read as (b) 'y is expressible iff it is metaphysically possible that there be some x which expresses y'; or it can be read as (c) 'y is expressible iff it is nomologically possible that there be some x which expresses y.' (a), (b), and (c) denote three very distinct extensions of 'can.' If we restrict our definition of expressibility to the nomological extension of 'can,' a nonlinguistic item y is expressible if it is nomologically possible for there to be a linguistic item x that expresses y. However, what if we are dealing with a highly complex nonlinguistic item, call it HC, whose expression is so complicated that it would take more than a human lifetime to express it? Then it would certainly be nomologically impossible to express HC and it would consequently count as ineffable. However, declaring a nonlinguistic item ineffable simply because of the complex structure its expression would require seems counterintuitive. Intuitively, there is also a clear sense in which HC is expressible, namely if only humans happened to live longer. Restricting our definition of expressibility to the nomological extension of 'can' seems too restrictive and is thus not a satisfactory definition.

What if we go for (c), the logical extension of 'can'? On that definition, HC would surely not count as ineffable because it is certainly logically possible that there be a being with a longer life-span than humans, that manages to express HC. However, I think that (c) is so permissive that it becomes vacuous; I cannot see how anything would turn out ineffable on that definition. It is always logically possible that there be an expression of any nonlinguistic item, unless, of course, the nonlinguistic item is already *defined* as ineffable—in this case, it is logically impossible to express it, but then it is also not an interesting kind of ineffability but a merely definitional one. It is not a case that provides any insight into the nature of ineffability.

In order to capture all the interesting instances of ineffability, our definition of expressibility should neither be vacuous nor too restrictive. It therefore seems to me that (b) employs the right extension of 'can': 'y is expressible iff it is metaphysically possible that there be some x which expresses y.' On that definition, a nonlinguistic item like HC would not count as ineffable merely because of the complexity of its expression.

Having clarified the difference between ineffability and indescribability, provided a definition of 'x expresses y', and explained the way in which the word 'can' is to be interpreted the sentence 'y is expressible if it can be expressed by some x,' we can now pin down the following definitions:

'x expresses y' x expresses y if and only if (i) x is a linguistic item with content that makes it either true or false, (ii) y is a nonlinguistic item with content that makes it either true or false, and (iii) the content of x nontrivially entails the content of y.

Expressibility x is expressible iff there exists an x such that x expresses y.

Ineffability A nonlinguistic item y is ineffable if and only if it is metaphysically impossible that there be a linguistic item x whose content nontrivially entails the content of y and whose content is, in principle, communicable to other finite beings by users of a finite language.[70]

It should be clear by now that what I will henceforth refer to as the 'philosophically interesting' or 'philosophically relevant' kinds of ineffability are all those cases in which an experience of ineffability is not due to trivial reasons (nescience, physical constraints, category mistakes). With the above definitions in place, we can now proceed to the examination of the metaphysical constitution of ineffability.

CHAPTER 3

INEFFABLE PROPERTIES AND OBJECTS

3.1 Why Ineffable Properties and Objects?

As we saw in the Introduction, it is not at all clear how we can give a metaphysical underpinning to the ways in which the concept of ineffability has been applied historically. This is because the term is used in slightly different ways that seem to point in different metaphysical directions. Sometimes, for example in religious contexts, a person's *experience* is called ineffable. This is ontologically noncommittal, given that we can think of all kinds of unmysterious, that is, ontologically neutral reasons for why an experience might be impossible to express. We can think here about the cases of irrelevant ineffability*: if someone has an experience of ineffability because he is temporarily out of words to articulate what he wants to say, but remembers the appropriate words after a few seconds and expresses whatever he wanted to express, then there is nothing mysterious about it. We wouldn't start wondering if some hitherto unknown entity, such as an ineffable property or an ineffable truth, were responsible for his lack of words.

The historical references to ineffability I am concerned with, however, are different. They carry much more ontological weight, for example when reality, some of its aspects, its essence, its entirety (referred to as 'the Absolute,' 'the One,' or 'the Whole'), its origin, or its first principle (God, 'the Will') are declared ineffable. Think of Laozi, who holds that the Dao, the world's fundamental principle and essence, is beyond any characterization, or Maimonides, who argues that no expression can ever capture the nature of God, or Adorno, who even goes so far as to claim that philosophy's only effort is to express the Nonidentical, the most important aspect of reality, which, however, remains forever beyond expression.

How are we to make sense of these ways of speaking? In what follows, I will begin with an examination of the term 'the Absolute' and I will assume that this concept is coextensive with 'the Whole,' the 'Infinite,' Plotinus' 'One,' Schopenhauer's 'Will,' etc. (More on this will follow shortly. Since I don't want to take theism as a given, I will leave open the question whether the Absolute is to be identified with God.)

The question now is: if there is such a thing as the Absolute, what does it mean for it to be ineffable? Aren't we calling it 'Absolute' and aren't we ascribing the property of absoluteness to it? More generally, what could it mean for an object or entity, no matter what size or material, to be ineffable? Didn't we establish in the Introduction that objects are not the kinds of entity that are expressible in the first place, so that calling them ineffable would be nothing but a category mistake?

In what follows, we will take a closer look at the historical references to the Absolute and we will try to get a rough idea of how to make sense of the respective ineffability claims. I suggest a reading on which calling the Absolute 'ineffable' is coherent with ascribing the descriptive property of absoluteness to it. The property of absoluteness then provides the segue to a more general discussion of what it could mean for an object to be ineffable.

I show that there are two principle ways in which the idea of an ineffable object can be fleshed out metaphysically: either there are properties that render their objects ineffable; or there are objects that are bare of any properties and therefore ineffable. The former notion is discussed within the context of contemporary theories of haecceity; the latter notion is examined with regard to some current debates about bare particulars.

I suggest that it is questionable whether such things as haecceities and bare particulars actually exist, and that, even if they could be shown to exist, they would be insufficient to account for a metaphysics of ineffability as experienced in aesthetic, religious, and philosophical contexts.

3.2 Absoluteness

Numerous philosophers throughout the long history of metaphysical speculation have invoked a most mysterious, capitalized object, an object instantiating an equally mysterious and unique property: absoluteness. Sometimes this object is referred to as 'the Absolute,' sometimes as 'the One,' 'the Whole,' 'the Infinite,' or even 'the Will'. It is possible that those who refer to the object as 'the One' would consider the term 'Absolute' a misnomer, and those who prefer calling it 'the Infinite' might reject the term 'the Whole'. However, their characterization of this most unique object are similar enough to justify the assumption that it is one and the same conception of an object that is being talked about, something that encompasses "everything there is." Thus, I will henceforth speak only of the 'Absolute' and its property of 'being absolute,' and I will consider it to be synonymous with 'the Whole,' 'the Infinite,' the 'One,' etc.

The roots of the word 'Absolute' are Latin, 'absolutus' being the past participle of 'absolvere' ('to loosen from,' 'to detach,' 'to complete'). It can be paraphrased as 'not dependent on,' 'not conditional on,' 'not relative to anything else,' 'not restricted by anything else,' and also as 'self-contained,' 'perfect' or 'complete'.[1] Since its first use as a noun in Nicolas of Cusa's work *De Docta Ignorantia* (1440), the term 'Absolutum' has sometimes been used as a transliteration equivalent to 'God'. More than 300 years later, German philosophers started to use the term also as a name for 'the ultimate reality as a whole.' Hegel, for example, thought that there must be something absolute, something that—unlike the rest of reality—is not dependent on anything else. For him, the Absolute is the philosophical expression of God, yet an expression without anthropomorphic connotations. Moreover, it is completely unconditioned: first, because it is independent of anything else, and second, because it overcomes all restrictions by unifying things (concepts, objects, ideas).

Let's look at a few examples illustrating the role that the Absolute plays in religious and aesthetic contexts:

> overcoming … all the usual barriers between the individual and the Absolute is the great mystic achievement. In mystic states we both become one with the Absolute and we become aware of our oneness. This is the everlasting and triumphant mystical tradition, hardly altered by differences of clime or creed. In Hinduism, in Neoplatonism, in Sufism, in Christian mysticism, in Whitmanism, we find the same recurring note, so that there is about mystical utterances an eternal unanimity which ought to make a critic stop and think, and which brings it about that the mystical classics have, as has been said, neither birthday nor native land.[2]

In this passage, William James points out the cross-cultural relevance of the Absolute as a mystical–religious concept. In religious contexts, the Absolute is often used synonymously with God. However, the concept is not only relevant in religious contexts. Also art, specifically music, is sometimes seen as an expression of the Absolute. We can think of Schopenhauer's boundless admiration for instrumental music, which he considers to be "an expression of the world" and therefore, a "universal language":

> to the man who gives himself up entirely to the impression of a symphony, it is as if he saw all the possible events of life and of the world passing by within himself. Yet *if he reflects, he cannot assert any likeness between that piece of music and the things that passed through his mind.* For, as we have said, music differs from all the other arts by the fact that it is not a copy of the phenomenon, or,

more exactly, of the [W]ill's adequate objectivity, but is directly a copy of the [W]ill itself, and therefore expresses the metaphysical to everything physical in the world, the thing-in-itself to every phenomenon. Accordingly, we could just as well call the world embodied music as embodied will.³

Note the implied ineffability claim (in italics). The capacity of expressing the otherwise inexpressible "quintessence of life" (the 'Will,' or in my preferred terminology, the 'Absolute') is the reason Schopenhauer considers music the most superior form of art.

These are only two small examples but they are representative for a whole class of references to an Absolute in philosophical and religious writings throughout hundreds of years of philosophical history.⁴ The crucial question now is: How are we to understand the claim that the Absolute is ineffable? After all, aren't we successfully referring to it as 'the Absolute,' and aren't we ascribing the property of absoluteness to it? If so, what does its ineffability consist in? In order to understand the ineffability claim involved here, a little bit of history will be helpful.

In Neoplatonic and Daoist writings we find the claim that there is an Absolute (Oneness/One/Whole, etc.), which *underlies* all metaphysical reality. Its ineffability is explained in terms of this unique metaphysical status. Laozi phrases this as follows:

> No characterization can fully capture Dao; the Dao would immediately transcend any characterization, so that it would not be identified with any thing or any aspect of things in the world. In this sense Dao is simply no-thing, beyond our conceptualization or delimination.⁵

Similarly Plotinus:

> The One is in truth beyond all statement: any affirmation is of a thing; but the all-transcending, resting above even the most august divine Mind, possesses alone of all true being, and is not a thing among things; we can give it no name because that would imply predication: we can but try to indicate, in our own feeble way, something concerning it.⁶

The basic assumption of these arguments is that everything there is is characterized by a metaphysical hierarchy of existence, that is, some form of priority-relation amongst all existing things: whatever existing things there are, their existence depends on the existence of other existing things. Only what lies at the very top⁷ of the metaphysical hierarchy, the Absolute, does not depend for its existence on anything else. It exists necessarily and grounds the existence of all other things. Ben-Ami Scharfstein puts it as follows: "The hierarchies therefore have a single basic direction, that of the power of existence passing 'down' from the absolute unity (if such it is conceived to be) to the variety of things successively 'below' it."[8]

To Neoplatonists like Plotinus, the Absolute (or the "One," as he calls it) is metaphysically prior to anything else. This is because a world in which Oneness is not fundamental is inconceivable. Without Oneness, it would be impossible to conceive of the unity and identity of the things that make up the world. It would also be impossible to conceive of numbers: since all numbers are multiples of the number one, it is impossible to conceive of any numbers at all without having first mastered the concept 'one.' However, this Oneness is considered ineffable because—so it is argued—

> words necessarily describe a world of differences and limitations, in which thought is possible only if the thinker is split from the object of his thought. ... The consequence is that every description we give of the One is inaccurate and must be understood as though modified by the words as if.[9]

The general thought here is that one cannot predicate anything of the thing that is supposedly composed of everything. This could be interpreted as follows: given that the Absolute is composed of everything there is, all predicates there are apply to the Absolute: if the Absolute contains an apple and a dog and the color green, then there is a sense in which the concepts of applehood, doghood, and greenness all apply to the Absolute. However, if all predicates apply to the Absolute, then for each predicate that applies to it, also its negation applies. Hence, assertions about the Absolute are necessarily contradictory.

Kant famously argues for a similar claim: he holds that we cannot meaningfully (i.e., consistently) speak of the Absolute (Kant actually speaks of the 'world as a whole') due to the way our cognitive apparatus is built:

> In whatever way and through whatever means a cognition may relate to objects, that through which it relates immediately to them, and at which all thought as a means is directed as an end, is intuition. This, however, takes place only insofar as the object is given to us; but this in turn, is possible only if it affects the mind in a certain way. The capacity (receptivity) to acquire representations through the way in which we are affected by objects is called sensibility. Objects are therefore given to us by means of sensibility, and it alone affords us intuitions; but they are thought through the understanding, and from it arise concepts. But all thought, whether straightaway (directe) or through a detour (indirecte), must ultimately be related to intuitions, thus, in our case, to sensibility, since there is no other way in which objects can be given to us.[10]

Kant here argues that, since we can only relate to objects via our intuition, the objects in the external world ("things-in-themselves") can only be objects of thought but not objects of knowledge. The thing in itself can be *thought of* as that which is causing our minds to have appearances but it cannot be *known* to play that role because we cannot relate to it in an unmediated way. Hence, we cannot know the mind-independent world "as it is." Kant does not mean to say that the external world is illusory or does not exist. It is perfectly real, for he defines the 'Real' as that which exercises "a degree of influence on sense."[11]

Kant's empirical realism thus preserves the ordinary independence and reality of objects of the world, while his transcendental idealism enables him to claim that properties of concrete objects (like their causal powers and their spatial and temporal properties) are determined by our minds. They are so determined because human understanding imposes "categories" like causality and dependence, unity and plurality upon the manifold of experience.[12] In addition to this, two forms of pure intuition structure our sensations into the experience of things in space and time.[13] Space and time are thus not features of the world as it is but they are *a priori* necessary conditions for any human experience whatsoever. Thus, the objects of ordinary experience are empirically real but transcendentally ideal: they are not to be identified with anything that lies beyond, and thus transcends, the bounds of possible experience.

It is on this background that we must understand Kant's claim that questions of metaphysics are legitimate only insofar as they don't relate to objects that transcend all possible experience. If we want to avoid illusory and contradictory claims, we must restrict metaphysics to objects we can intuit under the *a priori* conditions of space and time. This means that we have to resist the urge to make claims not only about things-in-themselves, but also about all other non-sensible objects, for example, the world as a whole.[14]

Applying this Kantian picture to our discussion of ineffability, we can now make sense of the claim that the Absolute is ineffable as follows: once we assert something of it, we necessarily utter a contradiction. We cannot make assertions about something that transcends all possible experience. Similarly for God: for Kant, God is a regulative ideal, an unconditional wholeness-principle of all conditioned things (in his practical philosophy also a "postulate"). As such, God can be defined as "ens realissimum," "ens entium," etc. Considered as a postulate, God is furthermore creator, author, judge, etc. Hence, according to Kant, *definitions* of these terms are possible, yet noncontradictory assertions about their objective existence or nonexistence are not.

It is now possible to dissolve the contradiction we identified at the beginning of this discussion: how can the Absolute be ineffable if we manage to refer to it and even know of one property that applies to it, that is, absoluteness? The answer is: we can define the Absolute as that to which all predicates apply. But since all predicates apply to it, none of them apply in a noncontradictory way: for each predicate, also its negation applies. Hence, we cannot assert anything meaningful about the Absolute, and we have thus found a coherent way to call a particular object, that is, the Absolute, ineffable without immediately contradicting ourselves.

In opposition to Kant, Hegel famously rejects the claim that we cannot meaningfully speak of the Absolute. He thinks it perfectly conceivable that cognition provides access to the Absolute, but given that, for him, the Absolute is a dynamic concept, it requires a lot of dialectical thinking to get a full grasp of it:

> Of the Absolute it must be said that it is essentially a result, that only in the end is it what it truly is; and that precisely in this consists its nature, viz. to be actual, subject, the spontaneous becoming itself. Though it may seem contradictory that the Absolute should be conceived essentially as a result, it needs little pondering to set this show of contradiction in its true light. The beginning, the principle, or the Absolute, as at first immediately enunciated, is only the universal. Just as when I say 'all animals,' this expression cannot pass for a zoology, so it is equally plain that the words, 'the Divine,' 'the Absolute,' 'the Eternal,' etc., do not express what is contained in them.[15]

Hegel's entire philosophical project can be understood as one long and intricate attempt of expressing the Absolute. As Michael Inwood puts it:

> Hegel concludes that the [A]bsolute is not something underlying the phenomenal world, but the conceptual system embedded in it. Since this conceptual system is not static, but develops, manifesting itself both at successively higher levels of nature and in the advance of human knowledge over history, the [A]bsolute is not static, but developing, and reaches its final stage in Hegel's own philosophy.[16]

The problem many philosophers have with Hegel's dialectical thinking is that it seems to require us to accept contradictory claims as true. In the *Encyclopaedia*, he gives the following description of his methodology:

> In point of form Logical doctrine has three sides: (α) the Abstract side, or that of understanding; (β) the Dialectical, or that of negative reason; (γ) the Speculative, or that of positive reason. (α) Thought, as Understanding, sticks to fixity of characters and their distinctness from one another: every such limited abstract it treats as having a subsistence and being of its own. ... (β) In the Dialectical stage these finite characterizations or formulae supersede themselves, and pass into their opposites. ... (γ) The Speculative stage, or stage of Positive Reason, apprehends the unity of terms (propositions) in their opposition—the affirmative, which is involved in their disintegration and in their transition.[17]

As we can see, the transition from (α) to (β) occurs in form of antinomies. For example, if one attempts to conceptualize the Absolute within the framework of Understanding (i.e., in conformance with the law of noncontradiction), the result will be an antinomy to the effect that both of the following two propositions hold: 'The Absolute is finite' and 'The Absolute is infinite'. Only on the next stage, the Dialectical stage, can these finite characterizations be superseded so that we can make sense of the antinomy: we understand that the Absolute is both finite and infinite. The transition from (β) to (γ) occurs in form of determinate negation, the step from negation to negation of negation, through which we overcome the contradictoriness of our experiences and thought determinations. If determinate negation didn't function in this essential role, our experiences would be nothing more than a continuous accumulation of perceptual facts. However, with the help of determinate negation, our experiences can go beyond the collection of perceptual facts: the discrepancies between concepts and truths together with their sublation lift our thought up to a higher level of knowledge. On the final level, we reach the Absolute.

Within the framework of Hegelian metaphysics, this dialectical method makes sense (perhaps). However, contemporary standards of logical stringency won't allow such Hegelian moves. In other words: if the Absolute can only be expressed by means of contradictory claims, as Hegel seems to argue, then this does not count as proper expression in the eyes of most contemporary philosophers. The reason for this is simply that contradictions are not taken to express anything definite (except falsehoods). In addition to that, it is well-known that everything follows from a contradiction. Logically speaking, then, everything can be inferred from a contradictory expression. And an expression from which everything (p, ¬p, the Absolute, the non-Absolute, etc.) can be inferred is not a meaningful expression. We can thus conclude that Hegel's claim that the Absolute is, in fact, expressible, does not meet the requirements for expression as we understand them today.

So as things stand now, we came up with a possible interpretation of the initial ineffability claim, namely, the idea that the Absolute might be considered ineffable because all possible predicates apply to it: if all possible predicates apply to an object, then for every predicate P also its negation ¬P applies to it, which makes meaningful predication impossible. This gives us a straightforward interpretation of the claim that there exists an Absolute that is ineffable.

I will now proceed to discuss a major problem for this interpretation. The problem is that it is reasonable to assume that the Absolute instantiates the property 'being absolute' or 'absoluteness'. And as a matter of definition, this property is only instantiated by one object, namely the

Absolute, which is the only object that does not stand in a metaphysical dependence-relation to anything else. However, this conflicts with the view that all predicates, and hence, their negations, apply to the Absolute. If the Absolute instantiates the property of absoluteness but not the property of not-absoluteness, then it instantiates at least one property without instantiating also its negation. Thus, meaningful predication is possible in at least one case. And this, in turn, means that the alleged ineffability of the Absolute cannot be accounted for by claiming that only contradictory, that is, meaningless, predications about it are possible.

A defender of an ineffable Absolute might grant that we can meaningfully predicate absoluteness to the Absolute. However, he could then rejoin that it is precisely this mysterious property that somehow accounts for the ineffability of the Absolute. Let's take a moment to try and spell out this idea. If the Absolute instantiates both P and its negation for all possible properties except the property of absoluteness, then absoluteness cannot be a qualitative property. This is because for all qualitative properties there exists a negation. Absoluteness can also not be a relational property because relational properties signify dependence, whereas absoluteness is the property of not standing in any dependence relation. So absoluteness must be a nonqualitative and nonrelational property.[18] At the same time, absoluteness is the predicate that uniquely picks out the Absolute: all other predicates arguably apply to other objects as well.

This brings us to the first intermediate result: the property of absoluteness must be a nonqualitative, nonrelational property, which uniquely identifies the Absolute and which somehow accounts for its alleged ineffability. For some, this characterization rings a familiar bell. There have indeed been attempts to argue for the existence of a class of nonqualitative properties that account for the unique individuality of particular objects. These properties have come to be known as 'haecceities'. Thus, it must be the Absolute's *haecceity* that somehow accounts for its ineffability.

The Absolute is, by definition, the existent that grounds (or crowns) the entire metaphysical hierarchy of existents. Precisely because it is prior to all other individuals, none of the predicates applicable to other existents are applicable to it, which is one reason why it can be considered ineffable. One might say that what distinguishes absoluteness from haecceities is that the former was not invented to individuate otherwise exactly similar objects. Rather, absoluteness implies that only one object can be the bearer of it. This, however, is equally true for all haecceities: each haecceity can only be instantiated by one particular object. Absoluteness is a property designed to single out one specific individual without making any reference to qualitative or relational properties. So it is reasonable to assume that absoluteness is nothing else but the haecceity of one particular object, namely, the Absolute. The fact that only one object instantiates the property of absoluteness can explain why we tend to find the individual singled out by it much more interesting than the individuals singled out by haecceities. But in the end, on this picture, absoluteness also is nothing but a haecceity.

In what follows, we will take a look at the concept of haecceities and raise the question whether the metaphysics of ineffability can be explained in terms of them. I will suggest a number of reasons why we should not believe in the existence of haecceities. Consequently, we should also not believe in an ineffable Absolute.

3.3 Haecceities

Haecceities are defined as those properties that account for an object's individuality. This is especially relevant in the absence of any other distinguishing features. In fact, even though defenders of haecceities believe that *all* objects have them, they were actually invented to account for the fact (if it is a fact) that indiscernible objects are not identical. The term 'haecceity' has first been introduced by Duns Scotus in his *Ordinatio II*. It stems from the Latin word *haec*, which means 'this'. Thus, haecceities are also sometimes referred to as 'thisnesses'. They are opposed to 'quiddities' (i.e., 'whatnesses'; from the Latin *quid*, meaning 'what'). Quiddities are those qualitative properties characterizing an object that can be shared by other objects. The term has since been picked up by other philosophers as well: Charles Sanders Peirce uses the term 'haecceity' to refer to an individual nondescriptively[19], David Kaplan uses the term to discuss questions of transworld-identity in the context of Leibniz's philosophy,[20] etc.

An object's haecceity individuates an object even if that object shares all of its qualitative and relational properties with other objects. We can define haecceities as follows:

Haecceitiy If object a and object b are two distinct objects, even if a and b have exactly the same qualitative and relational properties, a's haecceity is the property responsible for the fact that $a = a$ and $a \neq b$.[21]

This definition entails that haecceities are nonqualitative properties. Their nonqualitative nature accounts for the fact that haecceities are considered ineffable: it is impossible to determinately refer to something that doesn't have qualities—no predicate or negation of a predicate is suitable for that. Now, if it were possible to make a strong case for the existence of haecceities, then the nature of ineffability as experienced in aesthetic, religious, and philosophical contexts could potentially be explained in terms of them. The ineffable qualities of a Mahler symphony, it could be argued, or of a painting by Bacon might be due to their individual haecceities, that is, due to the specific property on which their very individuality rests.

Put differently, if haecceities existed, then, given the fact that they are incommunicable, explaining ineffability in terms of them would stand to reason. Of course, it would still remain to be shown that a theory of ineffability based on haecceities would actually manage to explain all the cases of ineffability that I have identified as the philosophically relevant ones. In other words, it would require an elaborate argument to the effect that it is *haecceities* that are ultimately accountable for ineffable aesthetic, religious, and philosophical experiences. However, in light of my arguments for the nonexistence of haecceities, taking this second step won't be necessary.

The strongest argument in favour of haecceities emerges from the debate about the principle of the Identity of Indiscernibles ($\forall F(Fx \leftrightarrow Fy) \rightarrow x = y$), and its converse, the principle of the Indiscernibility of Identicals ($x = y \rightarrow \forall F(Fx \leftrightarrow Fy)$). According to the former, two objects are identical if they share all their properties; according to the latter, if two objects are identical, then they share all of their properties. It is the conjunction of these two principles that has become known as Leibniz's Law.[22]

The above formulations don't tell us anything about what exactly is meant by a property, however. Philosophers have drawn distinctions between intrinsic and extrinsic properties, essential and accidental properties, pure and impure properties, qualitative and nonqualitative properties, etc. Properties can thus be distinguished in numerous (sometimes only subtly different) ways. However, nothing in my argument depends on how exactly these fine distinctions are drawn, so to keep things as simple as possible, I will henceforth distinguish between *qualitative* properties (such as the firmness of wood or the sweetness of sugar) and *relational* properties (such as being-left-of something or being-taller-than someone) without trying to provide definite answers for controversial cases such as, for example, having-a-proper-part or being-Obama's-daughter (which might be understood both as qualitative and relational properties) or being-a-cat-lover (which is relational but doesn't involve a relation to a *particular* cat).

The principle of the Identity of Indiscernibles, that is, the first part of Leibniz's Law, implies that, in order to be distinct, two objects must differ with regard to at least one property. Given the above distinction between qualitative and relational properties, this allows for at least three readings, namely that distinct objects must differ either with respect to (at least one of) their qualitative properties, or with respect to (at least one of) their relational properties, or both. Ordinary, medium-sized objects typically differ with regard to both qualitative and relational properties: cats and tables, for example, are made of different materials and occupy different spatiotemporal regions. However, we can imagine cases of qualitatively identical objects that differ only with respect to their relational properties (clones, for example, or other examples of completely identical replicas).[23] If we want Leibniz's Law to apply to these cases as well, then we must give it a weaker reading: in order to be distinct, two objects must differ either with regard to at least one qualitative or one relational property.

Its spatiotemporal location and other relational properties can help to uniquely identify a particular object. In fact, as Russell famously argues, nomic and causal relations are the main features in terms of which objects and events are characterized in physics.[24] Nevertheless, relational properties have the disadvantage of not providing solutions for symmetrical setups. The most famous example for such a case has been provided by Max Black, who argues as follows:

> Isn't it logically possible that the universe should have contained nothing but two exactly similar spheres? We might suppose that each was made of chemically pure iron, had a diameter of one mile, that they had the same temperature, colour, and so on, and that nothing else existed. Then every quality and relational characteristic of the one would also be a property of the other. Now if what I am describing is logically possible, it is not impossible for two things to have all their properties in common. This seems to me to refute the principle [of the Identity of Indiscernibles].[25]

Black suggests a particular example of a world in which the principle of the Identity of Indiscernibles does not apply, but clearly there is an entire class of worlds where it does not hold, namely all worlds composed of nothing but qualitatively identical objects (same size, temperature, color, material, etc.) whose shape and arrangement is perfectly symmetrical (e.g., three identical spheres arranged in an equilateral triangle, four identical cubes arranged cube-wise, 100 spheres arranged in a circle, etc.). In all of these worlds, the existing objects share all of their qualitative and all of their relational properties. Now, according to the principle of the Identity of Indiscernibles, objects that have no distinguishing features are identical—but we know, of course, that, by stipulation, there are more than one object in these worlds. We therefore need to find a distinguishing feature of these objects that will allow us to establish their numerical difference.

Haecceities provide a neat solution to this problem. They are, as it were, properties whose sole purpose is to ensure the nonidentity of two qualitatively indiscernible objects: if object a and object b are two distinct objects, and if a and b share all their qualitative and relational properties, a's haecceity is the property responsible for the fact that $a = a$ and $a \neq b$.

The case for haecceities can further be supported semantically by arguments from direct reference: given that we often succeed in referring to individuals without knowing any of their qualitative properties (e.g., by means of proper names or indexical expressions), shouldn't we believe that there is something over and above the sum of an individual's qualitative and relational properties that uniquely identifies it (and makes such direct reference possible)? Even though semantic arguments only provide ancillary support for the existence of metaphysically substantial haecceities (as Robert Adams points out, haecceities could very well be *semantic* primitives without being metaphysically primitive, i.e., they might ultimately be analyzable into standard qualitative properties),[26] it is worth being aware of this additional explanatory potential.

So we have good prima facie reasons to believe that haecceities exist because they seem to be the only way to distinguish numerically different yet otherwise identical objects. In what follows, I will go through a number of arguments against the existence of haecceities.

Starting with a consideration in a somewhat Ockhamian spirit, one may want to ask oneself what one really gains by the postulation of haecceities. As we have just seen, haecceities enable us to describe possible worlds made up of qualitatively and relationally indistinguishable objects. They achieve this by making every object uniquely identifiable, independently of their properties. This, in turn, guarantees that the objects can be considered numerically distinct, even under the principle of the Identity of Indiscernibles. Hence, haecceities provide a way to render qualitatively and relationally identical, numerically distinct objects coherent with the principle of the Identity of Indiscernibles. Without haecceities, the principle would seem to force us to consider the two spheres of Black's world as one and the same sphere because they are qualitatively and relationally indistinguishable.

The question is, however: should we really be so concerned about preserving the principle of the Identity of Indiscernibles for those worlds? What do we gain from that? Are haecceities the only way of squaring the principle with Black's world? The price we pay for the postulation of haecceities is quite substantial: we are not only postulating a whole new class of metaphysical entities (if haecceities exist, then every object has one!) for the sole purpose of describing a very small and outlandish subset of possible worlds; we are also postulating a new *type* of formerly unknown property, namely nonqualitative, indescribable properties. This seems like a huge effort for the—relatively—small gain of being able to give a metaphysical underpinning to a very small number of artificial possible worlds.

One way to avoid such a substantial commitment is, of course, to simply drop the principle of the Identity of Indiscernibles, or in other words, to allow the existence of distinct yet indistinguishable objects. One argument in favour of this strategy is that we are, after all, perfectly capable to give coherent descriptions of those worlds based on which our doubts about the principle arose in the first place, for example, Black's two-spheres world. And if we are able to give a coherent description of a world, shouldn't that be reason enough to allow the possible existence of such a world?

The problem with such a deflationary move is that it is unclear what a coherent description amounts to. To illuminate the problem, let's take a moment to think about the following world description: imagine a possible world where a team of archaeologists finds a very ancient cave in the middle of a rock in the middle of a desert. On the wall of that cave they find an ancient inscription, which turns out to be a logical proof of Frege's Basic Law V. The description of this world is perfectly coherent; we have no trouble imagining a proof inscribed on a cave wall. However, we know that this world is impossible because we know there can never be a logical proof of what has been shown to be contradictory. The point of this example is that we should be cautious when it comes to imagining and describing possible worlds: it may well be that we can give a coherent-sounding description of a world that actually contains a hidden incoherence.

The question now is whether Max Black's two-spheres world is indeed a world that contains a hidden incoherence, a question that is difficult to answer. It is much harder to come to a conclusion about whether something is metaphysically possible than whether something is logically possible: whatever is logically possible is logically provable, but there is no equivalent proof-method for metaphysical possibilities. Hence, whether we accept or reject a world like Black's world depends on whether our description of that world can withstand our metaphysical scrutiny. And whether Black's world does withstand metaphysical scrutiny depends, in turn, on our intuitions about the principle of the Identity of Indiscernibles.

We can thus note that haecceities might be unnecessary if we are willing to give up the principle of the Identity of Indiscernibles, which in turn depends on our metaphysical intuitions. For those who are reluctant to abandon the principle, I will now discuss two further worries about haecceities. These worries provide some reason to reject haecceities independently of the principle of the Identity of Indiscernibles.

The first worry is that haecceities lack the explanatory value they are supposed to have. The objection is that haecceities, though stipulated to enable individuation, in fact only achieve to *highlight* the problem they were supposed to *solve*. Recall that haecceities are defined as those entities that account for the individuality of numerically distinct objects in the absence of any other distinguishing features. In other words, haecceities account for the fact (if it is a fact) that two objects can be completely identical yet distinct.

Now, on closer inspection it seems unclear that haecceities actually provide a solution to the problem of individuation because of a well-hidden, but nevertheless vicious, circularity in the metaphysical order of things. Here it is:

1. (Premise) Properties are instantiated by individuals.
2. (Premise) If something instantiates a property, it is an individual.
3. (Premise) Haecceities are nonqualitative properties that guarantee individuality.
4. (From 3) If something instantiates a haecceity, it instantiates a property.
5. (From 2 and 3) If something instantiates a haecceity, it is an individual.
6. (From 4 and 5) Only individuals instantiate haecceities.
7. (From 3 and 6) Haecceities guarantee individuality to the individuals that instantiate them.
8. (Conclusion from 7) Haecceities presuppose what they are meant to account for.

The problem here is not that the property of being an individual and the haecceity property are necessarily co-instantiated. Rather, what we are facing here is a problem of metaphysical priority. Haecceities establish distinctness between otherwise indistinguishable individuals. Yet if haecceities can only be instantiated by individuals, then in order for us to be able to claim that an object instantiates an haecceity, *we already have to know* that the object is an individual. This is just a different way of saying that haecceities don't add significant information to the picture of individuation.

We can only posit that objects have distinct haecceities on the assumption that these objects are distinct. So the distinct haecceities can't then be a reason to think that the objects are distinct. That is, the distinct haecceities can't justify the conclusion that the objects are distinct if we can only attribute distinct haecceities to objects we've already presupposed to be distinct.

Imagine once again Max Black's two-spheres world, and imagine further a complete list of all the stuff in that world: a sphere made of solid iron, three metres away from a sphere made of solid iron, which is in turn three metres away from a sphere made of solid iron, which is in turn three metres away from a sphere made of solid iron, etc. (Note that the list does not contain any information on the number of objects in this world—providing that information in the descriptive list would beg the question, given that we are looking for whatever it is that establishes distinctness between otherwise indistinguishable objects.) Now, can we determine from such a list how many things there actually are in Black's world? No, we cannot. The descriptive list is true of all worlds with two, three, four, ..., infinite indistinguishable spheres.[27] In order to determine the actual number of objects in Black's world, we need the additional information that there are *two* spheres. But haecceities don't give us that information. Saying that their haecceities distinguish the individuals in Black's world from one another is only enlightening if this is read in conjunction with the postulation that there are two, rather than one, or one hundred, things. But establishing distinctness was precisely what haecceities were invoked for in the first place! Hence, the explanatory value of haecceities is questionable.

A second worry about haecceities relates to their indeterminacy. The worry is simply that haecceities cannot be distinguished from one another, that is, they cannot be individuated. Let's think of the world solely constituted of Black's two identical spheres again and let's refer to those spheres as A and B. Then the question arises whether the haecceities attributed to A and B can themselves be distinguished from one another. As it turns out, they cannot. Given that haecceities are, by definition, nonqualitative properties, a defender of haecceities can't evoke a qualitative property that distinguishes A's haecceity from B's haecceity. It is also not an option to distinguish A's haecceity from B's haecceity by reference to the individuals instantiating them, given that A and B, as a matter of metaphysical priority, only "receive" their individuality through their respective haecceities.

Yet without identifying a distinguishing mark, A's and B's haecceities cannot be meaningfully argued to be distinct entities, and thus, remain completely indeterminate: to the extent that we have any grasp at all of what is meant by an object's 'thisness,' every object possesses it.[28] In order to eliminate this indeterminacy, the only way left for a defender of haecceities would be to argue that A's and B's haecceities instantiate some sort of second-order haecceity themselves, which in turn guarantees their individuality. However, besides the fact that the mere notion of a second-order haecceity is bewildering, second-order haecceities would face the exact same problem as their first-order cousins: they would have to be individuated as well, yet we wouldn't have any qualitative property that could help us achieve that, and so forth, ad infinitum.

INEFFABLE PROPERTIES AND OBJECTS

These objections might not be considered fully decisive refutations of haecceities by someone who wanted to insist on their existence. However, they definitely manage to highlight that there are substantive ontological costs, and only questionable advantages, to such a postulation.

Where do these considerations leave us? I have outlined some reasons to believe that haecceities do not achieve their purpose of establishing individuality for otherwise indistinguishable objects. Examples like Max Black's two-spheres world are intuitively compelling cases for the need of haecceities. Yet, on a closer look, we can see that our descriptions of such worlds are either insufficient to pick out a definite world (this is true for descriptions not containing explicit information about the number of objects present), or they foreclose the number of objects present. Consequently, descriptions of Black-worlds are either incomplete and thus indeterminate, in which case also the postulation of haecceities does not add the desired information, or they are complete and determinate, in which case the postulation of haecceities is only a restatement of the initially given information of how many objects are present.

I shall conclude this section on haecceities with a quote by Ian Hacking:

> Whatever God might create, we are clever enough to describe it in such a way that the identity of indiscernibles is preserved. This is a fact not about God but about description, space, time, and the laws that we ascribe to nature.[29]

If we are looking for a way to make sense of the notion of an ineffable object, turning to haecceities does not look like a promising route. This also relates back to our initial example of an ineffable Absolute: if the property of absoluteness instantiated by the Absolute is, in fact, nothing but its haecceity (I have argued as to why it is reasonable to assume this), then absoluteness faces the same difficulties as any other haecceity. Consequently, haecceities don't provide the metaphysics for an ineffable Absolute, and neither for any other occurrences of ineffability.

However, as I mentioned at the beginning of this chapter, there is one further reason why an object might be called ineffable: it might not instantiate any property if at all. In the following section, I will examine a close relative of haecceities, bare particulars, and the potential of this notion of enlightening our search for a metaphysics of ineffability.

3.4 Bare Particulars

It should be clear by now that haecceities, and presumably any other conceivable non-qualitative, ineffable property, suffer from the defect of being indeterminate and hence, impossible to individuate. This renders the prospect of explaining the ineffability of allegedly ineffable objects in terms of ineffable properties unattractive. However, there is another potential reason, besides ineffable properties, why an object might be ineffable: it might not instantiate any properties at all. Hence, the object is ineffable because nothing can be predicated of it.

The idea of objects entirely devoid of properties has been discussed with regards to metaphysical questions about the relationship between objects and their properties. Defenders of what has come to be known as the *substratum theory* hold that objects and their properties, or more substantially, particulars and their universals, are separate entities: particulars instantiate universals. They are *characterized* but not *exhausted* by the universals they instantiate. Opponents of this view defend what is now commonly referred to as the *bundle theory* of universals, according to which particulars are exhausted by their universals: they are *nothing but* bundles of universals. The disagreement between substratum and bundle theorists is thus over the question of what is left of an object when we subtract its universals: according to the bundle theorist, nothing is left. According to the substratum theorist, a universal-free, completely naked particular is left. This particular, labelled 'bare particular,' 'naked particular,' or 'thin particular,' was invented to solve the problem of individuation of otherwise identical objects. In other words, bare particulars are the counterpart to haecceities, only on the level of objects instead of on the level of properties. These allegedly property-less particulars have been the cause of some controversy.

The main issue regarding bare particulars is whether one can make sense of a particular independently of the universals it instantiates. Bundle theorists think that this is impossible. Particulars are characterized by their universals, and nothing but their universals. Take those away, and the particular itself disappears. Substratum theorists, on the other hand, are convinced that there is no problem in thinking of a particular independently of its universals.

One of the most passionate recent defenders of bare particulars is Ted Sider.[30] He professes to be very annoyed with complaints about bare particulars[31] and then goes on to discuss several formulations of the central complaint, which is the alleged mysteriousness of their nature in the absence of any properties.[32]

He first rejects the complaint that bare particulars have no properties with what he calls a "flat-footed" response: bare particulars do have properties, namely those they instantiate (in their non-naked state). Hence, there is nothing mysterious about their nature.

This is, of course, a somewhat simplistic depiction of the bundle-theorist's argument. Sider knows this and proceeds to a formulation of the objection that comes somewhat closer to the real concern, which is that bare particulars have no properties *in themselves*.[33] Sider considers several versions of this worry, the first one being that bare particulars have no intrinsic nature. His answer to this is, again flat-footed, that the intrinsic nature of a particular is determined by the monadic universals it instantiates. This response, however, doesn't take into account a central point of the discussion, which is the question whether we can identify a particular's nature *independently of the universals instantiated by it*. To this question, Sider's flat-footed response is no response at all.

Finally, he reformulates the bundle theorist's worry as a worry about essence: how should we make sense of an essence if it is not characterized by properties? Sider's initial answer to this worry is, again, rather short: "could it not be part of a [bare] particular's essence that it instantiate certain universals?"[34] He poses the (rhetorical) question of what would be missing in a world where none of a bare particular's properties were part of what that particular is, that is, in a world where a bare particular's character is exhausted by the universals it instantiates. He seems to think that nothing would be missing, but it doesn't take a lot of effort to see that his answer misses the point of the initial question: can we make sense of a particular *independently of its universals*? Sider's flat-footed arguments don't address the independence-requirement. In this sense, his argument fails to address the central worry bundle theorists have with regard to substratum theory.

Let me try to spell out what exactly this worry is. It is not that bare particulars can't be identified while considering them *in conjunction with* the properties they instantiate: in conjunction with their properties, bare particulars can of course be identified *through* them: bare particular A is the one instantiating a cat-property, bare particular B is the one instantiating a table-property, etc.[35] The worry is, rather, that in order to make sense of substratum theory, we have to be able to make *independent* sense of a particular on the one side, and the universals instantiated by it on the other. If the particular can only be uniquely identified *via* its universals, then substratum theory collapses into bundle theory. So in order to defend the substratum theory, we need something like bare particulars.[36]

At this point, the attentive reader will probably already guess that the problems occurring for bare particulars parallel those occurring for haecceities: a bare particular considered apart from the universals it instantiates lacks explanatory power and is indeterminate.

The problem of explanatory power is that, just like in the case of haecceities, also bare particulars merely achieve to highlight the problem they were supposed to solve. The concept of bare particulars was intended by the substratum theorist to explain an object's individuality independently of its (qualitative) properties, that is, independently of the universals it instantiates. And again, as in the above case, it turns out that bare particulars don't have any explanatory value for the problem of individuation. This, again, becomes evident when we look at the special case of qualitatively and relationally indiscernible objects, that is, particulars instantiating the exact same monadic and relational universals. Recall Black's identical spheres A and B in a symmetrical universe and let's ask the defender of bare particulars: which one of the two spheres is A? None of A's properties can help answer this question, given that A shares all of its properties with B. The two bare particulars that are supposed to be the substrata instantiating A's and B's respective bundles of universals *and* to guarantee the individuality of A and B are as indistinguishable as their properties. In order to distinguish A's and B's bare particulars, they already have to be individuals, as a matter of metaphysical priority. But then they clearly don't explain what it is over and above A's and B's universals that makes them individual and numerically distinct objects. Hence, bare particulars fail to account for their objects' individuality.

The problem of indeterminacy is that bare particulars can't be individuated and are thus indeterminate objects. The substratum theory postulates bare particulars in order to enable us to consider an object and its properties separately. But the only way we can determine an object's bare particular is via its properties. So we are stuck in a vicious circle. Again, as in the case of haecceities, a last resort out of this circle would be some kind of higher-order property designed for the sole purpose of accounting for the numerical distinctness of two otherwise completely identical objects—an ad hoc move and as such, a high price to pay for keeping the concept of bare particulars alive.

Let me summarize my reservations about bare particulars as follows. The general worry about substratum theory is that the respective substrata, that is, the bare particulars, are superfluous: if (as the bundle theorist holds) objects are nothing over and above the conjunction of their (intrinsic) properties, then we don't need to postulate substrata as an additional entity instantiating those objects. The substratum theorist, on the other hand, worries that properties alone are not enough to make up an object. We need an object instantiating those properties in addition. The basic disagreement here seems to be a matter of intuitions. The point I have been trying to advance here is that the substratum view collapses into bundle theory if bare particulars can neither be shown to have any explanatory power, nor to be individuals: if bare particulars are so deflated that even the fact that we can't individuate them doesn't matter, then what difference remains between the bundle theorist and the substratum theorist? Put differently: if unique reference to bare particulars is impossible, that is, if we can't single them out as individuals, what good reason is there to believe in them at all?

INEFFABLE PROPERTIES AND OBJECTS 71

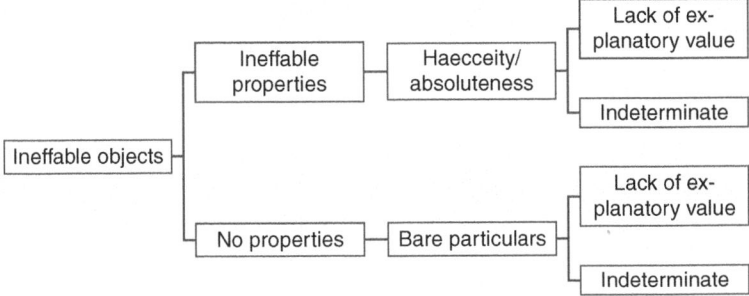

Figure 3.1 Possible reasons for the ineffability of an object

In this chapter, I have focused on the notion of an ineffable object and I have tried to find ways of making metaphysical sense of such objects. Drawing on historical references to an ineffable 'Absolute,' 'Whole,' 'One,' etc., I have argued that, if anything, it must be the property of absoluteness that accounts for the alleged ineffability of the Absolute. I then showed that the property of absoluteness, if it existed, would in fact be identical to the Absolute's haecceity. In the subsequent discussion, I outlined a number of reasons why belief in the existence of haecceities is not justified, thus rendering the belief in an ineffable Absolute questionable as well. In the final section, I examined the notion of a bare particular as an alternative way of giving a metaphysically coherent account of an ineffable object. As it turned out, however, the reasons to be doubtful about bare particulars run parallel to the reasons based on which I rejected the postulation of haecceities. The upshot of this chapter is, therefore, that the notions of ineffable objects and properties are unfounded. Explaining the metaphysical structure of ineffability in terms of such objects or properties is thus no promising way to go (Figure 3.1).

In the next chapter, we will turn our attention to another candidate for the metaphysics of ineffability: ineffable propositions.

CHAPTER 4

INEFFABLE PROPOSITIONS

4.1 Why Ineffable Propositions?

One of the main phenomenal characteristics of ineffable experiences is a feeling of meaningfulness: ineffable experiences often seem to afford some kind of insight. One way to make sense of this feeling is by arguing that such experiences consist in grasping an ineffable truth, or an ineffable proposition. In this chapter, we will examine whether there is reason to believe in ineffable propositions, and if so, whether ineffable propositions provide a good model for our three paradigmatic examples of ineffability: aesthetic ineffability (e.g., as experienced in the presence of a particular work of art), religious ineffability (e.g., as experienced during prayer), and philosophical ineffability (e.g., as experienced when reading the *Tractatus'* paragraphs on the limits of thought (§5.61) or solipsism (§5.62)).

Recall our definitions:

'x expresses y' x expresses y if and only if (i) x is a linguistic item with content that makes it either true or false, (ii) y is a nonlinguistic item with content that makes it either true or false, and (iii) the content of x nontrivially entails the content of y.

Expressibility x is expressible iff there exists an x such that x expresses y.

Ineffability A nonlinguistic item y is ineffable if and only if it is metaphysically impossible that there be a linguistic item x whose content nontrivially entails the content of y and whose content is, in principle, communicable to other finite beings by users of a finite language.

These definitions cover our paradigmatic examples while ruling out irrelevant cases of ineffability, where trivial circumstances such as nescience, physical constraints, or category mistakes are the cause of ineffability.

I will not engage with the larger controversy about the nature of propositions here, though it is worth keeping in mind that some take them to be sets of possible worlds, while others consider them to be structured entities with constituents (although there is no agreement as to what sort of things these constituents are, and as to what binds these constituents together). This is important for our discussion of Lewis' argument from functionalist access conditions, which depends on a picture of propositions as sets of possible worlds. If one believes, contrary to Lewis, that propositions are structured entities, so much the worse for ineffable propositions (more on this later).

The arguments for ineffable truths I will examine all use the terms 'truth' and 'true proposition' synonymously, but I refrain from claiming that propositions are the only kind of truth-bearers there are. There may be truth-bearers that are not propositional in form (it has been suggested, for example, that photographs convey truth). The question then arises whether nonpropositional contents can be transformed into propositional ones or not. Chapters 2 and 5 deal with this question. For now, let us focus on the concept of ineffable truths that are propositional in form.

The motivation to explain the metaphysical constitution of ineffability in terms of ineffable propositions arises as follows. Experiencing ineffability feels meaningful. We feel as if we understand or learn something. The things we ordinarily learn are truths; hence, it seems that we have good reason to think that experiencing ineffability consists in grasping an ineffable truth. Reasoning of this kind is the basis of many arguments for the ineffability of religious or mystical insights, aesthetic experiences, and so forth. In this chapter, I will examine four lines of argument for the existence of ineffable truths or propositions, and will then show why neither of them is a good model for our paradigmatic examples of ineffability. The chapter ends with the conclusion that the metaphysics of ineffability cannot be explained in terms of ineffable truths or propositions.

A note regarding possible underlying truth-theories: As explained, if we assume a deflationist theory of truth as our background theory, the very question whether there are or could be ineffable truths doesn't even get off the ground. According to deflationist theories of truth, propositions are by definition expressible, and truth is by definition a property of propositions only. Hence, the possibility of ineffable truths is ruled out from the beginning. However, this position evidently contains two substantial presuppositions: that all propositions are expressible and that truth is a property of propositions *only*. If one or both of these presuppositions are false, ineffable truths are prima facie possible. I will assume the possibility of ineffable truths for the sake of the argument in this chapter, and I will show them to be impossible by means of arguments independent of one's underlying theory of truth. If deflationists are right about truth, so much the worse for ineffable propositions.

4.2 Inaccessibility

Let us begin by clarifying the two principle reasons for a proposition's ineffability. The first reason is that the proposition could be empty, that is, lacking any content. The second reason could be that the proposition is inaccessible.[1] Provided the notion of an entirely empty, content-free proposition does not constitute a contradiction in terms, the resulting ineffability would nevertheless not fall into the category of philosophically relevant cases of ineffability as specified in the Introduction. An empty proposition would constitute a case of trivial ineffability. So the only philosophically relevant reason for a proposition to be ineffable would be if it was strictly inaccessible.

What does it mean for a proposition to be inaccessible? I propose that a proposition is inaccessible if no (possible) language user is capable of grasping it, even though one may have some idea of what the content of the proposition must be, and what its truth entails.[2] A proposition is strictly inaccessible if it is necessarily inaccessible, and not only contingently. What exactly does it mean for a proposition to be contingently inaccessible?

One example of contingently inaccessible propositions are *discovery-fugitive* propositions, and their existence can be argued for as follows. Given that physicists continuously discover truths about the world, it is reasonable to assume that there are truths "waiting" to be discovered in the future. For example, one of the chief goals of the Large Hadron Collider at CERN is to generate evidence for or against the hypothesis that there exists an elementary particle called the 'Higgs boson.' The research conducted at CERN is based on the assumption that there is a *truth* about the existence of the Higgs boson that can be discovered: either, the Higgs boson exists' or, the Higgs boson does not exist. Until recently, there was no evidence as to which one of the two sentences expresses the truth about the Higgs boson. In other words the truth about the Higgs boson was, up to then, ineffable. Now, however, the evidence seems to indicate that 'The Higgs boson exists' is true. We knew at all times that one of the two sentences expresses the truth about the Higgs boson, but we didn't know which one was true, so that the truth about the matter was ineffable until it was discovered. The inaccessibility of discovery-fugitive propositions is therefore due to nescience, that is, the "physical constraint" of being located at a certain point in time where the truth-value of a given proposition has not been determined yet.[3] The fact that they are inaccessible at a certain point in time is accidental, that is, contingent upon a certain point in time. Therefore, even though we may not know the truth-value of a discovery-fugitive proposition at a specific point in time, discovery-fugitive propositions do not fall under the definition of *in principle* ineffability I gave in Chapter 2 and are thus irrelevant for my examination.

A second example for contingently inaccessible propositions are *finitude-fugitive* propositions. Their inaccessibility is caused by a restriction common to all finite beings: we cannot express infinite propositions, for example, infinite propositional conjunctions, because expressing them would take an infinite amount of time. It may be perfectly possible to express each single instance of an infinite collection, but it will always be impossible to express its conjunction, that is, to express all single instances in a finite time. Examples of such propositions are the conjunction of all empirical true propositions of the past, present, and future,[4] the conjunction of all propositions expressing instances of the law of the excluded middle, and, more generally, the conjunction of all propositions representing instances of a schema. However, as Russell noted, the impossibility of performing infinitely many tasks in a finite time (such as writing down the complete decimal expansion of π), is not a logical impossibility but a merely 'medical' one.[5] Applying this argumentation to our case, finitude-fugitive propositions such as infinite conjunctions represent a case of philosophically irrelevant ineffability caused by the physical constraint of being a finite being. It is true that finitude is a kind of constraint that cannot be removed as easily as in the example mentioned in the Introduction of a gagged person; nevertheless, the example still does not seem relevant philosophically, partly because we have a pretty clear grasp of what it is that prevents us from expressing finitude-fugitive propositions (namely, our own finitude), and partly because it seems that each *single* numeral of the decimal expansion of π, or each single proposition of an infinite conjunction is, in principle, expressible. The fact that they are inaccessible *in practice* is accidental, that is, contingent upon our physical constraint of being finite. Thus, finitude-fugitive propositions also don't fall under my definition of philosophically relevant ineffability given in Chapter 2 and are thus irrelevant for my examination.

Now that we have some idea of *contingently* inaccessible propositions, we need to clarify when exactly a proposition can be said to be *strictly* inaccessible, and therefore ineffable. In the following, I will describe four classes of propositions that, at first glance, seem to be strictly inaccessible: propositions underlying semantically paradoxical self-referential sentences; unformulable mathematical propositions; excess propositions; and perspectival-fugitive propositions. I will then argue that the first three classes are in fact either only contingently inaccessible, or have no metaphysical import and are therefore not suitable to explain the philosophically interesting cases of ineffability. The fourth class, perspectival-fugitive propositions, are indeed metaphysically relevant, yet I will show that the notion is incoherent. The conclusion of this chapter is that there is no coherent, metaphysically relevant way of spelling out the notion of ineffable propositions. Therefore, the metaphysics of ineffability cannot be explained in terms of ineffable propositions.

4.3 Semantic Paradoxes

Paradoxes arise if a chain of logically valid reasoning based on apparently true premises leads to a contradiction. A classic case of ineffable propositions are the propositions giving the truth-value of semantically paradoxical, self-referential sentences such as:

Liar Paradox "This sentence is not true."

What is the truth-value of this sentence? If the sentence is true, then, according to what it states, it is false. If the sentence is false, then, according to what it states, it is true. Therefore, it seems that we are forced to say that the sentence is both true and false. But that is contradictory. One way of avoiding this contradiction is to say that the proposition stating the truth-value for the Liar sentence is ineffable.

Paradoxes like this arise when a sentence refers to itself (i.e., to its own referent) in a particular way. Besides the most well-known example of the Liar paradox, countless other paradoxes can be constructed using the tool of self-referentiality (in the case of sentences defining entities in terms of a set of other entities at least one of which is the entity being defined, we speak of *impredicative* definitions[6]). Here are a few more examples of sentences whose truth-value is indeterminate because arguably, both 'true' and 'false' are applicable:

Grelling's Paradox "The predicate 'heterological' is heterological."

Russell's Paradox "There exists a set of all sets not members of themselves."

Cantor's Paradox "The power set of the set of all sets has a bigger cardinality than the set of all sets."

In cases like these, it is impossible to state which truth-value the respective sentence has. Thus, the proposition stating the truth-value is ineffable. Self-referential sentences of this kind[7] are interesting because they seem to bring ineffability almost within our reach: even though we cannot construct the ineffable proposition itself, we can get quite close to it by constructing a sentence whose (indeterminate) truth-value is the truth-maker for the ineffable proposition. In this sense, the semantic paradoxes seem to give us at least some grip on the ineffable.

However, there are several good reasons why these cases are not very enlightening when it comes to examining the metaphysics of ineffability as defined in Chapter 2. First of all, none of the cases we defined as the relevant cases of ineffability involve semantic paradoxes. It seems very odd to try and explain, say, an ineffable religious experience in terms of a semantic paradox. Or the ineffable aspect of a piece of art. There just doesn't seem to be any relevant connection between these cases. This fact alone doesn't suffice, of course, to dismiss the semantic paradoxes as irrelevant. They are certainly interesting in their own right. However, they lack metaphysical import and can therefore not contribute much to an examination of the metaphysics of ineffability. Rather, possible solutions to the semantic paradoxes are mainly interesting in the context of formal semantics and formal theories of truth.[8]

The possibility of a way of dissolving the paradoxes then leads to another point: if a way to solve the paradoxes were found, that is, a way to determine their truth-value or to explain why they lack a truth-value, then the ineffability allegedly involved in the semantic paradoxes completely disappears. Take, for example, Graham Priest's proposed solution to the paradoxes, dialetheism, a paraconsistent logic according to which Liar sentences and other semantic paradoxes are both true and false at the same time.[9] This is clearly a possible (if nonorthodox) solution to the problem. On other views, the solution to the semantic paradoxes is dismissing the principle of bivalence (according to which every sentence is either true or false), so that Liar sentences can be considered paracomplete, that is, neither true nor false: they mark 'truth-value-gaps.'[10] If either one of these theories is correct, then the proposition stating the truth-value of a semantically paradoxical sentence is not ineffable: either, it would state that the truth-value is 'both true and false,' or it would state that the truth-value is 'neither true nor false'—both propositions would be perfectly expressible. Thus, the possibility of a solution to the semantic paradoxes makes it probable that the underlying propositions are merely contingently inaccessible, that is, they are a special case of discovery-fugitive propositions.

We can thus note that propositions giving the truth-value of semantically paradoxical, self-referential sentences would only come out strictly inaccessibly (and thus, relevantly ineffable according to our definition) if one wasn't ready to accept any of the proposed semantic solutions to the paradoxes (which would require a lot of argument and doesn't seem a

INEFFABLE PROPOSITIONS   79

very likely position to take). But even if one wasn't ready to accept the possibility of a solution to the semantic paradoxes and was therefore ready to accept them as strictly inaccessible, they wouldn't have any metaphysical implications for the relevant cases of ineffability. We may therefore safely conclude that, for an examination of the metaphysics of ineffability, the semantic paradoxes are not relevant.

4.4 Unformulable Mathematical Propositions

Besides the semantic paradoxes, other classic cases of ineffable propositions are found in mathematics. Here are two examples. The first one is related to the set-theoretic Axiom of Choice (AC), a widely used addition to the axioms of Zermelo-Fraenkel set theory (ZF), which has been shown by Kurt Gödel and Paul Cohen to be logically independent of ZF (i.e., it can neither be proven nor disproven from ZF). That axiom can be formulated as follows:[11]

Axiom of Choice: "For any x, if x is a set of nonempty disjoint sets (two sets are disjoint if nothing is a member of both), then there is a set, called a choice set for x, that contains exactly one member of each of the members of x."[12]

So if t is any family of disjoint sets, the axiom simply asserts that among the subsets of $\cup t$ (the union set of the members of t) there is a set that has as members and only as members one and only one member from each member of t. All the axiom asserts is the *existence* of such a set. It does *not* assert that such a set will be definable in the language of set theory. Indeed, it will in general not be. Intuitively it is easy to see why we know that certain key theorems are unprovable without the Axiom of Choice, for example, that the Real numbers can be well-ordered or that there is a Lebesgue nonmeasurable set (sets that can be assigned a volume are called Lebesgue-measurable). In these cases, if the set that the Axiom of Choice says exists were definable by a formula of the language of set theory, then we could simply use the Axiom of Separation[13] (the *Aussonderungsaxiom*) to obtain the necessary subset of $\cup t$. However, we know that this is impossible since the Axiom of Choice is essential to the proof, which implies that there must be some sets that are not definable in the language of set theory (if they were definable, they could be picked out using the Axiom of Separation). Applied to the example of the Reals, this means that, assuming the Axiom of Choice, there is a well-ordering of the Reals (indeed there are many), and thus, many 'propositional contents,' which we know to be inexpressible in any language adequate for mathematics.

Of course, the Axiom of Choice is not so much an *argument* for ineffable mathematical propositions; rather, they simply follow from it. But there is also a more straightforward method of constructing ineffable mathematical propositions, used by intuitionists in order to argue that only constructible mathematical objects are legitimate mathematical objects. Let's say that S is a sequence of rational numbers and let's define S as follows: If by the nth place in the decimal expansion of the number π, no sequence of the form 9999999999 has occurred, S(n) = $(-\frac{1}{2})$n. If by the kth place in the decimal expansion of the number π, a sequence of the form 3333333333 has occurred (with k being the place at which the last member of the sequence occurs, and n ≠ k), S(n) = $(-\frac{1}{2})$k. We have thus generated a real number, which lies between 0 and 1, but we don't know which relation the number has to the number $\frac{1}{2}$. S oscillates left and right of $\frac{1}{2}$, approaching it from both sides, as long as the sequence 9999999999 doesn't occur. However, if it occurs, the sequence will stop at a certain distance from $\frac{1}{2}$. The stopping point will be either less or greater than $\frac{1}{2}$, depending on whether k is odd or even.[14] Real numbers of this kind are indeterminate because their calculability is directly dependent on an unknown factor, in this case whether there does or doesn't exist a particular sequence in the decimal expansion of π. Propositions referring to them can thus be argued to be ineffable because even though we know the general way to construct the number, we cannot determine it until we determine whether or not the decimal expansion of π includes the sequence 9999999999.

There are countless other examples of ineffable propositions in mathematics, namely the propositions stating the truth-value of the many hitherto unsolved problems in mathematics, such as the Goldbach conjecture (asserting that every integer greater than 2 is equivalent to the sum of two prime numbers); the Continuum Hypothesis (which states that there is no set whose cardinality is strictly larger than that of the integers and strictly smaller than that of the real numbers); the Riemann Hypothesis which states that all 'nonobvious' zeros of the zeta-function—a function that plays a central role in examining the distribution of prime numbers—are complex numbers with real part $\frac{1}{2}$; and many more.

Moreover, there is the problem of consistency. A system of thought is internally consistent if it doesn't contain contradictions. For an abstract system of thought AS, this can mean that it is impossible to derive both P and not-P from AS's axioms (syntactic definition) or that there is at least one model under which all theorems of AS come out true (semantic definition). A system is complete relative to a certain property A if every formula instantiating that property is a theorem of that system, that is, can be derived from its axioms via the respective rules of deduction. And this, in turn, is most interesting for the case of the property of truth:

Gödel showed in his first incompleteness theorem that all axiomatic systems (except trivial ones) capable of doing arithmetic are incomplete, that is, there are arithmetical truths about the relations of the natural numbers that are unprovable in a given system, such as Peano Arithmetic (PA). In his second incompleteness theorem, Gödel showed that by extension of his first incompleteness theorem, if PA is consistent, it cannot prove its own consistency. This has been widely accepted as a proof that it is impossible to give a complete and consistent set of axioms for all of mathematics. Only very few, such as Edward Nelson and Vladimir Voevodsky at Princeton, have seriously considered the *further* implication following from this, which is that mathematics is possibly inconsistent.[15]

It is true that it is generally assumed that mathematics is, in fact, consistent. This assumption is intuitively justified given that the natural numbers provide a model for PA (rendering PA at least logically *possible*), and given that the standard inference rules of first-order logic seem to be sound, that is, they make it impossible to derive a contradiction from any description of a logically possible state of affairs. Yet without being disproved, the inconsistency of mathematics remains at least a logical possibility. If mathematics is indeed consistent, as is commonly assumed, the language of mathematics is incapable of proving this—in which case the consistency of mathematics could be considered an ineffable truth.

How should we evaluate these examples of ineffable mathematical propositions? What follows from their existence? Is there any consequence to be drawn that is relevant for our examination of ineffability?

First of all, we need to recall the distinction between contingently and necessarily inaccessible propositions. As I have explained, contingently inaccessible propositions are only contingently ineffable and hence, do not count toward the relevant cases of ineffability. And in fact, most of the above mentioned ineffable mathematical truths fall into the irrelevant category: the intuitionist examples of ineffable propositions, the Goldbach Conjecture, the Continuum Hypothesis, and the Riemann Hypothesis, are all cases of contingently inaccessible propositions whose truth value will be definite once mathematicians find the respective proofs. Hence, these propositions are not inherently ineffable.

What about the ineffable propositions implied by the Axiom of Choice and Gödel's incompleteness theorems? Their inaccessibility is not contingent but necessary, just as the resulting ineffability. So prima facie, we are facing ineffable propositions of the relevant kind. However, we now need to ask ourselves if our three paradigmatic examples of ineffability—the ineffability experienced in the presence of a particular work of art, the ineffability of a religious experience during prayer, and the ineffability of solipsistic philosophical intuitions—could be explained in terms of this kind of necessarily ineffable proposition. And I think it is quite obvious that there is no detectable connection between those examples and necessarily ineffable mathematical propositions: the Axiom of Choice or Gödel's incompleteness theorem can neither account for the ineffable quality of Rachmaninov's Third Symphony, nor for one's ineffable experience of God, nor for the ineffability of one's solipsistic intuitions. It is important to take note of the existence of ineffable mathematical propositions, but it is equally important to be clear about the limits of their explanatory role when it comes to the metaphysics of aesthetic, religious, and philosophical ineffability.

4.5 Excess Propositions

Another way of arguing for ineffable truths can be extracted from an argument for excess propositions provided by David Lewis. In *On the Plurality of Worlds*, Lewis argues that propositions are sets of possible worlds. On this view, any subset of possible worlds constitutes a proposition that would be expressed by a thought or sentence, which was true exactly in every world of that subset and in no other world. A Lewisian proposition thus divides the set of all possible worlds into two classes, so that a sentence expressing the proposition is true in all and only one half of worlds and false in all and only the other half of worlds.[16]

Before getting into the examination Lewis' argument, it is important to note the following. The fact that this section deals with a notion of expressibility defined in terms of the *equivalence* of expressions and propositions marks a departure from the definition of expression I gave before. Recall that, according to clause (iii) of my definition, it would suffice for a sentence S to count as an expression of proposition P if S *entailed* P (in which case S would not be true in *all* the possible worlds that constitute P but only in a specific *subset* of those worlds). My definition does not require that S be *equivalent* to P. According to my definition, the sentence 'Lemons are yellow and oranges are orange' counts as an expression of the proposition that lemons are yellow.[17] Lewis' argument, on the other hand, assumes a stronger notion of expression. For him, a sentence S expresses a proposition P just in case S is *equivalent* to P. I will explain in due course why it is important to keep this distinction in mind.

Lewis bases his argument for excess propositions on a paradox, known as 'Kaplan's Paradox,'[18] which emerges as follows:

1. We assume that the cardinality of the set of all possible worlds is K.
2. If propositions are sets of possible worlds, then each subset of the set of all possible worlds constitutes a proposition.

3. Since a set of size K has 2^K subsets, there are 2^K propositions. 2^K is strictly greater than K.
4. Every proposition can possibly constitute the sole content of a being's thought at a given time.
5. For each such scenario, there is a possible world.
6. Therefore, there are at least 2^K possible worlds. This contradicts (1).[19]

Since Lewis wants to defend the notion that propositions are sets of possible worlds, he needs to find a way to avoid this paradox. He chooses to avoid it by denying (4), that is, by holding that not every but only a very specific, very small subset of all propositions can possibly constitute the content of a being's thought. All other propositions, although they exist, *cannot possibly* constitute the content of a being's thought. Therefore, they can also never be expressed and are thus, ineffable propositions.[20] They are 'excess propositions,' as it were.

Lewis thus suggests restricting possible thought contents to a small number of propositions only. He proposes the following functionalist restriction criterion:

> A man or a beast or a god, or anything that is a thinker at all, has a thought with a certain content in virtue of being in a state which occupies a certain functional role. This definitive functional role has to do with the causal relations of that state to the thinker's sensory input, his behavioural output, and his other states.[21]

His idea is this. Imagine any thinking being B. B's having a thought is directly dependent on B's being in a state with a certain functional role. In other words, the functional role of B's state determines the content of B's thought. Thus, Lewis claims, "there can be only as many different possible contents of thought as there are different definitive functional roles."[22] What does Lewis understand by a 'functional role'? He explains them as "the relevantly different ways of thinking."[23] According to Lewis' theory of content,[24] an assignment of content to states must *fit* the functional role of that state. Whether a content fits the functional role of a state depends on certain principles of rationality. For example, if a person A is in a state s that is assigned content c (where c consists of some system of propositional attitudes such as beliefs, desires, etc.), then the assignment of c to s fits the functional role of s iff s tends to produce conduct that is conducive to the aim of the relevant propositional attitude.

Lewis thus argues, in line with standard rational choice theory, that we can assign beliefs and desires to people according to their behavior. If we assume that people are rational and that rational beings tend to act in order to satisfy their preferences by maximizing the expected utility of their actions, then it is likely that rational beings have a preference ordering among possible actions. What we know about human behavior provides a fairly full picture of this preference ordering. On this picture, it is possible to employ some mathematical representation theorem (like Savage's representation theorem[25]) to conclude that an action is rational if and only if, relative to the subject's beliefs and desires, it has the highest subjective expected utility of all available options. From this rational preference structure of actions, we can now assign relevantly belief-like things (credences such that the higher the credence, the more believed the proposition/the higher the degree of belief) and relevantly desire-like things (utilities or values assigned to outcomes, such that the higher the utility, the more desired the outcome) to rational agents. On this way of characterizing propositional attitudes, allowing an arbitrary proposition to be the sole content of a belief will require a respective arbitrary stream of behavior. However, assuming that we don't want to accept arbitrary streams of behavior as rational, we must rule out all propositions for which belief in them couldn't be assigned a stream of rational behavior. Hence, we must rule out all propositions that consist in arbitrary sets of possible worlds.

Put less abstractly, if I am in a certain state to which a certain content consisting of the desire expressed by 'I want ice-cream' is assigned, then that content fits my state iff my state tends to produce action conducive to my getting ice-cream (e.g., sending my father to the nearest ice cream parlor). The content would *not* fit my state if it tended to produce action conducive to something other than getting ice-cream (e.g., going to the gym). However, the tricky thing is that there are plenty of absurd content assignment scenarios that qualify as 'fitting' according to this criterion. For example, rather than thinking that I can get ice-cream at the next door ice-cream parlor, we could construe a completely absurd assignment, for instance that I desire a cactus and, due to a strange yet valid chain of inductive reasoning supported by all my previous experiences with ice-cream parlors, I expect the ice-cream parlor to serve me cactus. In order to rule out such absurd yet valid assignments, Lewis suggests a 'principle of humanity' for content assignments, that is, a principle designed to somehow rule out unreasonable cases. It is those ruled out content assignments that are, according to Lewis, examples for inexpressible propositions:

> They are ineligible contents of thought because they are utterly unpatterned and miscellaneous. I suggest that an unthinkable content is one that can never be correctly assigned because, whenever it fits the functional roles of the thinker's states, some more favoured content also fits.[26]

Lewis has thus provided an argument from functionalist access conditions for a kind of proposition that is strictly inaccessible due to the ineligibility of its contents to be contents of thought. In the following, I will first discuss possible objections to his argument, and then turn to the implications of his account for the metaphysics of aesthetic, religious, and philosophical ineffability.

There are several reservations one might have about the setup of Lewis' argument. After all, hardly anyone fully endorses Lewis' metaphysical framework. The first objection that can be brought forward is against the notion that propositions are *sets* of possible worlds, rather than, say, disjunctions of ways things might be. However, that objection won't help to refute Lewis' argument. The reason is that Kaplan's paradox does not only arise if propositions are taken to be sets of worlds; it arises for anyone who believes that, for any disjunction of ways worlds could be, there is a proposition that is true in all and only those worlds.

One can also argue that propositions slice logical space more finely than possible worlds by considering distinct propositions picking out the exact same set of possible worlds. Consider, for example, the propositions 'Louis' kite is rectangular' and 'There is a 90-degree-angle between all four sides of Louis' kite.' Both propositions are true in exactly the same possible worlds but, given that they provide slightly different pieces of information, they are distinct. However, even if such arguments falsify Lewis' premise that for K possible worlds, there are 2^K propositions, it doesn't get rid of Kaplan's paradox. Actually, it only makes things worse by multiplying the number of propositions and, thereby, the number of worlds.

Another possibility to object to the setup of Lewis' argument is to claim that the cardinality of the set of possible worlds is not K but 1 because there is only one actual world. However, that wouldn't help either. The paradox is not a paradox about *worlds* but a paradox about *descriptions of possibilities*. Hence, it also arises if the cardinality of worlds is assumed to be 1 and possibilities are taken to be maximal descriptions ('ersatz worlds') of ways things might be. If the assumption is that the cardinality of the set of maximal descriptions of the way things might be is D, then there are 2^D non-maximal descriptions of ways things might be, and thus, 2^D possible settings in which a lonely thinker thinks one of those non-maximal descriptions. To avoid the paradox, one either has to deny that there are such maximal descriptions of possible worlds, or deny that they can be thought, as Lewis does. I agree with Lewis that denying the existence of maximal descriptions of the way things might be is not the right way to go. This is because, as I mentioned, meaningful disagreement is only possible if we assume the unity of both the actual world and each possible world (or maximal description of possibilities), and thereby, the consistency of the respective associated propositions. Thus, the way to avoid Kaplan's paradox is to find a way to deny that completely arbitrary propositions can constitute the content of a thinker's thought.

A simple solution is to deny that unthinkable propositions are propositions at all. If a proposition is defined as the kind of thing that could be thought or uttered, then arguably those excess propositions Lewis invokes won't even count as propositions because they are neither thinkable nor utterable. This would entail that all propositions *can* be thought. However, given that Lewisian excess propositions are nothing but (arbitrary) disjunctions of descriptions of ways things might be, it is difficult to make sense of the idea that a 'non-arbitrary' disjunction of propositions would qualify as a proposition while an 'arbitrary' disjunction wouldn't. Again, this does not seem to be the right way to object to Lewis' argument.

Lewis attacks premise (4) of Kaplan' paradox, that is, the claim that every proposition can possibly constitute the sole content of a being's thought at a given time. His attack can be converted into an argument for ineffable propositions. However, maybe he could have challenged premise (4) in a way that did not depend on the strange notion of ineffable propositions? Maybe one could challenge premise (4) by arguing that it is impossible that a being thinks exactly one proposition at a given time.

Recall that Kaplan's paradox arises because it is assumed that every proposition can possibly constitute the *sole* content of a lonely thinker's thought at a given time. However, on second thought, it is unclear whether a thinker can really think one proposition alone (i.e., have one propositional attitude) at a given time. Take beliefs for example.[27] Arguably, all beliefs we hold are embedded in a network of other beliefs. We hold beliefs on the basis of other beliefs, we know that belief b_1 entails belief b_2, we make inferences from one belief to another, etc. Therefore, holding one belief arguably implies that one holds several other beliefs at the same time (in the "back" of one's mind, as it were) and thus, that lonely-thinker-scenarios aren't real possibilities. Arguments of this kind show that there are not as many worlds as Kaplan's paradox establishes. However, this strategy can easily be countered. It may well be that we never actually think about one proposition only at a given time. However, we can simply reformulate Kaplan's paradox in terms of a lonely writer, that is, someone who writes down exactly one proposition at a given time. This would reestablish that, for K possible worlds, there are 2^K propositions the lonely writer could write down, and thus, 2^K possible worlds we can infer from those scenarios.

I have considered several different ways of attacking Lewis' argument, but none of them succeed in resisting it if the underlying definition of expression is one of equivalence rather than entailment. This is an interesting philosophical result. However, for some people it might also be a motivation for adopting a definition of expressibility in terms of entailment rather than equivalence. The notion of ineligible contents of thought, which I converted into the notion of ineffable propositions, obviously depends on Lewis' definition of expression according to which an expression must be *equivalent* to a proposition. On my definition of expression (see earlier), an expression need only *entail* a proposition. This is for the simple reason that I want a sentence like 'Lemons are yellow and oranges are orange' to count as an expression both of the proposition that lemons are yellow and oranges are orange and of the proposition that lemons are yellow. This is reasonable because the sentence picks out a set of possible worlds in which lemons are yellow and oranges are orange. However, given that the set of all possible world in which lemons are yellow and oranges are orange is a subset of the set of all possible worlds in which lemons are yellow, the expression 'Lemons are yellow and oranges are orange' also entails the set of all possible worlds in which lemons are yellow, and therefore, counts as an expression of the proposition that lemons are yellow.

Hence, a Lewisian ineffable proposition does in fact not come out ineffable on my definition because it is possible that there be an expression picking out a subset of the set of all possible worlds constituting the proposition that entails the set of all possible worlds constituting the proposition. Nevertheless, I think Lewis' argument deserves its place in my discussion, first, because it is an interesting attempt to motivate the notion of ineffable propositions, and second, because there may be some philosophers who reject clause (iii) of my definition of 'expression.' On my definition of ineffability, however, Lewis's account cannot be considered an argument for ineffable propositions. Yet even if it could, we would have to ask ourselves whether Lewisian excess propositions provide a suitable account for explaining the metaphysics of ineffability as encountered in aesthetic, religious, and philosophical contexts. The ineffable quality of Rachmaninov's Third Symphony is very likely not due to the fact that it somehow communicates a Lewisian excess proposition. The same holds for religious experience and philosophical intuitions. If we want to continue looking for an eligible account of ineffable propositions, we must turn elsewhere.

4.6 Perspectival Propositions

Besides discovery-fugitive and finitude-fugitive propositions, which were discussed at the beginning of this chapter, there is a third kind of fugitive proposition, which I will call *perspectival-fugitive*. Here the alleged ineffability of a proposition is due to a subjective perspective, or a point of view, which is argued to be embedded in the proposition and is therefore only accessible to beings with a matching perspective. The most famous example for an argument of this kind is probably Thomas Nagel's. In 'What is it like to be a bat?,' he famously argues that a successful account of the mind-body-problem must be able to accommodate the subjective character of conscious experience; the conscious experience of a bat serves as the main example to support his point.[28] Also in *The View from Nowhere*, he states that

> not everything there is can be gathered into a uniform conception of the universe from nowhere within it. If certain perspectives evidently exist which cannot be analyzed in physical terms, we must modify our idea of objective reality to include them. If that is not enough, we must admit to reality some things that cannot be objectively understood.[29]

In his view, reductionist accounts of the mind, like physicalism, fail to acknowledge the fact that providing an objective account of reality requires both an abstraction from and an accommodation of something that could be called 'perspectival fact.' The general structure of his arguments is something like this:[30]

- Just as human beings have conscious experience, other organisms, for example bats, have conscious experience as well.
- For a bat to have conscious experience means that there is *something* it is like to be a bat. (Nagel refers to this 'something' as "the subjective character of experience" (p. 436); "the phenomenological features of experience" (p. 437); "Facts about what it is like to be an X" (p. 437); "facts that embody a particular point of view" (p. 441).
- The human sensory apparatus is unsuitable to form representations of such nonhuman perspectival facts. Consequently, humans cannot form conceptions of such perspectival facts—they are "beyond the reach of human concepts" (p. 441).

Nagel is thus arguing for a class of perspectival facts that obtain, or put differently, that constitute parts of the furniture of the world, without being expressible by human concepts. On the assumption that to each fact f there exists a corresponding proposition p that is made true by f, Nagel's argument intends to show that propositions corresponding to (i.e., made true by) perspectival facts are ineffable. He writes:

> Reflection on what it is like to be a bat seems to lead us, therefore, to the conclusion that there are facts that do not consist in the truth of propositions expressible in a human language. We can be compelled to recognize the existence of such facts without being able to state or comprehend them.[31]

A similar line of thought has been provided by Frank Jackson. It has come to be known as the 'Knowledge Argument' but I think it would be more accurate to describe it as a demonstration of our deep-rooted intuitions regarding phenomenal knowledge. Jackson argues for the existence of certain features that are taken to be the phenomenal aspects of our mental lives in the following way:

> I think that there are certain features of the bodily sensations especially, but also of certain perceptual experiences, which no amount of purely physical information includes. Tell me everything physical there is to tell about what is going on in a living brain, the kind of states, their functional role, their relation to what goes on at other times and in other brains, and so on and so forth, and be I as clever as can be in fitting it all together, you won't have told me about the hurtfulness of pains, the itchiness of itches, pangs of jealousy, or about the characteristic experience of tasting a lemon, smelling a rose, hearing a loud noise or seeing the sky.[32]

In order to illustrate his point, he asks the reader to imagine Mary, a poor creature confined to a black-and-white room, who (through black-and-white books and a black-and-white TV) learns everything physics can tell us about the world.[33] Specifically, she learns all the physical facts so far known about color perception, including facts about wavelengths, retina receptors, etc. A physicalist would have to say that she knows all there is to know about the world, and specifically about color perception. However, as Jackson argues, there is an intuitive sense in which Mary seems to learn something *new*, something *in addition* to the physical facts, when she sees the color red for the first time. Jackson argues that the intuition that Mary acquires an extra piece of knowledge when seeing red for the first time is strong enough to reject physicalism, that is, the view that everything that exists (objects, minds, etc.) exists physically (or supervenes on the physical). In addition to its implications for physicalism, Jackson's argument has been interpreted as an attempt to establish the point that there are perspectival-fugitive propositions accommodating facts such as what it is like for Mary to see the color red.

Working out the common structure of the above lines of argument will help us identify the weak points of any such theory of ineffable propositions or truths. Here are the crucial argumentative steps:

1. Phenomenal experiences such as seeing red or being a bat contain an irreducibly subjective element.
2. The irreducibly subjective element of those experiences corresponds to a perspectival fact.

3. Perspectival facts are only accessible to the subjects of those experiences.
4. To each fact there exists a corresponding proposition representing that fact.
5. If a fact is perspectival, its corresponding proposition is perspectival as well.
6. From 3, 4, 5: For each perspectival fact there exists a corresponding perspectival-fugitive proposition, or truth. A perspectival-fugitive proposition t(P) can only be grasped from the respective perspective P of the subject undergoing the subjective experience, such that for all perspectival-fugitive propositions t, there is only one perspective P from which t can be grasped. From every perspective other than P, t is ungraspable.
7. Only graspable propositions are expressible.
8. From 6, 7: Perspectival-fugitive propositions are inexpressible.[34]

We noted earlier that the only philosophically relevant reason for a proposition to be ineffable is strict inaccessibility; the central question was which conditions have to be fulfilled in order for a proposition to be strictly inaccessible. Nagel's and Jackson's arguments provided us with two examples of strictly inaccessible propositions. Generalizing these cases, we can call this class of strictly inaccessible propositions perspectival-fugitive propositions, that is, propositions that correspond to perspectival facts, that is, facts accommodating the phenomenal character of a subjective perspective or point of view. Ineffable propositions of this kind are inaccessible to all beings without a matching perspective. On first sight, the possibility of ineffable propositions of this kind seems quite straightforward. In the following sections, however, I will raise two principal objections against them, one of them a linguistic objection, the other a metaphysical one. The first objection is rejected, the second one endorsed. I argue on the basis of the second objection that the notion of perspectival-fugitive propositions is incoherent.

4.6.1 Linguistic Objections

Let's start with the first objection according to which the concept of 'truth' implies the possibility of being expressed. If truth implied expressibility, ineffable truths would be impossible. The classical defenders of this view are deflationists about truth, according to whom truth is a metaphysically thin concept implicit in all instances of the equivalence schema "$\langle p \rangle$ is true iff p," where $\langle p \rangle$ stands for any proposition.[35] As discussed in Chapter 2, on the assumption of a deflationist theory of truth, ineffable truths are

INEFFABLE PROPOSITIONS 91

impossible by definition. Yet even if we don't assume deflationism about truth, there is another way to argue for the expressibility of all truths on linguistic grounds.

A. W. Moore, for example, argues that we cannot make sense of the concept of a 'truth' independently of the concept of 'linguistic expression.'[36] His argument is that any truth is expressible in one way or another, and that therefore, any truth is expressible linguistically. It runs as follows:

1. For any truth *t*, there is at least one possible corresponding true representation *r* of *t*. [This is because, arguably, talking about truth implies that there be some identifiable entity that can be said to be true. For example, if I say that there is a truth in the witness' testimony, this either means that the witness' testimony contains a true sentence (or utterance), or that there is the possibility of someone making a claim that is entailed in one way or another by the testimony, that is true. There cannot be a truth in the witness' testimony unless some such possibility of expression obtains. That possibility *just is* the possibility of the truth's being expressed.]
2. A possible corresponding true representation *r* of *t* is identical to a possible (not necessarily linguistic) expression *e* of *t*.
3. Thus, for any truth *t*, there is a possible (not necessarily linguistic) expression *e* of *t*.
4. Representations have content that answers to reality and in virtue of which they are either true or false.
5. For any (arbitrarily chosen) true representation r_1 and for any (arbitrarily chosen) true representation r_2, there must be an integrating possible true representation r_3 whose content is either identical to, or at the least includes, the contents of r_1 and r_2 taken together. [This holds on the assumption that representations are made true by a single, unified reality. Imagine any two true representations: a true representation produced by an owl when detecting a mouse in a dark grass field, and another true representation produced by a piano teacher when hearing her student's agonizing rendition of Schubert. On the assumption that both representations are made true by a single, unified reality, there will be some linking content "between" these two representations, namely, an integrating representation r_3.]
6. The content of r_3 will supply a truth that, like any other truth, is expressible, yet only abstractly. [There are radical differences of type and content between some representations.[37] The type of a representation is determined by the role it plays in the psychology and phenomenology of the subject that produces it if it informs a belief

of that very subject, while the content is determined by its subject matter. An integrating representation like r_3 can only integrate r_1 and r_2 abstractly. That is, in order to merge the contents of two true representations r_1 and r_2, an integrating true representation r_3 must abstract from the points of view from which r_1 and r_2 were produced.]
7. A sufficiently high degree of abstraction can be provided only by linguistic expressions.
8. Therefore, for any true representation r corresponding to truth t, there is a linguistic expression e_l which expresses r.

What is interesting about this argument is that it tries to refute the notion of ineffable truths on a linguistic basis without resorting to a deflationary theory of truth.[38] The crucial assumption is that every truth can possibly be represented *somehow*, and the key move is to argue that every representation must be expressible linguistically because only language affords the required degree of abstraction necessary to integrate radically different representations into a unified picture of reality. Unfortunately, however, the argument is flawed. Let's see why.

I do not intend to challenge Moore's initial assumptions (1–3) according to which the concept 'truth' implies that every truth can be expressed somehow, for example, simply by being represented by a conscious being. In this sense, a representation already counts as an expression. As I explained earlier, countless things besides language could be argued to be "expressions" of this kind—dances, melodies, gestures, etc. I have no worries about the possibility that the concept 'truth' implies expressibility understood in this very broad way of representation because whether or not this is true has no bearing on the kind of ineffability which is the topic of this book. A truth that is expressible by nonlinguistic means *only* is still ineffable according to my definition, which is a definition of linguistic ineffability.

Rather, it is the second part of Moore's argument I have reservations about, specifically premises (5), (6), and (7). Premise (5) states that for any two true representations, there is a third representation connecting them, that is, their content in some way. Premise (6) states that, in order to merge the contents of two such representations r_1 and r_2, an integrating representation r_3 must abstract from the points of view from which r_1 and r_2 were produced. Premise (7) then adds that a sufficiently high degree of abstraction can be provided only by linguistic expressions. Let's discuss them one by one.

Premise (7) immediately begs the question: why is only language capable of making abstractions? Couldn't there also be other forms of expression that are, like language, independent of specific perceptual perspectives and therefore suitable for abstraction purposes, such as melodies, certain movements, etc.? It seems perhaps a little funny to think that the laws of physics, for example, could be rendered in something other than language, but there is no principled reason why that should not be possible (or at least, if there are such reasons, Moore hasn't stated them). Likewise, on the assumption that objects count as representations of themselves, there is arguably at least one integrating representation that manages to merge the contents of any two true representations r_1 and r_2 nonlinguistically, namely the world or reality itself. Of course, these examples raise the general question of what counts as a language, and I have no intention, of getting into that subject matter here. Suffice it to say that in order to establish the claim that only language is a form of expression capable of making abstractions, additional argument is required.

However, even if we assume that language is the only form of expression capable of making abstractions, another question arises: How do we know that the level of abstraction achieved by language is abstract enough? After all, the abstraction achieved by language is, in the end, also only a means of coding information into a system of signs that we only understand by drawing parallels between whatever is represented in abstract form, and our own, familiar phenomenal lives. This is because language relies heavily on conceptual metaphors, which tacitly rely on a human perspective. Traditionally, metaphors have been considered features of language rather than features of thought.[39] Recently, however, cognitive scientists have argued that some metaphors are not mere literal embellishments but actively shape our cognition. This capability of influencing our thought processes is attributed to a particular subclass of metaphors, that is, conceptual metaphors. Conceptual metaphors are instruments of our cognitive faculty used to conceptualize the world. This is achieved by mapping-processes across conceptual domains, enabling us to understand one domain by reference to another, often the more abstract by reference to the more concrete. A good example is the metaphorical way in which we grasp the highly abstract concept of a theory by means of the rather concrete concept of a building:

> Is that the *foundation* for your theory? The theory needs more *support*. The argument is *shaky*. We need some more facts or the arguments will *fall apart*. We need to *construct* a *strong* argument for that. I haven't figured out yet what the *form* of the argument will be. We need some more facts to *shore up* the theory. We need to *buttress* the theory with solid arguments. The theory will *stand* or *fall* on the *strength* of that argument. The argument *collapsed*. They *exploded* his latest theory. We will show that theory is *without foundation*. So far we have only put together the *framework* of the theory.[40]

Conceptual metaphors help us grasp highly abstract concepts that we cannot grasp directly, without the use of expressions that rely on the human sensory apparatus. Such conceptual metaphors are both indispensable for human cognition and not paraphrasable in a nonmetaphorical way.

What this means is that language is not as perspective-free as it first sounded, and this brings up the question whether the abstraction achieved by language is abstract enough at all. If the answer is that even language cannot abstract to the extent required in order to express representations that differ radically in type and content, then the possibility of ineffable truths reappears. Moore does not address this issue, and until he doesn't do so, his linguistic refutation of the possibility of ineffable truths is unsuccessful.

In addition to the difficulties with regard to premise (7), also premises (5) and (6) are problematic. Premise (5) begs the question. Why must there be an integrating *representation* r_3 integrating representations r_1 and r_2? A representation implies a conscious being that is entertaining that very representation, which in turn implies that every representation is entertained by a conscious being. And this is, of course, absurd. Perhaps what Moore had in mind is that between each two arbitrary facts f_1 and f_2, there is an integrating fact f_3 "between" them that "links" f_1 and f_2. This is a perfectly logical assumption, especially on the assumption of, as Moore writes, "a single conception of reality."[41] However, if this is what he meant then nothing follows for the *representation* of these facts. There may very well be facts about the world that are unrepresentable—such as perspectival facts, which will be discussed later. The existence of unrepresentable facts would mean that they are never represented by a conscious being, and so the question of whether their representations are expressible or not does not even occur.

Premise (6), the claim that in order to merge the contents of two such representations r_1 and r_2, an integrating representation r_3 must abstract from the points of view from which r_1 and r_2 were produced, suffers from a similar error. How do we know that between any two representations a third, connective representation exists at all? Moore writes:

> Given any true representation r_1, it must be possible, however indirectly, to integrate it with any other true representation r_2. That is, it must be possible to produce a third true representation r_3 whose content either is or in some sense includes the product of r_1's and r_2's. For r_1 and r_2 will between them have content, and this content will furnish a truth which, like any other, must be expressible.[42]

Again, it seems to me that representations are being confused with facts here. While it makes no sense to assume that for every fact there exists a representation of that fact, it makes a lot of sense to assume that between each two facts, there exists a third fact "connecting" the two. Yet in order to achieve that result, no abstraction has to take place because abstraction does not happen on the level of facts (but rather, on the level of expressions and representations).

As we have seen, Moore's attempt at a linguistic refutation of the possibility of ineffable truths is, though an interesting idea, unsuccessful. For all we know up to now, ineffable truths or propositions understood as perspectival propositions are still possible.

4.6.2 Metaphysical Objections

Besides linguistic considerations, there are also metaphysical worries about the notion of ineffable perspectival truths. The core intuition of this view is that perspective, in addition to being a feature of *representations* of reality, is a feature of reality *itself*. This, however, leads to incoherence. Moore summarizes this view, which he calls the 'Specious View,' as follows:

> Perspective is [assumed to be] a characteristic not only of representations but also of what is represented. There are perspectival features of reality, which figure in perspectival facts. Perspectival facts are like any other facts in that for them to obtain is for the world to be a certain way. But they are unlike other facts in that their obtaining is itself relative to a point of view.[43] The perspectival facts that obtain from one point of view are different from those that obtain from another. What makes (some) true perspectival representations true is, precisely, the obtaining of perspectival facts.[44]

As we have seen earlier, one adherent to this view is Nagel (recall the example of the bat), another one is Jackson (recall the example of Mary's seeing red for the first time). According to their arguments for the existence of perspectival facts, these facts (e.g., facts about how the world looks/sounds/feels from specific perspectives) obtain relative to a point of view. This distinguishes perspectival facts from objective facts (e.g., facts about the number of siblings I have, facts about physical laws, etc.): absolute facts do not obtain relative to specific points of view only, but from any point of view. Consequently, according to the perspectivalist, perspectival representations are made true by the obtaining of perspectival facts in the same way that objective representations are made true by objective facts.

But now we must note the following: the argument of the perspectivalist is perhaps intuitively appealing when we talk about bats or Mary-scenarios. However, there are countless structurally equivalent examples that are a lot less appealing. For example, imagine two people, Ernie and Bert, standing in the vicinity of Carfax Tower in the center of Oxford. Ernie is standing 200 meters away of the tower in front of Christchurch College.

Bert is standing one meter away, right at the bottom of Carfax Tower on Cornmarket Street. Ernie says: 'Carfax Tower is 200 meters to the right.' Bert says: 'Carfax Tower is one meter to the left.' A perspectivalist is committed to say that both representations are true because of the obtaining of their respective perspectival facts. I doubt anyone finds this argument convincing. If what Ernie says is true because it is a fact that Carfax Tower is 200 meters to the right, and if what Bert says is true because it is a fact that Carfax Tower is one meter to the left, then Carfax tower is both 200 meters to the right and one meter to the left, which is contradictory.

However, the exact same refutation can be used for bat-cases and Mary-scenarios. Instead of assuming a location-dependent perspectival fact as in the example of Ernie and Bert, we assume a perspectival fact dependent on a specific sensory apparatus. Imagine a bat using its sonar technique, thus producing a representation of a tree through sound propagation. Let's call the bat's representation of the tree r_B. Imagine further a human being looking at the tree and, through her human sensory system, producing a representation of the tree, call it r_H. Let's suppose that the content of both representations is that there is a tree. The adherent to the Specious View would have to say that r_B is true because it corresponds to a perspectival fact obtaining for the bat, call it f_B, and that r_H is true because it corresponds to a perspectival fact obtaining for the human, call it f_H. Consequently, although both representations have the same content, they are made true by different facts—a paradoxical result. No matter how we try to motivate the perspectivalist view, be it with arguments from different sensory apparatuses or less appealing cases of spatial relativity, they lead to contradiction.

Of course, the perspectivalist could now argue that the given examples rely on our intuitive grasp of the notion of a 'point of view,' yet what exactly points of view are supposed to be remains very blurry. Moore's definition, according to which a point of view is a "location in the broadest possible sense,"[45] is formulated in a way that suggests that the different examples have something substantial in common, namely, their perspectivalness. The perspectivalist could raise a doubt as to whether the idea of a point of view could be made any more specific without losing its ability to cover both cases like Nagel's bat and cases like Ernie and Bert. However, I don't see how the concept of a point of view could be defined in such a way as to include bat-perspectives while excluding Ernie-and-Bert-perspectives without distorting the concept beyond recognition. If such an argument were to be attempted in order to save perspectivalism, the burden of proof would be on the perspectivalist to show that such a modification of the concept 'point of view' is indeed possible.

A more common way in which perspectivalists try to remove contradiction is by claiming that perspectval facts are only "accessible" from the respective points of view of bats, humans, etc. However, it is difficult to make sense of what exactly restricted accessibility consists in: Do perspectival facts only exist relative to certain perspectives? But then we end up with the highly unattractive notion of relative existence. If perspectival facts do not exist relative to a specific perspective, then they exist simpliciter. But, as we have seen with Ernie and Bert, this means that they stand in contradiction.

One way to avoid this is by claiming that the conjunction of all perspectival facts obtaining from a specific point of view constitutes a world. Indexing perspectival facts to their respective perspectives by indexing them to separate perspectival worlds avoids contradiction but also commits us to the existence of as many worlds as there are points of view—a number far exceeding the number of possible worlds, since every possible world contains infinitely many points of view. Again, the perspectivalist is left with a rather unattractive ontology.

However, even if the perspectivalist were ready to accept such a vast number of worlds (perhaps by arguing that the objective world is ontologically privileged whereas perspectival worlds are deflationary entities whose ontological weight is somehow insignificant), there remains another problem. The perspectivalist would have to tell some story about the relations between perspectival worlds and the objective world (i.e., the world described by physics), since every person inhabits both of the objective world and at least one (but possibly many more) perspectival worlds. Denying the existence of the objective world is obviously not an option, at least not for anyone who believes that true representations are made true by one and the same unified reality.[46] Let's go back to Ernie and Bert and their respective claims that Carfax tower is 200 meters to the right and one meter to the left. In order to resolve the blatant contradiction, Ernie and Bert must find a way to integrate both their representations into one picture, and the way to do this is by transcending their subjective points of view. A way of transcending their points of view in order to accommodate their contradictory beliefs about the location of Carfax Tower is to point out that Ernie and Bert both inhabit the same world but occupy different spatial locations of that world. In order to interpret Ernie's claim that Carfax Tower is 200 meters to the right correctly, we must take into account Ernie's spatial location. The same goes for Bert's claim that Carfax Tower is one meter to the left. If we do this, we will see that both of their claims are true relative to their spatial location. The point is that, for any number of true representations, it must be possible, not only for each single one of them, but for all of them taken together, to be true.

In other words: there must be a single, unified world of which all true representations are true. Whoever denies this rules out the possibility of meaningful disagreement: if there wasn't a single, unified world, it wouldn't even be possible to identify a contradiction in Ernie's and Bert's claims.

Another problem for perspectivalism is that one needs to explain the individuation of, and the relations between, different perspectival worlds. This is difficult since there is both overlap of perspectival worlds and interaction between them. For example, although Ernie's and Bert's perspectival worlds differ with regard to the truths about Carfax Tower, they are the same (i.e., they overlap) with regard to other truths, for example, about physical laws (if $E = mc^2$ is true in Ernie's world, it is true in Bert's world as well). Does this overlap mean that Ernie and Bert "share" a world with regard to physical laws but live in separate worlds with regard to Carfax Tower? That seems absurd. The perspectivalist could try to argue that there isn't strictly speaking any overlap of perspectival worlds but rather some kind of *correspondence* between the truths in one world and truths in other worlds. On this view, truth T_E ($E = mc^2$) is a truth of Ernie's world and corresponds to a counterpart-truth T_B ($E = mc^{2*}$) which is true in Bert's world. This view avoids the problem of overlap. However, it also creates new ones. For example, the perspectivalist would have to explain what the correspondence relation between truths like T_E and T_B consists in. A natural answer would be that it consists in the fact that T_E and T_B have the same content (namely, $E = mc^2$). However, they don't. T_E and T_B are true of two different worlds and therefore cannot have the same content. I don't see how a correspondence relation could be explained without some sort of appeal to content, and therefore, I consider the strategy of invoking correspondence relations between perspectival worlds unconvincing. Given that different perspectival worlds are factually incompatible, the enterprise of trying to accommodate all perspectival worlds in such a way that interaction between them is possible and mutual exclusion is unproblematic seems bound to fail.

A final attempt for the perspectivalist to save his theory from contradiction involves embracing some form of truth-relativism, that is, some form of the view that truth is relative to frameworks such as points of view, perspectives, etc. However, as Plato already noted in the *Theaetetus*,[47] solutions of this kind suffer from the defect of self-refutation: either, the claim that all truths are relative to a specific framework is itself a truth relative to a specific framework (and thus not universally applicable); or, the claim that all truths are relative to a specific framework constitutes an exception to the rule that all truths are relative to a specific framework, in which case one could readily ask how this exception can be motivated and whether there are further exceptions to the rule. The perspectivalist could,

INEFFABLE PROPOSITIONS 99

of course, cheerfully admit that he is operating in a particular framework, which may be inaccessible to people not working in that framework. However, as noted earlier, it seems to me that this isn't really an option if we want to allow for the possibility of meaningful disagreement between the perspectivalist and his opponent.

To sum up, the notion of ineffable truths as inferred from perspectival facts must be rejected because the attempt to accommodate the perspectival

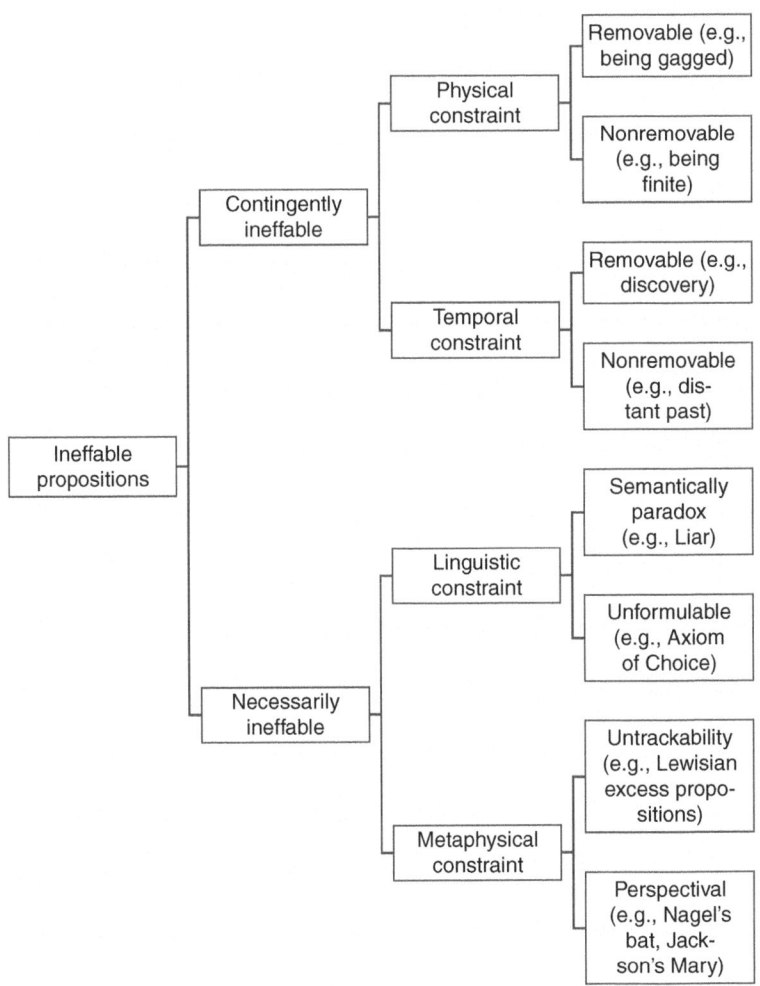

Figure 4.1 Varieties of ineffable propositions

facts corresponding to ineffable truths in one's ontology leads to an incoherent picture of reality. The only way of rendering the notion of perspectival truths coherent is by assuming relativism about truth, which is a self-refuting doctrine.

In this chapter, I have examined the concept of ineffable propositions (see Figure 4.1). I have raised the question whether the metaphysics of ineffability as experienced in aesthetic, religious, and philosophical contexts can be explained in terms of ineffable propositions and have answered this question negatively. I have argued that for a proposition to be ineffable without being trivially empty, it must be strictly rather than contingently inaccessible. Two cases of contingently inaccessible propositions were considered—self-referentiality and inaccessible mathematical truths—and their metaphysical relevance was dismissed. I have then outlined two ways of arguing for strict propositional inaccessibility via functionalist access conditions and perspectival access conditions. On the former account, the accessibility of a proposition depends on the functional role the proposition plays for its subject. On the latter account, the accessibility of a proposition depends on the perspective from which it can be accessed, that is, it depends on the spatiotemporal location and/or the psycho-physical constitution of the subject. I have demonstrated why neither functional nor perspectival access conditions provide a model of ineffable propositions that can be used to explain the metaphysics of ineffability. Hence, even though there are coherent ways of making sense of the notion of an ineffable proposition, these ways are unsuitable to explain the metaphysical underpinnings of aesthetic, religious, and philosophical ineffability. I will now proceed to examine whether ineffability can be explained in terms of 'ineffable content.'

CHAPTER 5

INEFFABLE CONTENT

5.1 Why Ineffable Content?

The idea of ineffable content—in the context of the philosophy of perception the term 'nonconceptual content' has become standard—appears primarily in the context of three different explanatory projects: the characterization of the contents of perceptual, aesthetic, and religious experience.

Recall our definition of mental content:[1]

Content A piece of mental content c is what informs and characterizes the mental state of a subject S at a given time t. It consists in the informational data contained in a subject's mental state at time t and on the basis of which S cognitively classifies the informational data.

Defenders of nonconceptual content challenge the widely held view that a person's mental contents are functions of the concepts she possesses. This view puts a conceptual constraint on mental contents. If all of a person's mental contents are functions of the concepts she possesses, then, on the assumption that we can express (linguistically) everything we can conceptualize, all of a person's mental contents are expressible. If, on the other hand, a person's mental contents are at least partly nonconceptual, then some mental contents are ineffable. As José Luis Bermúdez puts it, "Although few proponents of the idea of non-conceptual content explicitly adhere to an ineffability claim, the debate ... is best seen as a debate about ineffability."[2]

The central question behind the notion of nonconceptual content is whether it is possible for someone to be in a mental state with content without possessing the concepts needed to express the content of that state. If we can make sense of such nonconceptual content, the question is then whether it is nonconceptual *simpliciter* or whether it is nonconceptual for a particular being only. Tasting chestnut tea for the first time in her life, Claire might not be in possession of the concept 'chestnut tea'. Therefore, the content of her experience could be called nonconceptual *for her*. Georgie, on the other hand, has been drinking chestnut tea for years and is therefore in possession of the concept. In other words, nothing in the concept of chestnut tea is necessarily nonconceptual, so this would not be a case of interestingly ineffable content.[3] I am interested in the question whether there is a category of content that *necessarily* resists expression. In other words, is there a kind of nonconceptual content that is *strictly* inexpressible? Before we start the discussion of possible ways of arguing for such content, let's get clear on the meaning of 'concept'.

Following Christopher Peacocke, I take concepts to be "constituents of those intentional contents which can be the complete, truth-evaluable, contents of judgment and belief."[4] Besides 'ordinary' concepts like 'red' or 'wooden', I take it that there are also demonstrative concepts like 'this' or 'that' as well as indexical concepts like 'here' or 'there', which need to be supplemented by demonstrative gestures such as fingerpointing.[5] Concepts are individuated according to their content, so that two concepts C and D are distinct

> if and only if there is some completing content Σ such that the complete content $\Sigma(C)$ is distinct from the complete content (D); or, in other words, if and only if there is some content $\Sigma(C)$ such that someone for whom the question arises can rationally judge $\Sigma(C)$ without judging $\Sigma(D)$.[6]

The case of nonconceptual content constitutes a challenge to theories according to which the way in which a sentient being experiences the world depends on her conceptual capacities. Assuming that any content expressible by a proposition is conceptual, proponents of nonconceptual content then hold that conceptual and nonconceptual content are two different types of content, distinguished by the fact that only one of them can be brought into propositional form.

At this point it is important to note that there is a difference between mere sensations and perceptual content. The sensational component of perceptual experiences (their 'what-it-is-like-ness'/'raw feel'/'phenomenal quality'/'qualia') is *trivially* ineffable: no concept is able to communicate the subjective phenomenal quality of a sensation. No matter how rich Georgie's vocabulary is, she won't be able to induce the taste of chestnut tea in Claire by means of a concept. Only drinking chestnut tea provides Claire with a full understanding of the taste of chestnut tea. This is another way of saying that only the representational components of perceptual experiences are communicable: the fact that Claire is drinking chestnut tea is represented by Georgie's belief that Claire is drinking chestnut tea, whereas the sensational component of Claire's tasting chestnut tea is unrepresentable and therefore ineffable.

The trivial ineffability of sensations is different from the ineffability of nonconceptual content. This is because nonconceptual content is supposed to be representational:

> If a given perceptual experience has a nonconceptual content that ϕ, this means that the experience represents ϕ as holding in the world. Conceptual and nonconceptual contents are distinguished not by whether they are representational but according to how they represent. They are distinguished according to whether, in specifying how they represent the environment as being, we need to restrict ourselves to concepts possessed by the perceiver. This is in stark contrast to the traditional distinction between sensation and belief, according to which the sensational component has no role to play in explaining how the experience represents the world as being.[7]

Thus, what we are looking for is a category of representational mental content that is strictly nonconceptual. I will now proceed to examine whether there is such content, and if so, whether it provides a good model for our paradigmatic examples of ineffability.

5.2 Nonconceptual Content in Perception

The debate about nonconceptual content revolves around a constraint, call it the 'conceptual constraint', which conceptualists impose on all mental contents and which nonconceptualists intend to lift. Put simply, conceptualists hold that all mental contents are conceptual, whereas nonconceptualists deny this. Accounts of nonconceptual perceptual content differ with regard to how they attempt to lift the conceptual constraint: the conceptual constraint can be lifted 'globally', so that a subject's mental contents come out as entirely independent of the concepts she possesses, or it can be lifted 'locally', so that a subject's mental contents come out as partly independent of the concepts she possesses.

One way of lifting the conceptual constraint for all mental contents is to assume a realist possible-worlds-semantics according to which propositions are functions from sets of worlds to truth-values. On such a view, all mental contents are trivially nonconceptual because propositions are defined as sets of worlds rather than structured entities composed of concepts and functions. But even without assuming possible-worlds-semantics, it is possible to hold that all mental contents are trivially nonconceptual. Robert Stalnaker, for example, argues that nothing in the way we think of concepts precludes thinking of concepts as means to *refer to* informational content rather than constituents *of* informational content:

> Let us grant (without looking too hard at what this means) that states of belief and judgment are essentially conceptual—states and acts that require the capacity to deploy concepts, and that manifest the exercise of this capacity. That does not by itself imply that the concepts that subjects deploy and are disposed to deploy when they are in such states or perform such acts are thereby constitutive of the contents that are used to describe the states and acts.[8]

It is quite clear that an account on which *all* mental contents come out nonconceptual renders the notion of nonconceptual content quite uninteresting. In other words, there is no way of distinguishing between trivially ineffable and interestingly ineffable content on a picture where simply all contents are ineffable. Put differently, on the assumption of possible-worlds-semantics, the question of nonconceptual content as a model of significantly ineffable experiences does not even get off the ground.

Thus, in order to avoid a trivial solution to the question whether mental contents are necessarily conceptual, I will set such global lifting strategies aside and focus on local lifting strategies. According to those accounts, some parts of a person's mental content are not functions of the concepts she possesses, which amounts to the claim that only *some* mental contents are ineffable.

In general, if we want to lift the conceptual constraint for some parts of our mental content, we must find a way to argue that those parts of our mental content are, for some reason x, beyond the reach of our conceptual apparatus. What could be such a reason?[9]

5.2.1 Contradictory Content

Recent research in neurobiology has shown that illusory motions can be induced in the human sense of vision and touch. This phenomenon is called the 'motion-after-effect'. If we look at a waterfall (or any other constant downward movement) for about 30 seconds and then shift our gaze to a still object in our vicinity (a tree, a bench), then it seems for a brief moment that that object is moving upward, in the opposite direction. It is assumed that the reasons for this phenomenon is our brain's adaptation to a given movement: it compensates for movement in one direction, which can cause us momentarily to see an actually non-moving object as moving. The same effect can also be induced in our tactile senses, a phenomenon known as 'cutaneous saltation', whereby a tactile illusion is induced by tapping two separate regions of a person's skin, for example, on her forearm, in rapid succession. This induces the illusion of continuous taps between both areas of tapping (sometimes referred to as the cutaneous "rabbit" hopping up one's arm), even in those areas where no taps were applied. Finally, perceptual illusions like these can also be induced across senses, so that visual stimuli can induce a tactile motion-after-effect, and vice versa.[10]

Some philosophers, most notably Tim Crane, have tried to infer the existence of contradictory, and therefore, nonconceptual content from these phenomena:

> If you stare for a period of time at a scene which contains movement in one direction, and then turn your attention to an object in a scene which contains no movement, this object will appear to move in the opposite direction to that of the original movement. ...But the above description is not quite right. For although the stationary object *does* appear to move, it does not appear to move relative to the background of the scene. That is, there is a clear sense in which it also *appears to stay still.*[11]

Crane holds that the contents of mental representations of this kind are contradictory: it is logically impossible for something to be both moving and not moving. On the assumption that conceptual content must be consistent—inconsistent conceptual content is incapable of realization in a possible world—Crane concludes that such contradictory perceptual content is nonconceptual.

The strategy of inferring nonconceptual content from allegedly contradictory perceptual content is question-begging, however, since contradictions *imply* concepts. It is propositions that stand in contradiction to one another, and propositions are conceptual. We can only detect a contradiction if we are already operating on the level of concepts. In order to determine that the content of one's perceptual experience is contradictory because it represents an object as both moving and not moving, one needs to employ the concept 'moving'. If we didn't possess the relevant concepts, we wouldn't be able to detect the contradiction.[12]

Now Crane could argue that this is the whole point, that is, the minute we start talking about concepts, we are playing the wrong game. As long as content is taken to be conceptual, it has to be consistent, of course. But given that experience tells us otherwise in cases of waterfalls etc., we should assume that content is nonconceptual.

The problem with this line of argument is, however, that we simply don't experience inconsistent content. We receive content *simpliciter* through perception, and sometimes (as in the waterfall case), when we try to describe that content, we end up using contradictory concepts ("The object is both moving and not moving"). This doesn't establish that the content itself is contradictory.

Arguments from contradictory perceptual content are thus not successful in establishing the existence of nonconceptual content. Let's see what other ways there are of motivating nonconceptual content.

5.2.2 *Analog Content*

Perhaps nonconceptual content is all that content that doesn't make it into a propositional thought or assertion, but which is still there, lurking in the background, as it were. An argument of this kind has been made by Fred Dretske. He claims that in cases of perception, we must distinguish between 'analog' and 'digital' perceptual content. The former, he argues, characterizes the contents of one's perception, whereas the latter characterizes the contents of one's propositional attitudes.[13] He illustrates his view with the following example:

> I see a red apple in a white bowl surrounded by a variety of other objects. I recognize it as an apple. I come to believe that it is an apple. The belief has a content that we express with the words, 'That is an apple.' The content of this belief does not represent the apple as red, as large, or as lying next to an orange. I may have (other) beliefs about these matters, but the belief in question abstracts from the concreteness of the sensory representation (icon, sensory information store, experience) in order to represent it simply as an apple. However, these additional pieces of information are contained in the sensory experience of the apple.[14]

Dretske argues that our transition from the sensory representation of an apple (i.e., seeing it) to the cognitive representation of an apple (i.e., forming a belief about it) is characterized by "a systematic stripping away of components of information ... in order to feature *one* component of the information."[15] He calls this procedure of exposing one particular component to the exclusion of all others 'digitalization' and argues that all propositional attitudes, being conceptual, are necessarily digital representations. The perceptual experience itself, on the other hand, constitutes an analog representation, which carries much richer information than any proposition could express. Thus, it is concluded, analog content must be nonconceptual.

The problem with Dretske's description of propositional attitude formation on the basis of rich (analog) perceptual content is that it seems at least possible for every piece of analog information to become the object of our selective attention and thus, to feature in a propositional attitude with digital content: instead of forming the belief 'That is an apple', I could shift my attention to its colour and form the belief 'That is a red apple' or 'That is a bright shade of red' or 'The apple is lying next to an orange.' In other words, nothing in Dretske's argument proves that some components of analog content are intrinsically nonconceptual. Their nonconceptuality is accidental and in principle removable.

In fact, Dretske's account is even compatible with the idea that perception is *nothing else* but the constant acquisition of propositional beliefs (i.e., conceptual contents) about one's environment, even if those beliefs fade away almost immediately.[16] In Dretske's apple-scenario, for example, it is arguably possible that we acquire many more beliefs than 'That is an apple,' including beliefs about the specific features of that very apple ('The apple is half-red half-green'; 'The apple has a dent right next to its stalk'), about the close environment of the apple ('The apple is in a white bowl'; 'The white bowl is made of porcelain'), etc. It may be the case that we never pay conscious attention to these beliefs because we focus on one specific belief only. Yet it may very well be that perception consists in a continuous formation of numerous beliefs, all of which could *potentially* figure in a propositional attitude. Simply postulating superfluent perceptual content does not make a case for nonconceptual content. If we want to be able to infer nonconceptual content from our perceptual experience, then we must give a reason why some parts of our perceptual contents are *necessarily* beyond the reach of our conceptual apparatus. Arguments to this effect are known as 'fineness-of-grain' arguments.

5.2.3 *Fineness of Grain*

The account that has provoked most discussion in recent years has initially been triggered by Gareth Evans. In *The Varieties of Reference*, he raises the following question: "Do we really understand the proposal that we have as many colour concepts as there are shades of colour that we can sensibly discriminate?"[17]

Evans' question is a rhetorical one, suggesting that we can perceptually discriminate many more shades of color than we can conceptualize. Peacocke picks up on Evans' question and argues that our conceptual resources are insufficient to capture the fineness of grain of the perceptual input we receive (or in other words, that our discriminative abilities outstrip our conceptual abilities).[18]

One way of answering Evans' question is to argue that our ability to discriminate F's from G's is enough for us to say that we possess a concept of F and a concept of G, so that the answer to Evans' question would be, trivially, yes: as soon as we can discriminate a particular shade of color, we can reasonably say that we possess the concept of that color shade—otherwise, we would not be able to discriminate it. The strategy of avoiding nonconceptual content is thus to align our conceptual abilities with our discriminative abilities. For example, an opponent of nonconceptual content could argue for the existence of 'demonstrative concepts,' which are exactly as fine-grained as the contents we receive perceptually.

John McDowell argues in this vein that our conceptual capacities are determined by our perceptual experiences. He suggests a strategy that has sometimes been referred to as the 'kidnapping strategy'.[19] The key move of this strategy is to invoke 'short-lived recognitional capacities' in order to capture the exact content of a person's perceptual experience:

> It is possible to acquire the concept of a shade of a color, and most of us have done so. Why not say that one is thereby equipped to embrace shades of color within one's conceptual thinking with the very same determinateness with which they are presented in one's visual experience, so that one's concepts can capture colors no less sharply than one's experience presents them? In the throes of an experience of the kind that putatively transcends one's conceptual powers—an experience that *ex hypothesi* affords a suitable example—one can give linguistic expression to a concept that is exactly as fine-grained as the experience by uttering a phrase like 'that shade,' in which the demonstrative exploits the presence of the sample.[20]

McDowell is thus arguing that recognizing a certain content implies having the concept to recognize it.[21] By invoking a higher-order sortal like 'shade', and combining it with a demonstrative like 'that', we can give expression to whichever shade we want by using the concept 'that shade'. More generally, the combination of demonstrative concepts (probably including the relevant gestures) with higher order sortals enables the expression of all perceptual contents, no matter how fine-grained.

The question whether we can count such demonstrative capacities as concepts at all, McDowell answers as follows:

> In the presence of the original sample, 'that shade' can give expression to a concept of a shade; what ensures that it is a concept—that thoughts that exploit it have the necessary distance from what would determine them to be true—is that the associated capacity can persist into the future, if only for a short time, and that, having persisted, it can be used also in thoughts about what is by then the past, if only the recent past. What is in play here is a recognitional capacity, possibly quite short-lived, that sets in with the experience.[22]

At the same time, however, one need not be in possession of a *linguistic* expression for a concept in order to possess the concept. An important aspect highlighted by this argument is that for something to be expressible, the subject need not be in possession of a canonical expression. As long as a person has *some kind* of demonstrative resource ("this", "that"), a higher-order sortal to pick out the general category of that which is picked out by the demonstrative (a color shade, a sound, a smell, etc.), and as long as she is situated in the near vicinity of the respective object or property, all perceptual contents that can be discriminated by our perceptual apparatus can also be expressed in just the same way that ordinary shades and other phenomenal concepts are expressed.[23]

Christopher Peacocke, a defender of nonconceptual content, admits that the McDowellian strategy rules out fineness-of-grain arguments for nonconceptual content. He only points out that one should not use a supplemented demonstrative like 'that shade' to make a case against nonconceptual content. The demonstrative 'that' should not be supplemented by a sortal like 'shade' if it is to capture the exact fineness-level of the relevant experience. This is because supplemented demonstrative concepts already cut too finely:

> Both the person who has the concept scarlet, and has an experience whose content he expresses using the phrase 'that scarlet', and someone who merely has the more general concept red, can be seeing a given scarf as having the same finely-individuated shade.[24]

According to Peacocke, the conceptualist should rather use unsupplemented demonstrative concepts like 'this' or 'that' to make sure every nuance of the perceptual experience is covered by the demonstrative.

This way of thinking about demonstrative concepts is problematic, however. When we use demonstrative concepts, we must take care to ensure that, despite the lack of a canonical expression for what we want to express, our interlocutor knows the general direction of our demonstrative gesture. If I point at a particular shade of red instantiated by an apple, saying "That!," it is unclear whether I intend to express the apple's color, or its shape, or its smell, etc. I have to add some sortal to direct my interlocutor's attention in the right direction, for example, "The color shade instantiated by this apple." This point will become relevant in Chapter 7, when I will have to explain why instances of ineffable knowledge *cannot* be expressed using demonstratives. One of the reasons I shall give is that there is no suitable higher-order sortal that we could use in order to point our interlocutor into the right direction.

For the cases of ordinary perceptual experiences, however, demonstrative concepts supplemented by higher-order sortals can be invoked to capture the most fine-grained properties, so that fineness-of-grain arguments can be ruled out as strategies to establish the existence of nonconceptual content.[25]

5.2.4 Animal Perception

Far from giving up his conviction of the existence of nonconceptual perceptual content, Peacocke then submits an argument for nonconceptual content himself, an argument from animal perception: "If the lower animals do not have states with conceptual content, but some of their perceptual states have contents in common with human perceptions, it follows that some perceptual representational content is nonconceptual."[26]

We can imagine a human being, Jane, in a perceptual state with content that Jane would express with the sentence 'There is a mushroom' and a cow in a perceptual state with the same content. Arguably, Jane and the cow are in states with the same perceptual content. In other words, the content of Jane's perceptual state can be shared by the cow. Jane has the concepts to express it, the cow presumably doesn't. If we follow Peacocke's line of argument, then, given that Jane and the cow can share the content of a perceptual experience, we must conclude that Jane is in a perceptual state with nonconceptual content.

Peacocke's argument depends on the assumption that animals are never in mental states with conceptual content. Aside from the complication that we can never be sure of what is going on in the minds of animals, Peacocke's assumption is only reasonable if we take concept possession to be a matter of verbal expression: given that cows don't talk, and given that talking is essential to having concepts, we can assume that the mental concept of cows is not conceptual. But this is a very strong way of defining concept possession. Cows and humans clearly differ with regard to their expressive capacities, but cows and humans are equally clearly capable of distinguishing, say, a flower from a tree (a cow eats flowers but would never attempt to eat a tree). If we don't want to deny the cow the capacity of recognizing what's a flower and what's a tree, we have to grant that it is sufficient for a person, or a cow, to possess a given concept F to be able to *discriminate* F's from the rest of the perceptually received content.

Given that both animals and humans are able to discriminate F's from non-F's, flowers from trees, etc., Peacocke's argument for nonconceptual content is unsuccessful. Unless he provides a plausible argument to the effect that concept possession requires more than being able to discriminate F's from non-F's, his argument from animal perception fails to establish the existence of nonconceptual perceptual content.

We may conclude at this point that arguments for nonconceptual content in perception, if successful at all, do not provide good models for a category of ineffable content suitable to explain the metaphysical underpinnings of our paradigmatic cases of ineffability. Recall that we are looking for a category of mental content that is both representational (as opposed to merely sensational) and strictly nonconceptual. As the above discussion has revealed, however, arguments for nonconceptual content in perception either cannot show that the relevant content is *necessarily* beyond the reach of concepts (Crane, Dretske), or they are based on the denial of a correlation between perceptual discrimination-capacities and concept-possession (Evans, Peacocke). None of these arguments manage to establish the existence of mental content, that is both representational and strictly (but nontrivially[27]) nonconceptual.

So let's turn our attention to an entirely different explanatory project and see if we can find a good argument for the existence of strictly nonconceptual, representational content there: the contents of aesthetic experiences.

5.3 The Contents of Aesthetic Experience

Works of art afford aesthetic experiences, some (perhaps all) of which are evaluated as meaningful or insightful. However, some (perhaps all) of these meanings or insights resist linguistic formulation. Most people feel that the content of a work of art cannot be paraphrased (without remainder) into language. This aesthetic ineffability has been the source of much fascination with the expressive powers of art.

If, for example, a friend invited us to enjoy Maria Abramovic's *The Artist is Present* together, we would find ourselves rather disappointed if we found out that our friend didn't mean visiting the *Museum of Modern Art* but reading a description of the performance. Likewise, we would find it odd if someone told us that, instead of listening to Mahler's Symphony N. 8, we could equally well read a review of it.

The reason why we wouldn't accept a description of an artwork instead of the artwork itself is that, intuitively, the content we receive through an aesthetic experience is inextricably linked to the form in which the content is presented, where the form of an artwork could be characterized as "the ensemble of choices intended to realize the point or purpose of an artwork."[28] Therefore, it seems impossible to most of us to render a painting, a melody, a poem, or even a metaphor, in literal language. In that sense, content transported through aesthetic experience is ineffable. Wittgenstein phrases the point as follows:

> I should like to say: 'These notes say something glorious, but I do not know what.' These notes are a powerful gesture, but I cannot put anything side

by side with it that will serve as an explanation. A grave nod. James: 'Our vocabulary is inadequate.'[29]

Defenders of the concept of aesthetic content as an independent category of content hold that aesthetic content is *intrinsically* unparaphrasable, which means that at least some parts of it are nonconceptual. The goal in this section is to examine whether we can make sense of such aesthetic content as nonconceptual, and therefore ineffable, content. If the notion is coherent, ineffability could possibly be explained in terms of such content.

Here are some reasons philosophers have given for assuming that aesthetic content is a specific kind of content that can only be communicated through the respective artworks and cannot be rendered in (literal) language:

> If all meanings could be adequately expressed by words, the arts of painting and music would not exist. There are values and meanings that can be expressed only by immediately visible and audible qualities, and to ask what they mean in the sense of something that can be put into words is to deny their distinctive existence.[30]

Dewey thus maintains that value and meaning of a piece of art are inextricably linked to its perceptual form, that is, its visible and audible qualities. The specific value of an artwork, that is, its aesthetic content, lies in its perceptual qualities.

> I think every work of art expresses, more or less purely, more or less subtly, not feelings and emotions which the artist has, but feelings and emotions which the artist knows; his insight into the nature of sentience, his picture of vital experience, physical and emotive and fantastic. [...] Such knowledge is not expressible in ordinary discourse. The reason for this ineffability is not that the ideas to be expressed are too high, too spiritual, or too anything-else, but that the forms of feeling and the forms of discursive expression are logically incommensurate, so that any exact concepts of feeling and emotion cannot be projected into the logical form of literal language. Verbal statement [...] is almost useless for conveying knowledge about the precise character of our affective life.[31]

Langer argues that aesthetic content is essentially sensual and emotional, and that the logical form of language is not suitable to express contents of this kind. Art thus expresses feelings and emotions more aptly than language.

> Certain works of high imagination bewitch the understanding [...], provoking a response which consists in venturing a coherent interpretation of the work which we know in advance to be inadequate, for we also know the value of the interpretation lies in the fact that it escapes us.[32]

Danto argues that aesthetic content is necessarily beyond the reach of our concepts, even though our understanding is constantly trying to capture it—aesthetic content is somehow too intricate for our understanding. The continuous impossibility of providing a coherent interpretation of it, then, is what accounts for an artwork's aesthetic value.

The above quotations suggest that there are at least two principal ways of accounting for the ineffability of aesthetic content: to argue that aesthetic content is *intrinsically different* from ordinary content, and to argue that it is more complex, or more fleeting, than ordinary content, but not necessarily intrinsically different from it. In the following, I will examine three accounts of aesthetic content, each one of which tries to explain its ineffability along one of these lines. According to the first account we will look at, aesthetic ineffability is due to a twofold structure within our awareness.

5.3.1 A Twofold Structure of Awareness

Rafael De Clercq applies the idea of a twofold structure of awareness, which he ascribes to Michael Polanyi,[33] to aesthetic perception. De Clercq begins his argument by stating that the discussion of art definitely requires specific skills, yet even provided these skills,

> there is some point at which even our best efforts run up against the limits of language. That is, at some point we must recognize that much of what we find of significance in art, and in aesthetic objects in general, cannot be rendered in words (without remainder) and so can never become fully our own. This observation, which I take to be in line with common sense, could also be phrased as follows: language, at least in its literal mode, is not able to capture fully the content of an aesthetic experience; aesthetic experience, therefore, may be said to put us in touch with the unsayable or "ineffable."[34]

De Clercq identifies three questions that any account of aesthetic ineffability should be able to answer. The first one is why the content of an aesthetic experience cannot be fully articulated. The second is why we would experience this inarticulable content as ineffable. The third is why we attach importance to what we fail to express in aesthetic experience.[35] He credits Polanyi's account of awareness with being capable of answering the first two of these questions. According to Polanyi, perceptual attention (or perceptual awareness—he uses them synonymously) has a twofold structure: there is focal awareness and there is subsidiary awareness. A perceptual experience consists of sensory elements, some of which we attend to focally and some of which we attend to subsidiarily.

We attend to an artwork like Beethoven's *Moonlight Sonata* by focussing on certain elements (the key, the rhythm, etc.), while leaving other, subsidiary elements in the background. A subsidiary element of an aesthetic experience is unspecifiable (and thus ineffable) because "as soon as we shift our attention to it, and start to examine it focally, its meaning changes, that meaning being, in fact, the focus upon which it used to bear."[36] In other words, as soon as we try to focus on the subsidiary elements, they stop being subsidiary and thus, change their character (this fact might also account for the often reported feeling of 'elusiveness' of aesthetic experiences). Consequently, it is impossible to attend to an object both focally and subsidiarily; focal and subsidiary attention are mutually exclusive.

What is ineffable about an aesthetic experience, on his account, is thus not a particular aspect of the aesthetic content in question (such as the bass line, the melody, the brush strokes, the rhyme, etc.) which we attend to merely subsidiarily. Rather, it is "the way these various parts contribute to and are integrated into a whole that can move us deeply."[37]

In other words, it is the composition of an artwork's parts into a whole that we cannot attend to focally, at least not without changing its character. The impossibility of turning our focal attention to the composition of an artwork's parts into a whole, then, is what accounts for our inability to express the content of the respective artwork.

What is appealing in De Clercq's account is that it offers a clear explanation of what exactly it is about an artwork that causes the experienced ineffability. What is problematic, however, is that nothing in De Clercq's description of aesthetic experiences is unique to *aesthetic* experiences: if his description of a twofold structure of aesthetic awareness is correct, it arguably applies to ordinary perceptual experiences as well (indeed, Polanyi's original account was intended to describe ordinary perceptual experiences). Consequently, De Clercq's account also fails to explain why it is that we credit only aesthetic (but not ordinary perceptual) experiences with extraordinary importance.

Moreover, the claim that we cannot attend to the composition of an artwork's parts into a whole focally without changing its character remains unsupported by argument. Why should it not be possible to attend to each composite part of an artwork and to the way these parts interact to form a whole? It may be true that we typically don't attend to these things focally when apprehending a piece of art (typically we focus on specific details rather than the interplay between all parts of an artwork), but this does not mean that we cannot attend to them in principle.

Finally, DeClercq's account, if successful, would entail that the ineffability experienced in the presence of a work of art is a direct consequence of the way we process sense perceptions. Ineffability would thus not be a feature of a specific kind of content. While there is nothing wrong with attempting to explain ineffability in such a way, it is not an argument for a specific kind of ineffable content. Hence, accounting for aesthetic ineffability in terms of a twofold structure of awareness is not a promising route to argue for the existence of ineffable aesthetic content.

In the next section we will look at an account of aesthetic content according to which aesthetic content is ineffable because it cannot be employed inferentially.

5.3.2 Non-inferential Content

Michael Luntley makes a case for the existence of nonconceptual content in music by arguing that musical experience features content that does not function in the way conceptual content does.[38] His account is designed specifically to resist McDowell's 'kidnapping strategy', which we discussed earlier.

Luntley argues that the content of a person's perceptual experience can only be 'kidnapped' by a demonstrative concept if it has the potential to figure in a person's 'space of reasons', that is, if it has the potential to be employed in the body of rational inferences which inform a person's reasons for action.

According to Luntley, the distinguishing mark of conceptual content is that it figures in a subject's reasons that are deployed for belief and action. Nonconceptual content, though representational, cannot perform this function. He writes:

> If subject S has a conceptual capacity for discriminating F-ness (their experience represents F-ness in some way), the representation of F-ness must be capable of contributing to the rational organization of their behaviour by figuring in their inferential reasons for belief/action. ... The capacity to discriminate F-ness as contributing to the content of the subject's experience is nonconceptual if and only if the capacity cannot contribute to the subject's rational organization of their behaviour.[39]

He then proceeds to identify a confirmation condition for nonconceptual content:

> Confirmation condition: A representation of F-ness will be nonconceptual if (a) the subject can discriminate F-ness, (b) the subject is a novice with respect to the sortal concepts required for generating demonstrative kidnapping concepts, (c) the subject fails to treat transparently the validity of inferences that exploit a conceptual representation of F-ness.[40]

Luntley finds examples of nonconceptual, representational content in musical experiences. His prime example is the sense of tonality invoked in a musical novice, that is, an inexperienced hearer unfamiliar with music theory, upon hearing a dominant 7th chord for the first time.[41] Unlike the novice, an experienced musician would know that hearing a dominant 7th chord has the quality of, as it were, 'pulling towards the resolution' provided by the tonic. A novice will be unable to describe the quality of the dominant 7th chord; but of course he will experience it just as any other listener would. Now the five basic steps of Luntley's argument can be rendered as follows:

1. A novice experiences the quality of pulling-towards-resolution upon hearing the dominant 7th (V7) chord.
2. If it is correct to say that he experiences this quality, then we are justified in claiming that the novice discriminates the V7-ness of the music.
3. Therefore, an *external observer* can render the representational content of the novice's experience through the proposition "That sounds V7-ish."
4. The novice himself, on the other hand, cannot conceptualize the content of his experience because he lacks the concepts to do so. A McDowellian demonstrative or recognitional concept won't help him either because the content of the novice's experience is unavailable to his inferential reasoning (recall that Luntley identified unavailability to inferential reasoning as the characteristic mark of nonconceptual content earlier).
5. Therefore, the content of the novice's experience is an example of nonconceptual representational content.[42]

Luntley's argument for the existence of nonconceptual content is compelling at first sight: most of our experiences serve to provide perceptual information, which we will then use in order to rationally organize our thought and behavior. Contents that cannot be used in this way are nonconceptual precisely because of their unsuitability for rational inference.

The problem with Luntley's account is that, despite his prime example being a musical one, his account does not explain what distinguishes the case of aesthetic nonconceptual content from ordinary perceptual cases. In fact, he suggests that another example for nonconceptual content is the puzzlement we experience when we enter a familiar room whose furniture has been subtly rearranged: we feel that something in the room is not quite right, but we cannot say what it is.[43]

Luntley's goal is to provide a case for nonconceptual content by means of an argument that is not susceptible to McDowell's demonstrative 'kidnapping strategy.' And insofar as we are considering only a particular point in time, for example, the point in time where the novice still lacks the concept of a dominant 7th, Luntley succeeds in showing why McDowell's strategy won't work. This is because Luntley presents a case where the subject in question wouldn't even know where or at what to point demonstratively—the received content is still entirely unlocated. In the same way, we would not manage to point out immediately exactly where the difference in the rearranged furniture is.

The word 'immediately' reveals another problem with Luntley's argument, however: he has not presented us with a case of necessarily nonconceptual content. As soon as the novice learns the concept of a dominant 7th, he can employ it in his rational inferences. And as soon as a piece of content can be employed in rational inference, according to Luntley, it ceases to be nonconceptual. For the same reason, a piece of content may be nonconceptual for one person but perfectly expressible for another: the musical content the novice receives when hearing the V7, though expressible from an external point of view as 'This sounds V7', is inexpressible for the novice himself. As in the case of De Clercq's subsidiary awareness, also the nonconceptual content Luntley argues for is merely a case of relative nonconceptuality, and hence, relative ineffability. It is therefore unsuitable as a model for the metaphysics of absolute ineffability.

5.3.3 Phenomenal Ineffability

The final and most promising way of arguing that aesthetic content is intrinsically different from propositional content is by claiming that it is nonrepresentational, that is, purely phenomenal. William Kennick, for example, argues that we experience works of art in a way in which we can never "experience" a proposition. This is because, he explains, "poems and paintings have meanings and values that ordinary prose descriptions do not have. Pictures have color, depth, balance, chiaroscuro, design; propositions do not. Poems have measured rhythm and rhyme, striking images and involved metaphors; ordinary prose statements do not."[44]

In other words, it is the phenomenal qualities of artworks that account for the aesthetic experience they afford: the color of a painting stimulates our visual perception, the rhythm of a poem stimulates our auditory perception, etc. Propositions, on the other hand, don't have perceptual qualities and hence, don't stimulate our perceptual apparatus. Propositions are purely cognitive entities. As a consequence, claiming that the content of an artwork is ineffable because it cannot be translated into literal language is misleading.

Kennick uses the example of a protractor to support his argument that there is no reason to think that an artwork's "informative content"[45] could not be rendered in literal language. He asks us to imagine a man complaining about the fact that his protractor didn't draw square circles and inferring from this that his protractor must be broken. He compares this case with the case of aesthetic content, and our puzzlement about the fact that words don't seem to be able to capture the contents of art. Kennick's view is that complaints of these sorts "do not strike at remediable difficulties, and hence they do not strike at inadequacies or defects of language at all; they do not point to something that language cannot do or that art can do better than language can."[46]

In his view, the sensational components of a work of art are ineffable by definition, that is, they are ineffable for the same reason that all sensations are ineffable: they are merely phenomenal, not representational. Calling the specific perceptual qualities of a work of art ineffable is a category mistake. The perceptual qualities of a work of art are simply not the kind of thing that could be expressed linguistically, in the same way that the smell of coffee cannot be expressed. Hence, Kennick holds, the reason we feel that works of art cannot be paraphrased is not because they communicate a specific kind of aesthetic content, but because they afford a specific kind of perceptual experience that lacks representational content altogether.[47]

In a similar vein, also Stephen Davies argues against the idea that the ineffability of aesthetic content is in any way significant. Using the example of music, he identifies a common temptation to associate aesthetic content with ineffable truths, and a further temptation to think that "such truths are somehow more important or vital than those language can capture."[48]

Davies argues that this temptation should be resisted, and explains the ineffability of musical content with "a degree of detail and resolution in auditory expressions that exceeds the possibility of verbal description or specification, and not some new dimension of the eternal verities."[49]

The ineffability of aesthetic experiences is thus nothing but a lack of descriptive resources to capture all the nuances of a perceptual experience to the full extent. In other words, the ineffability of aesthetic experiences is not due to a specific kind of content whose nature is such that it necessarily resists linguistic expression, but due to a lack of fine-grained-ness of our expressive resources. Thus, since this kind of ineffability is not restricted to aesthetic contexts but can be found in ordinary perception as well, Davies concludes that we have no reason to consider aesthetic ineffability any more interesting than ordinary perceptual ineffability.

The view that the ineffability attributed to artworks originates trivially in the limitations of our cognitive apparatus, not in the aesthetic content itself, is also defended by Diana Raffman, who explores the relationship between human memory capabilities and verbalization within the context of tonal music.[50] She argues that musical perception consists in the computation of abstract mental representations of musical signals.[51] Certain aspects of these musical signals, notably the shallowest levels of pitch, cannot be mentally categorized ("type-identified") in a way that allows for the development of appropriate vocabulary. This is because, she argues, our mental categories or schemas are not as fine-grained as our perceptual abilities.[52]

Raffman's argument is structurally akin to Evans' argument for the fineness of grain: all the argument manages to show is that some aspects of a work of art are ineffable *relative to* our immediately available expressive resources. As we have seen already in the case of McDowell's argument about nonconceptual content, however, relative ineffability is not absolute ineffability. McDowell's strategy of invoking higher-order sortals and demonstrative concepts will solve the issue also in Raffman's case: even if there is no canonical expression for a given pitch or any other aspect of musical content, pointing at it ('*That* pitch!') will be the first step to develop an appropriate vocabulary. But this also means that nothing in the concept of musical content can be said to be *in principle* ineffable.

The attentive reader will have noticed that this line of argument is structurally similar to those given in Chapter 4, where the goal was to argue for ineffable propositions: just as there is nothing interesting in propositions that happen to be ineffable due to a 'merely medical'[53] constraint of human beings (such as the constraint of being finite and therefore incapable of expressing infinite propositions), there is nothing interesting in contents that are ineffable due to the 'merely medical' constraint of our being unable to describe them on the appropriate level of detail.

Explaining aesthetic ineffability in terms of the ineffability of an artwork's phenomenal qualities has one great advantage: it doesn't force us to posit a separate category of content (i.e., aesthetic content), which must then be brought into one coherent picture with ordinary content. Phenomenal ineffability is unmysterious and ontologically undemanding. The problem with such accounts, however, is that they fail to account for the feeling of *significance*, *meaningfulness*, or *importance* that is typically associated with ineffable aesthetic experiences, but never with ordinary perceptual experiences. The impossibility of expressing the phenomenal character of tomato salad is much less likely to arouse our curiosity than the impossibility to express the content of a symphony by Mahler. And even if we had the conceptual resources to express all nuances of an artwork (say, the exact color and position of a painting's brush strokes), we would still not feel that we had managed to express its specifically *aesthetic* content. Accounts explaining the ineffability of aesthetic content by pointing out the ineffability common to all sensory experiences fail to explain what is special and intriguing about *aesthetic* ineffability.

We have examined three different accounts of ineffable content in the context of aesthetic experiences, but none of them managed to show that aesthetic content is an independent category of content that is intrinsically ineffable. This should not be taken as an indication that there is, after all, nothing especially interesting or even mysterious about aesthetic ineffability. All it shows is that the ineffability found in aesthetic contexts is unlikely to be a matter of a specific kind of content.

5.4 The Contents of Religious Experience

In the preceding sections, I have demonstrated that attempts to argue for a specific category of content over and above perceptual and propositional content are unsuccessful. Another way of motivating the existence of ineffable content is by reference to the language we use when we attempt to express such content. The paradigm example here are religious experiences.

We have seen above that the content of a work of art is believed to be fully expressible only by the artwork itself. In the case of religious experience, we are facing a similar belief. People who report having had a religious experience typically hold that their experience defies (literal) expression. William James even lists ineffability as the number one distinctive characteristic of religious experiences. The second characteristic is that they are perceived as meaningful:

> Although so similar to states of feeling, mystical states seem to those who experience them to be also states of knowledge. They are states of insight into depths of truth unplumbed by the discursive intellect. They are illuminations, revelations, full of significance and importance, all inarticulate though they remain; and as a rule they carry with them a curious sense of authority for aftertime.[54]

So religious content is not *trivially* ineffable, which is what distinguishes it from sense perceptions. The intuition shared by all people who have had religious experiences is that they were meaningful, even if attempts to explain what their meaning consists in necessarily fail.

For thousands of years, religious scholars and philosophers have tried to answer the question whether religious experiences feature ineffable religious content. Aquinas, for example, argues in his *Summa Theologica* that he has been granted beatific vision, which allowed him to directly perceive God. He claims that words cannot describe his perception because God is ineffable.

On the other hand, there clearly is extensive talk of God and other aspects of religion—how can we square that fact with the view that religious content is ineffable? The answer given by defenders of such a view is that the respective religious language is necessarily metaphorical. In general, attempts to express religious experiences typically result in a highly idiosyncratic language full of more or less enlightening metaphors. We can see this when we look at the language used by mystics, for example, which is always characterized by a high degree of metaphoricity. Meister Eckhard claims that his eye and God's eye are one and the same, Saint Augustine compares the world to a book, and claims that "those who do not travel read only one page," St Teresa of Avila explains prayer as "being on terms of friendship with God," etc. Attempts to describe religious experience thus seem to lead inevitably into metaphor. Indeed, Meister Eckhard is famous for his statement that "Theologians may quarrel, but the mystics of the world speak the same language." And this common language seems to be irreducibly metaphorical.

There are two possible reactions to the claim that religious language is irreducibly metaphorical. The first is that religious experience features unparaphrasable content that manifests itself, or is reflected in, the metaphorical language used to describe the experience. In other words, it is the specifically religious aspect of its content that is responsible for the irreducible metaphoricity of religious language. Such a view has been suggested, for example, by C.S. Gurrey. He argues that the nonliteral concepts used in religious language might be understood as providing "intimations of depth... which take the individual beyond ordinary language, the directly communicable."[55] The idea is thus that the contents of religious experience can only be rendered (exhaustively) by means of nonliteral concepts.

A second way to deal with the metaphoricity of religious language is to be skeptical about the claim of irreducibility, that is, to ask the question whether we really have any good reason to believe that religious language cannot be rendered in literal terms. In other words, we need to ask ourselves: "Just how far can we push this idea of the irreducibly personal meaning, the necessarily individual content to such a moral or religious concept? Can we, in the end, give it an acceptable and unequivocal logical form?"[56]

If it turned out that religious language could in principle be rendered in a nonmetaphorical way, there would be no reason to believe that religious experience features ineffable content. In what follows, I provide an argument against ineffable religious content by refuting the claim that religious language is irreducibly metaphorical. Let us begin by getting clear on the concept of a metaphor. We can define it roughly as follows:

Metaphor A figure of speech whereby a name, a descriptive term, or a descriptive sentence is applied to an object, action, or event, which is different from that to which the name, term, or sentence is literally applicable. This figure of speech is often used to highlight a particular analogy between two seemingly unrelated domains.

What would be a reason to believe in irreducible metaphors? Traditionally, metaphors have been considered features of language rather than features of thought.[57] Recently, however, cognitive scientists have argued that a particular subclass of metaphors, 'conceptual metaphors,' are not mere literal embellishments. Understood as instruments of our cognitive faculties, conceptual metaphors actively shape our cognition. This is achieved through mapping-processes across conceptual domains, which enable us to understand one domain by reference to another, often the more abstract by reference to the more concrete.

Research conducted on conceptual metaphors shows that our conceptual systems function as a tool defining reality for us. Normally we are not aware of these processes but rather conceptualize our environment along certain lines without giving it a second thought. Lakoff and Johnson, who have conducted extensive research on conceptual metaphors in the area of cognitive linguistics, even go as far as to claim that "most of our ordinary conceptual system is metaphorical in nature."[58] An example for this is the metaphorical way in which we grasp the abstract concept of a *theory* by means of the concrete concept of a *building*:

> Is that the *foundation* for your theory? The theory needs more *support*. The argument is *shaky*. We need some more facts or the arguments will *fall apart*. We need to *construct* a *strong* argument for that. I haven't figured out yet what the *form* of the argument will be. We need some more facts to *shore up* the theory. We need to *buttress* the theory with solid arguments. The theory will *stand* or *fall* on the *strength* of that argument. The argument *collapsed*. They *exploded* his latest theory. We will show that theory is *without foundation*. So far we have only put together the *framework* of the theory.[59]

Conceptual metaphors thus help us grasp abstract concepts. There is no other way for us to grasp those directly, without the use of certain metaphors from the concrete domain of visual, perceptible things. In this sense, conceptual metaphors can be said to be indispensable for human cognition and therefore not paraphrasable.

Also Max Black argues that there are different classes of metaphors. 'Substitution metaphors,' which use a metaphorical expression in place of an equivalent literal expression, and 'comparison metaphors', which are explicit statements of comparison, are easily translatable into literal language, he argues. The only price we pay for such a translation is a loss of "charm, vivacity, or wit of the original,"[60] but none of the informational, cognitive content is lost. A third class of metaphors, however, are indispensable in natural language and hence, not translatable into nonmetaphorical language. Black calls these metaphors 'interaction metaphors.' Interaction metaphors can only be understood on the basis of a system of interrelated commonplaces associated with the metaphorical expression. He uses the example of 'Man is a wolf', which could be understood as 'Man is a scavenger', 'Man is an animal', 'Man is engaged in constant struggle', etc. There is no exhaustive list of possible associated meanings (this is sometimes referred to as the 'open-endedness' of a metaphor), and yet we understand the associated meaning if we understand the meaning of 'wolf.' A person insufficiently acquainted with wolves, on the other hand, will not understand the expression. Metaphors that cannot be rendered in literal language

> use a system of implications (a system of 'commonplaces'—or a special system established for the purpose in hand) as a means for selecting, emphasizing, and organizing relations in a different field. This use of a 'subsidiary subject' to foster insight into a 'principal subject' is a distinctive intellectual operation (though one familiar enough through our experiences of learning anything whatever), demanding simultaneous awareness of both subjects but not reducible to any comparison between the two.[61]

These examples by Lakoff, Johnson, and Black show how deeply entrenched metaphors are in our everyday language. So deeply, in fact, that our language can seem irreducibly metaphorical. The question then arises, of course, whether an irreducible metaphor should still count as a metaphor at all. Once an expression becomes a primary, that is, canonical, designator for a particular object, it arguably ceases to be an alternative designator for that object—and metaphors are by definition alternative, not primary, designators. In this sense, the question whether there are irreducible metaphors is a purely terminological one. On the other hand, we do, as a matter of fact, distinguish between regular expressions and metaphors, regardless of whether the latter have become part of the canonical way of talking about a subject. And as long as the metaphoricity of an expression is recognizable, it should reasonably count as a metaphor.

Let's now bring back into focus our primary concern, which is the language used to describe the content of religious experience, and the associated question whether irreducibly metaphorical talk ought to be understood as an indicator of a specific kind of literally ineffable content. We can find good reasons to believe that metaphors have the power to express otherwise inexpressible contents when we turn our attention to science.

Scientific theories often introduce metaphors that are constitutive for a particular theory: they describe and attempt to explain hitherto inexplicable phenomena by metaphorical extension of the scientific language. In the neurosciences, for example, a lot of talk about the brain makes use of computer-related metaphors. This talk has created a whole terminology in which neuroscientific discourse is now commonly framed: the brain is 'programmed', it receives 'input', provides 'output' and 'feedback', etc. Metaphors in science are thus a way of describing something that is not (yet) fully understood in terms of something else that is already fully understood. In this sense, a metaphor can provide a model for something still largely unknown. Janet Soskice uses the example of 'genes' to make a similar point:

> Terms like 'gene' are introduced with fixed senses (say, 'the mechanism responsible for the inheritance of acquired characteristics') but this sense, while guiding investigations, does not necessarily determine what it is that, in practice, the term is used to refer to. As the theory is improved, the original sense of the term may be altered (say by deleting 'acquired'), or in some cases (e.g., 'phlogiston') it may be decided that a term fails to refer. So the sense of the terms is important, not in tying one to a direct and exhaustive description of the referent, but rather in providing access to a referent, which access it is then the task of science to refine.[62]

The use of metaphors in science allows us to point at something in a reality-depicting way without giving a precise and exhaustive description of the thing we are pointing at. The explanatory potential of such metaphors is crucial to scientific progress.

Drawing an analogy with science, a religious person could now argue that the metaphors of his religious language point at aspects of reality that are not well understood yet but form parts of reality nevertheless. Just like the scientist can claim that the metaphorical predicates his model has generated can be seen as reality-depicting even prior to having definite knowledge to that effect, a religious believer can argue that his talk of, say, God is reality-depicting, even if the language used is highly metaphorical, and even if we don't have an entirely clear understanding of the term 'God' yet.[63] A metaphor may thus allow us to *refer* to a particular object without being suitable for *defining* that very object.

Taking this line of argument one step further, I submit that any metaphorical expression is in principle capable of being rendered literally. This may not be possible immediately—just like scientists use abstract terms as placeholders for not fully understood phenomena, religious believers can use metaphorical expressions in order to refer to objects or facts that are not (yet) fully understood (in scientific terms) but nevertheless constitute reality for the believer. And in fact, there are arguments that support my claim.

William Alston, for example, provides a forceful rejection of the view that metaphors in religious contexts are irreducible. He raises the question whether there can be irreducible metaphors in the specific context of divine predication, and if so, what status they have:

> if no term can be literally applied to God, our metaphorical talk about God will be irreducible. A metaphor is irreducible if what is said in the metaphorical utterance cannot be said, even in part, in literal terms. Obviously, if no term can be literally applied to God, we cannot do anything to spell out in literal terms what is said metaphorically about God.[64]

He argues that whether what is expressed by a metaphor can be expressed literally depends on whether the *propositional content* of a metaphorical statement[65] can be expressed literally. Given that he takes metaphors to be open-ended (recall the wolf example above), this should not be confused with the evidently impossible task of providing *exhaustive* literal paraphrases of metaphorical statements. He argues that we may be able to provide one literal expression of the propositional content of a metaphorical statement, while many different expressions may be possible. This, however, does not mean that the metaphorical expression is irreducible to literal language. In fact, he argues, the notion of irreducible metaphors is incoherent.

He identifies two kinds of truth-claims contained in metaphorical statements. The first one is the unspecific claim that the exemplar (i.e., the source of the metaphor: the object the metaphorical expression would apply to in a literal context) is in some way sufficiently similar to the subject (i.e., the target of the metaphor: what the metaphorical expression is applied to), such that the exemplar is a useful model of the latter. He calls this unspecific claim 'M-similarity' and argues that the unspecific truth-claims contained in metaphorical statements provide a basis of 'guaranteed literal paraphrasability' because the predicate 'M-similar' will always be true both of the exemplar and the subject of the metaphorical statement. In other words, every metaphorical expression can be "paraphrased" in literal terms as follows: 'God is my rock' can be translated as 'God is M-similar to a rock' (in general terms: 'S is M-similar to P'). From this, Alston concludes that "the literal expressibility of that much of the propositional content unquestionably holds for any metaphorical statement whatever."[66]

The second kind of truth-claim contained in metaphorical statements is a somewhat more specific attribution, which is usually derived from one or more particular points of resemblance. Alston considers the example: 'God is my rock' and argues as follows:

1. When a speaker asserts the metaphorical statement 'God is my rock,' he means to attribute a property P to God.
2. If a speaker means to attribute a property P to God, he must have formed a concept of P (i.e., have cognitive access to P).
3. If a property is cognitively accessible to one person, it is in principle cognitively accessible to other persons.
4. If it is possible for members of a linguistic community to form a concept of P, it is in principle possible that P will become the meaning of a predicate term in their language.
5. Therefore, it is in principle possible that a word signifies the property in literal language.

Alston furthermore argues that "a statement cannot possess a propositional content unless it is, in principle, possible that a language should contain words that have the meanings required for the literal expression of that content."[67] Hence, a metaphor that is not in principle expressible in literal terms has no propositional content and is therefore meaningless. The argument demonstrates clearly why metaphorical language in religious contexts is always in principle reducible to literal language.

Thus, arguing for the existence of ineffable religious content via the claim that religious language is irreducibly metaphorical, and that this metaphoricity reflects a specific kind of content, is a fruitless enterprise. First, because there is no reason to believe in a class of metaphors that can never be expressed literally. This is what Alson's argument shows us. Second, even if some religious metaphors are irreducible *at this moment*, the question is whether that allows us to infer that there is ineffable religious content. And the answer is no. Just like scientific metaphors are placeholders for phenomena that need to be better understood, religious metaphors are constituents of strongly held beliefs that are not fully understood by those who don't share those beliefs. Perhaps one day the atheist will understand better what people refer to when they say 'God,' so that, just like in science, the metaphorical way of speaking about God can be replaced with literal expressions. Perhaps we will eventually get rid of the central religious concepts, such as 'God' or 'miracle', because we will find that the phenomena they were designed to explain can now be explained better in terms of science. In any case, there is no reason to believe that there is ineffable content eternally hidden behind religious metaphors. However, this does not mean that language grasps everything

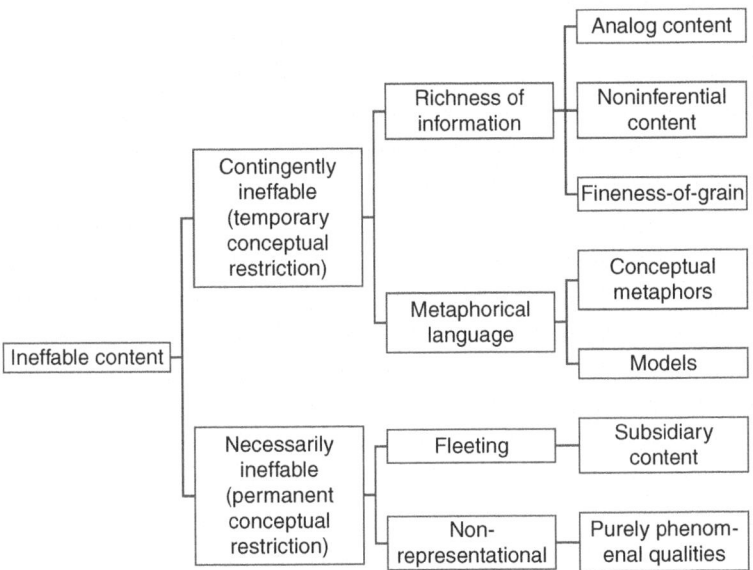

Figure 5.1 Varieties of ineffable content

there is to grasp about religious experience: Aquinas famously compared all of his writings to straw after he had a mystical experience. All the above arguments show is that there is no reason to assume that the metaphorical language used in religious contexts points toward a special kind of ineffable content.

In this chapter, we have examined three different explanatory projects in which the concept of ineffable, or nonconceptual, content plays a central role, but we have not found a good argument for the existence of ineffable content in either one of them. A sound argument for ineffable content requires a demonstration to the effect that the content of perceptual, aesthetic, or religious experiences is not analyzable without remainder into a combination of phenomenal quality and conceptual content. This has not been achieved in either one of the three examined contexts. Attempts to motivate nonconceptual content in perception are bound to be refuted by McDowell's 'kidnapping' strategy: invoking a higher-order sortal and combining it with a demonstrative like 'that' conceptualizes pretty much every perceptual object out there, no matter how finely grained.

Attempts to motivate ineffable content in the context of aesthetic experiences at most manage to establish the (trivial) claim that the sensory, nonrepresentational aspects of works of art are ineffable—a fact we were aware of all along, given that the phenomenal qualities of *all* sense perceptions are ineffable. So in this sense, aesthetic experiences are indistinguishable from ordinary perceptual experiences. Consequently, the ineffability of their sensory qualities cannot account for the meaningfulness felt in the presence of the respective work of art. Regarding their cognitive contents, none of the discussed arguments provide conclusive reasons to believe that the informational, that is, representational content of a work of art is not communicable.

Searching for ineffable content behind the metaphorical language used to express religious experiences did also not provide us with a cogent argument for the existence of ineffable content. This is because all metaphors, and therefore also all religious metaphors, are ultimately expressible in literal terms. Even if some metaphors cannot be expressed literally at a given moment in time, nothing in the concept of a metaphor supports the claim that some metaphors are eternally irreducible to language. Just like there are some propositions we cannot express at this moment (see Chapter 4) but which we will be able to express in the future, there are some metaphorical expressions that will either become literal expressions, or that will be translatable into literal terms in the future. Hence, we have no reason to believe that there are contents that are eternally hidden behind the metaphorical language found in religious contexts.

We can thus conclude that neither perceptual, nor aesthetic, nor religious experiences feature ineffable content. Even though at times it can seem as though some contents are inexpressible, this impression disappears as soon as we exploit all the conceptual resources available to us, including demonstrative concepts, as soon as we distinguish carefully between the phenomenal and the cognitive aspects of a piece of art, and as soon as we clear up our understanding of the expressive role played by metaphorical language.

One final thing needs to be said here. It is of course true that there remains a sense of ineffability hovering about aesthetic and religious experiences, no matter how elegantly we manage to analyze their contents. The feeling of meaningfulness and insight that characterizes aesthetic and religious experiences is not captured by any of the arguments discussed. All this chapter shows is that the ineffability we feel so keenly cannot be accounted for by means of a new metaphysical category called 'ineffable content'. It does not show that there is nothing ineffable to be found in aesthetic and religious experience. All this means is that *content* is not the right category to look for the metaphysical underpinnings of ineffability.

In the next two chapters, we will finally turn our attention to the only metaphysical category capable of explaining our prime examples of ineffability without running into ontological quandaries. This is the category of ineffable knowledge.

CHAPTER 6

INEFFABLE KNOWLEDGE I

6.1 Why Ineffable Knowledge?

So far, I have argued that ineffability can neither be explained in terms of ineffable objects, nor in terms of ineffable truths or propositions, nor in terms of ineffable content. As we have seen, each of these explanatory accounts eventually runs into metaphysical incoherence. By successively ruling out those theories of ineffability, my examination has now come close to what I consider the correct metaphysical account of the philosophically relevant examples of ineffability. In this chapter, I introduce three kinds of ineffable knowledge and thereby establish the category of ineffable knowledge as an independent epistemological category. I first discuss the concept of knowledge-how, then Frege's views on the foundations of logical thought, and finally, A. W. Moore's Wittgensteinian account of ineffable knowledge. The discussion of these three accounts constitutes the basis for my theory of ineffability, which I develop in Chapter 7.

6.2 Objective Ineffable knowledge

That there are different kinds of knowledge out there is a truism. Different areas of thought yield different kinds of knowledge: scientific knowledge, mathematical knowledge, historical knowledge, sociological knowledge, and so forth. What connects these different kinds of knowledge, however, is that they are all examples of propositional knowledge, that is, of knowledge that can be expressed. And this, in turn, means that it can be passed on from person to person in written or spoken form.

However, besides the class of propositional knowledge, under which mathematical, scientific, historical, and sociological knowledge fall, there is an entirely different class of ineffable knowledge, that is, of knowledge that cannot be passed on from person to person in written or spoken form: knowledge-how, logical knowledge, indexical knowledge, and phenomenal knowledge.

This class of ineffable knowledge can, in turn, be divided again into two groups, the first of which I call the group of objective ineffable knowledge, and the second of which I call subjective ineffable knowledge. This is not a clear-cut distinction, as all four kinds of ineffable knowledge can be used to generate knowledge both about the realm of objects and about the realm of the subjective. All the distinction is meant to highlight is a slight difference in focus: objective kinds of ineffable knowledge such as knowledge-how and logical knowledge enable us to interact with and have thought about whatever lies outside of us, whereas subjective kinds of knowledge such as indexical and phenomenal knowledge capture how whatever lies outside of us relates and feels to us subjectively. Nothing in my argument hangs on the distinction between objective and subjective ineffable knowledge, but I think it is a useful categorization of the different kinds of ineffable knowledge.

Let's take a look, then, at the first kind of ineffable knowledge, knowledge-how, and some of the arguments that have been brought forward against the view that it constitutes an independent epistemological category. This debate is also known as the debate about knowledge-how versus knowledge-that (propositional knowledge).

6.3 Knowledge-How

The knowledge-how/knowledge-that debate is directly relevant to our discussion of ineffability. Proponents of knowledge-how (sometimes referred to as 'anti-intellectualists') argue that there is a fundamental difference between knowledge-how and knowledge-that, that is, both constitute independent epistemological categories. The alleged difference is that knowledge-that is *propositional*, meaning it can be rendered in propositional form, whereas knowledge-how is *non-propositional*, meaning it cannot be reduced to propositional form.

If there is a category of knowledge that is irreducibly nonpropositional, then given that no linguistic item can express it, this knowledge is ineffable. Intellectualists reject the idea that knowledge-how and knowledge-that are different species of knowledge: they argue that knowledge-how is nothing but a particular subclass of knowledge-that.

The *locus classicus* of the knowledge-how/knowledge-that debate can be found in chapter two of Ryle's *The Concept of Mind*. Ryle argues that, while knowledge-that is clearly propositional knowledge, knowledge-how is nonpropositional knowledge, which is best described as an ability, a skill, a competence, or a capacity. He writes:

> [Opponents of knowledge-how] are apt to try to reassimilate knowing *how* to knowing *that* by arguing that intelligent performance involves the observance of rules, or the application of criteria. It follows that the operation which is characterized as intelligent must be preceded by an intellectual acknowledgment of these rules or criteria; that is, the agent must first go through the internal process of avowing to himself certain propositions about what is to be done.[1]

Ryle rejects this view, arguing that it entails a vicious regress:

> The consideration of propositions is itself an operation the execution of which can be more or less intelligent, less or more stupid. But if, for any operation to be intelligently executed, a prior theoretical operation had first to be performed and performed intelligently, it would be a logical impossibility for anyone ever to break into the circle.[2]

In other words, Ryle holds that it is absurd to assume that engaging in an intelligent action[3] or performance requires the consideration of an infinite number of propositions. His argument is a reductio ad absurdum. The assumption for reductio is that knowledge-how to ϕ is knowledge-that $p(\phi)$. Assuming that considering a proposition is a kind of action, the argument runs as follows:

1. If a person S engages in an intentional action ϕ, then S knows how to ϕ.
2. Knowing how to ϕ involves considering the proposition $p(\phi)$.
3. If S considers the proposition $p(\phi)$, S engages in an intentional action; she knows how to consider $p(\phi)$.
4. Knowing how to consider $p(\phi)$ involves considering the proposition $q(p(\phi))$.
5. If S considers the proposition $q(p(\phi))$, S engages in an intentional action; she knows how to consider $q(p(\phi))$, etc.

Since the chain of reasoning could in principle go on forever, we end up with a vicious regress. Ryle's argument, and variations thereof, form the basis for most anti-intellectualist accounts.

Intellectualists like Jason Stanley and Timothy Williamson disagree with Ryle's argument. Their intention is to show that all knowledge-how is, in fact, reducible to knowledge-that, pointing out that ascriptions of knowledge-that and ascriptions of knowledge-how neither differ with regard to their syntactic structure nor with regard to their semantics.

Here is their main line of argument.
Ryle's argument rests on two premises:

(1) For any intentional action ϕ, by ϕ-ing one employs knowledge *how* to ϕ.
(2) Employing knowledge *that* p, one considers the proposition that p.

Now, Stanley/Williamson argue that Ryle's argument is unsound because there is no uniform reading of the two basic premises (1 and 2) on which both turn out true. Given that we perform many actions without intentionally considering a corresponding proposition, premise (2) can only be true if 'considering a proposition' is interpreted as some kind of unintentional action. However, premise (1) can only be true if it is restricted to intentional actions. Therefore, Stanley/Williamson conclude, Ryle's argument for the fundamental difference between knowledge-*how* and knowledge-*that* cannot get off the ground.

They then present a reductive account of knowledge-how, which can be summarized as follows: for any proposition r ascribing knowledge-how to a person S—let's use the proposition 'Sophie knows how to strike the right note' for example—the following holds:

SW r is true iff, for some contextually relevant way w, which is a way for Sophie to strike the right note, there is a practical mode of presentation m, such that Sophie knows under m that w is a way for her to strike the right note.[4]

A general worry about thinking of knowledge-how in this way is that there are conceivable cases where, either someone has knowledge-how of the relevant sort without being able to perform accordingly, or someone knows how to perform without having the respective knowledge.[5] The worry is that ascribing propositional knowledge-that to a person who knows how to ϕ seems wrong in cases where the person would herself not be able to make that ascription, and in cases where the ascription would be correct but the person still unable to act according to the ascription. The first part of the worry only holds, however, on the assumption that a person needs to know that she knows a particular proposition in order to know it. This seems unjustified, particularly in cases of propositions ascribing practical knowledge: sometimes one "just knows" without being able to state *that* one knows. The second part of the worry holds in cases where a person is obstructed from acting on her knowledge-how for reasons independent of that particular piece of knowledge. A definition of knowledge-how could certainly be amended to exclude cases like that. So there is nothing wrong per se with the attempt to express knowledge-how in terms of knowledge-that.

So let's go back to examine the Stanley/Williamson account of knowledge-how. Clearly, the practical mode of presentation m is the most interesting part of this account. It is supposed to capture that which is peculiar about knowledge-how. When we say 'Sophie knows how to strike the right note,' we don't mean that Sophie has watched a number of choir singers for some time, listened to their explanations about pitch, and now knows certain facts about how to strike the right note. What we mean is that she herself, when singing, is able to strike the right note. This is what Stanley/Williamson intend to capture in the clause 'there is a practical mode of presentation m' under which Sophie knows how to strike the right note. I think this must be understood as follows.

In order to grasp w as the way to ϕ, a subject S must be in a specific receptive state of mind that allows her to identify w as the way to ϕ. This receptive state is the practical mode of presentation m under which S grasps that w is a way to ϕ, and under which S can demonstrate ('*that* is a way to ϕ') and attempt to describe ('w is a way to ϕ') her knowledge how to ϕ. The role that Stanley/Williamson assign to m thus seems to be that of enabling the demonstration and communication of that aspect of knowledge-how that is otherwise not formulable in language, that is, the ineffable aspect. Williamson even goes so far as to claim that "No verbal description of ... w is needed; one's grasp of the propositional content may be distinctively practical ('ϕ now!'; 'ϕ like this!')."[6]

What Stanley/Williamson's account lacks, though, is a further elucidation of m. In fact, they even concede that providing a nontrivial characterization of a practical mode of presentation might be very difficult![7] Hence, they are not concerned by the worry that an analysis of these practical modes of presentation might require appealing to a knowledge-how *primitive*, since they are "not engaged in the reductive project of reducing talk of knowledge-how to talk that does not involve knowledge-how." Rather, their only aim is to show "that knowledge-how is a species of knowledge-that."[8] Thus it seems like they are willing to pay a high price for a relatively modest goal, namely the price of introducing to their account the concept of a practical mode of presentation as a primitive. By doing that, whether or not one concludes that they achieve their goal of translating all knowledge-how into knowledge-that ascriptions, their account fails to explain the crucial and most puzzling aspect of knowledge-how. The only indication Stanley/Williamson provide as to what they mean by 'knowing something under a practical mode of presentation' is that it "undoubtedly entails the possession of certain complex dispositions."[9] Yet what else would these dispositions be if not those that ascribe to a person S the ability/skill/competence to ϕ? If it is granted that this is what these dispositions come down to, then Stanley/Williamson's account of knowledge-how suddenly looks sufficiently similar to Ryle's account of knowledge-how to justify the conclusion that

> All that Stanley's and Williamson's arguments show is that expressions of the form 'a knows how to F' are ambiguous between a reading in which we ascribe some propositional knowledge and one in which we want to say that a has a certain ability.[10]

We might even go one step further. Stanley/Williamson's account does not highlight an *ambiguity* between a propositional reading and an ability reading of knowledge-how ascriptions; rather, it simply highlights that every ascription of knowledge-how contains *both aspects*. However, from the fact that knowledge-how ascriptions contain both a propositional aspect and an ability aspect, it does not follow that knowledge-how ascriptions can be subsumed under knowledge-that ascriptions. Moreover, given that the irreducible aspect of knowledge-how ascriptions remains an integral part of knowledge-that ascriptions on their account, Stanley/Williamson fail to 'explain away' what strikes us as ineffable in knowledge-how ascriptions. The consequence of this is that knowledge-how reappears as a precondition of identifying the relevant way w as a way to ϕ:

> Once we appreciate the difficulty of supposing that knowing the way to V (knowing it practically, that is) can be fully accounted for without knowing-how-to-V's itself reappearing as a precondition for w's being identified as the w that verifies the proposition 'w is a/the way by which one V's'—once we appreciate everything that would be involved in this—examples [for the reappearance of the ineffable aspect of knowledge-how] will multiply.[11]

What Wiggins points out further is that, for the practical mode of presentation to have the desired effect of demonstrating and communicating the relevant piece of knowledge, there must be some sort of incipient knowledge-how in the hearer. For someone to grasp the meaning of the sentence 'w is a way to ϕ,' it is necessary that that person receive the information under a practical mode of presentation; which, in turn, requires her to be in the relevant receptive state of mind that allows her to receive the information that w is a way to ϕ, which then allows her to understand that w is a way to ϕ. To put it bluntly: a person won't come to know that w is a way to ϕ unless she already knows that w is a way to ϕ. I won't understand that w ('*that* way') is a way to strike the right note unless

I already know how to strike the right note. That is just what it means to know how to do something.

On the face of it, then, Stanley/Williamson's account of knowledge-how succeeds in reformulating knowledge-how ascriptions like 'knowing how to ride a bicycle' or 'knowing how to play the violin' in terms of knowledge-that ascriptions at the cost of adding an epistemic primitive, the 'practical mode of presentation'. I have argued that the practical mode of presentation is the most interesting aspect of such knowledge-that ascriptions because it is the ineffable aspect; yet Stanley/Williamson fail to shed further light on this aspect. Even if this is—doubtfully—taken to be unproblematic in the context of 'ordinary' knowledge-how ascriptions like knowing how to play the violin, knowing how to ride a bicycle, etc., there are additional kinds of knowledge, which will be elucidated in what follows, that seem to be knowledge-how, even though we cannot say what the correct knowledge-how ascription is. Yet if we cannot say what the correct knowledge-how ascription is, we also cannot reformulate it as a knowledge-that ascription. Therefore, Stanley/Williamson's account doesn't manage to rule out knowledge-how as a genuine case of ineffable knowledge.

Knowledge-how is crucial for countless areas of our lives. We can think, for example, of our general motor skills that enable us to walk, run, bend, etc., but also of more specialized kinds of knowledge-how such as playing violins, riding bikes, striking the right note, etc. What connects all examples of knowledge-how is that they enable us to interact with and within the world surrounding us.

We will now proceed to a discussion of another kind of ineffable knowledge, namely, logical knowledge. Logical knowledge does not enable us to ride bikes or play violins but it bestows another invaluable ability upon us: the ability to sort all the propositional knowledge we gain every day into one big, coherent, and unified picture, which can then serve as a basis for our thoughts, our emotions, our decision-making processes, etc. Taking the argument Frege develops in his *Foundations of Arithmetic* as an example, I thus show that ineffable knowledge not only forms an essential part of human actions, but also of human thought.

6.4 Basic Logical Knowledge

In his paper 'What the Tortoise Said to Achilles',[12] Lewis Carroll argues that *modus ponens* faces a regress problem. The problem is depicted in a dialogue between Achilles and a Tortoise. Carroll's tortoise argues that if we assume both A→B and A, then we consider it valid to infer B. However, the tortoise then claims that such an inference requires an additional principle, call it C, according to which B follows from the truth of A→B and A. Yet if we assume such a principle C in order to infer B from A→B, A, and C, that inference will require *yet another* additional principle, call it D, according to which B follows from the truth of A→B, A, and C. And so forth, ad infinitum.

This is, of course, not what we do when we employ *modus ponens*. Rather, we take *modus ponens* to have axiomatic status, that is, to fall under the class of principles, which, as Frege puts it, "neither need nor admit of proof."[13] Before addressing the question what 'neither needing nor admitting of proof' comes down to, let me briefly introduce Frege's account of logical thought as developed in the *Foundations of Arithmetic*.

We can start with the following passage, which illustrates a core element of Frege's philosophy:

> Thought is in essentials the same everywhere: *it is not true that there are different kinds of laws of thought to suit the different kinds of objects thought about*. Such differences as there are consist only in this, that the thought is more pure or less pure, less dependent or more upon psychological influences and on external aids such as words or numerals, and further to some extent too in the finer or coarser structure of the concepts involved; but it is precisely in this respect that mathematics claims to surpass all other sciences, even philosophy.[14]

The idea expressed in this passage is that the human mode of thinking is a constant, that is, there are universal laws of thought that determine our way of thinking. The circumstances in which thinking takes place may vary, yet the 'mode of thinking' itself always remains the same.

Frege's goal is to create a system of formal logic that will make this mode of thinking visible and that will enable us to formulate and exhibit every step in a chain of reasoning from premises to conclusion. The importance Frege assigned to his project is due to his conviction that "the laws of logic ought to be guiding principles for thought in the attainment of truth."[15]

He intends to show that within the framework of his logical system, the deployment of Kantian spatial and temporal intuition is irrelevant to understanding both the nature of reasoning and our knowledge of number. To this end, Frege invented a system of symbolic logic in order to formulate every single step in a chain of reasoning and was convinced that his *Begriffsschrift* and his *Basic Laws of Arithmetic*[16] constituted a successful realization of his goal, for mathematical inference in general and for arithmetic in particular. His conviction lasted until Russell inferred two contradictory propositions from Frege's Basic Law V, thus proving it to be inconsistent (cf. Russell 1902). What is nowadays referred to as Russell's Paradox (i.e., the existence, on the basis of Basic Law V, of the class of all classes not members of themselves) turned out to be an insoluble problem for Frege's project of deriving the Peano-Dedekind axioms of arithmetic from logical axioms alone.

Frege's role as one of the most outstanding logicians of all times remains uncontested, however. I now want to discuss a question that, though never explicitly formulated, nevertheless resonates in Frege's work. This is the question whether, in order to think logically, we need to assume the existence of a universal, a priori, ineffable knowledge that enables us to understand the most basic logical propositions in the first place.

Three reasons indicate that Frege would have answered this question positively. The first reason is that, although Frege's main interests lie elsewhere (namely, in finding a system in which to exhibit scientific, gap-free reasoning in order to prove the basic laws of arithmetic without the help of a Kantian form of intuition), he is in fact aware of the lack of an ultimate epistemic justification of his logical system:

> The question why and with what right we acknowledge a law of logic to be true, logic can answer only by reducing it to another law of logic. Where that is not possible, logic can give no answer.[17]

In other words, the final point of every chain of justification is a basic logical law. There are no further justifications for the most basic logical laws.

Frege is concerned with generating indubitable mathematical knowledge by reformulating the laws of arithmetic in purely logical terms. To that end, he invents a formal language suitable for scientific reasoning:

> [The Begriffsschrift's] first purpose, therefore, is to provide us with the most reliable test of the validity of a chain of inferences and to point out every presupposition that tries to sneak in unnoticed, so that its origin can be investigated.[18]

In the *Grundlagen*, Frege aims at giving a description of the natural numbers by means of classes,[19] and in the *Grundgesetze*, he provides a formal theory of classes by formulating his Basic Laws of Arithmetic, one of which is Basic Law V. This shows that Frege considers logic epistemically prior to mathematics. The way he sees it, every mathematical truth can be reduced to a logical truth, provided that we employ suitable definitions. Frege thus considers logic to be the epistemic foundation of mathematics. But what is the foundation of logic? Nothing that can be expressed in terms of logic, and hence (given that logic is the foundation of all thought), nothing that can be expressed at all:

The problem becomes, in fact, that of finding the proof of the proposition, and of following it up right back to the primitive truths. ... [If] its proof can be derived exclusively from general laws, which themselves neither need nor admit of proof, then the truth is a priori.[20]

Frege thus holds that we can generate a priori knowledge using nothing but the most general logical laws. These laws, in turn, neither need nor admit of proof. This is clearly a characterization of ineffable knowledge.

For those who are not yet convinced that Frege implicitly argues for ineffable knowledge, here is a second indication, namely that Frege depicts logic as superior to any given science:

> The most reliable way of carrying out a proof, obviously, is to follow pure logic, a way that, disregarding the particular characteristics of objects [Dinge;], depends solely on those laws upon which all knowledge [Erkenntnis] rests.[21]

Ranking sciences according to priority (or superiority), as Frege does, presupposes an epistemic foundation that forms the basis for such a ranking. However, Frege leaves this foundation unexplained. Without further ado, he claims that there are laws upon which all knowledge rests, and that these laws are so obvious to everybody that it is unnecessary (in fact: impossible) to elaborate on them any further. Frege thus assumes two things for his logical principles:

> First, these principles must be universally applicable to reasoning on any topic whatsoever. Second, the principles of logic must be immediately applicable without presupposition. Application of logical principles should enable us to determine implicational relationships antecedently to the investigation of any question in any special science.[22]

This is certainly right. The way we think about logic is that it applies equally to all contexts. Moreover, the way in which we apply the laws of logic is immediate; once we know what the laws of logic are, no further questions need to be asked. But why is this so? Why don't we challenge the fundamental logical laws? Couldn't we ask why 'If p and q, then p' holds?

I submit that the reason why most of us find this particular question unnecessary is that we all, just like Frege, presuppose an epistemic foundation, or basis, of our logical thinking. However, since logic cannot answer the question of its own epistemic grounds, the question of how we come to know that Frege's logical system is true is a question that can only be answered from a point of view outside the logical system. As Philip Kitcher puts it, if the significance of his program consists in the reform of mathematical knowledge then it is obviously required that there be a source of logical knowledge which can produce knowledge superior to that which we obtain in other ways.[23]

For Frege, psychology defines concepts in terms of the human mind[24] and can therefore only provide completely subjective explanations of how we come to know things, whereas logic is completely objective because its laws are universal. He makes a sharp distinction between psychology and logic,[25] and explicitly places his interest with the latter. The reason he considers logic superior to any given science is because of the level of epistemic certitude that can be achieved through logical proofs. Moreover, for him logic provides a universally applicable system of gap-free reasoning, which is something that other sciences do not provide.

A third reason for thinking that Frege's logicism is based on ineffable knowledge is the following. When referring to "general laws, which... neither need nor admit of proof"[26] it seems that Frege claims his Basic Laws to be self-evident; yet the concept of self-evidence entails the question: self-evident on what basis? Concerning the notion of self-evidence in Frege's theory, Tyler Burge correctly points out one important aspect:

> Although no one has remarked it, as far as I know, the term 'self-evident' that appears in the standard English translations does not translate a single German counterpart. Sometimes Frege uses '*einleuchtend*' (and grammatical variants); sometimes he uses '*selbstverständlich*'; and occasionally he uses '*evident*' and '*unmittelbar klar*'[27]

The fact that Frege does not always use the same word for *self-evident* indicates that he did not consider it necessary to give an explicit definition of self-evidence. Kitcher accounts for Frege's reticence by suggesting that he implicitly adopts concepts and distinctions (such as the concept of 'proof') from Kant's theory of human knowledge. Several passages in the *Grundlagen*, for example, suggest that Frege agrees with Kant on the three sources of knowledge: the latter introduces: sensory perception as the source of synthetic a posteriori knowledge; conceptual analysis as the source of analytic a priori knowledge, and pure intuition as the source of synthetic a priori knowledge.[28]

Instead of Kant's pure intuition, which could be called an *empirical intuition*, Frege makes use of something that might be called *rational intuition*, and refers to it as self-evidence. Self-evidence can be understood as an immediate awareness of the truth of an assertion without having to think about the reasons for its truth. This seems to be a sufficiently general definition of the concept. It is widely accepted that 'If p and q then p' falls into the category 'self-evident'. And, as the Russell paradox shows, Basic Law V does not fall into the category of self-evidence (even though it looked like it for a while).

Referring back to the quotation given at the beginning of this section, we can now ask: if a constant mode of thinking implies an epistemic foundation, but at the same time, no epistemic presuppositions are to be made in an argument of gap-free reasoning, what kind of epistemic foundation does human thought rest on? The answer, I suggest, is that logical thought rests on a foundation of ineffable knowledge. Let's take a closer look on what exactly it is that we call 'thought'.

Very roughly, we can say that thought consists in reflecting on the truth and falsity of propositions, and on the validity or invalidity of inferences. When we reflect on the truth of a proposition or on the validity of a formal inference, we examine whether the proposition or the inference can be coherently placed into our worldview. A state of knowledge always stands in logical relations with other states of knowledge. In other words: critical reflection leads to abstraction and ultimately, to the recognition of something that has come to be referred to as 'the logical space of reasons.'[29] The crucial question now is:

> why should different states of knowledge cohere (let alone be such that we can understand how they cohere)? Why should there not be incompatible states of knowledge, each of which holds in its own domain? Critical reflection supplies answers to these questions, by indicating that there is a single domain—a single world—to which any given item of knowledge is answerable. This ensures that, given any other item of knowledge, there must be a possible world to which that, and the original item, are both faithful, namely this world: the world. The reflective insight which leads one to recognise this is, I suggest, a central and fundamental example of ineffability.[30]

Applying this question to Frege's logicism, we can ask: Why *can't* we say 'If p and q then not p'? The answer is: because we cannot conceive of a possible world in which this inference is valid. Furthermore, one might want to know: how can my understanding of the truth of the proposition 'If p and q then p' be an example of ineffable knowledge? Haven't I just expressed my knowledge by writing 'If p and q then p'?

The answer is that the ineffable knowledge in question is not contained in what is expressed by the proposition 'If p and q then p'. Our capability to understand what is being expressed through 'If p and q then p' is *conditional upon* ineffable knowledge, that is, an ineffable epistemic foundation on the basis of which we place a proposition coherently into the 'logical space of reasons,' identify a paradox, or dismiss the notion of a concept without an intension.

Three reasons indicate that this is exactly what Frege had in mind as well: (i) The foundation of his logical system cannot be expressed within the realms of logic. (ii) For Frege, natural languages are plainly inconsistent and thus also not helpful to formulate the foundations of logic.[31] (iii) Self-evidence (which Frege claims for the basic laws of logic) denotes an immediate awareness of the truth of something without prior reasoning, and since the reasoning is the effable part of coming to know a truth, Frege must presuppose an ineffable way of grasping the self-evidence of basic logical laws. In one of his posthumously published works, Frege illuminates the circularity of the attempt to define what it means for a logical law to be true:

> Now it would be futile to employ a definition in order to make it clearer what is to be understood by 'true'. If, for example, we wished to say 'an idea is true if it agrees with reality' nothing would have been achieved, since in order to apply this definition we should have to decide whether some idea or other did agree with reality. Thus we should have to presuppose the very thing that is being defined.[32]

It seems that, by denying the possibility of defining truth in any noncircular way, Frege himself took the foundation of his logical axioms and laws to be ineffable.

I have raised two questions about the very foundations of Frege's logicism. The first question, whether there is reason to believe that Frege's logical system rests on an epistemic foundation, I have answered positively by giving three reasons: that Frege himself draws the attention to the epistemic foundations of logic that logic itself cannot give; that he ranks scientific methods of reasoning according to their epistemic priority; and that he makes use of the epistemic notion of self-evidence with regard to his Basic Laws.

The second question, whether the foundations of Frege's logicism are ineffable, I have answered positively by arguing that the foundations can neither be expressed in formal nor in natural languages, and by pointing out that self-evidence, which Frege claims for his basic logical laws, cannot be expressed in words and is therefore ineffable.

What conclusion follows from knowing that Frege's theory rests on an ineffable epistemic foundation? I think through knowing that we have gained a deeper understanding of three issues. First, we now understand better why Frege did not elaborate on the epistemic foundation of his logical system: he considered the Basic Laws to be self-evident and took it for granted that everyone else would agree. Second, it helps us understand that the attempt to elaborate on the epistemic foundations of logical thought is such a difficult enterprise because the knowledge involved is ineffable and hence, impossible to define or describe in language. And third, it provides us with a vivid example of ineffable knowledge that neither involves riding bikes nor playing violins. Finally, it is worth noting that the claim that logical knowledge rests on an ineffable epistemic foundation doesn't have any consequences for Frege's project. However, for an examination of the metaphysics of ineffability, it is extremely insightful to see that the notion of ineffability does not lie far away from the notion of 'maximally effable' logical thinking.

6.5 Nonrepresentational Knowledge

I will now introduce the account of ineffable knowledge, which I call 'nonrepresentational knowledge', developed by A. W. Moore. He does this in two steps. First, he argues that the concept 'knowledge' is in principle compatible with the concept 'ineffable'. Then, he positively motivates the concept of ineffable knowledge by means of a philosophical puzzle. His account will provide us with a first indication of the fact that subjectivity plays a central role in examples of meaningful ineffability.

Moore begins by arguing that states of knowledge are dispositional states capable of explaining purposive behavior. This is an important precondition for an argument for ineffable knowledge because it circumvents the condition that knowledge must be knowledge *of something*, that is, of a fact or of a truth.

> The structure of a given state of knowledge is a matter of how the knowledge guides the knower. That very same structure may be realized in some independent state of affairs or configuration of objects—which the knower, in virtue of his or her knowledge, is able to navigate.[33]

Moore uses Hugh Mellor's 'Specification Argument' to show how and when ineffable knowledge is possible.[34] Roughly, the Specification Argument intends to show that every state of knowledge x has utility conditions (enabling the knower to act on his desires) which must be expressible in a set of propositions; by stating x's utility set one specifies x—the specification becomes more and more complete the more inclusive the list of propositions is. Therefore, the Specification Argument can be used to argue that it is possible to make all states of knowledge explicit because all states of knowledge can be expressed through stating their utility sets.

Moore then argues against Mellor that "there are states of knowledge which are not answerable to anything, and whose success conditions are simply the conditions in which their subjects are in those states."[35]

To illuminate this notion and to explain the relation between ineffable knowledge and other kinds of knowledge, Moore distinguishes four kinds of knowledge.[36]

Propositional knowledge (knowledge-that) can either be absolute or perspectival ('absolute' meaning that it can be known from every possible point of view or even from no point of view).... As an example for absolute propositional knowledge, he suggests the physical formula $e = mc^2$. Other examples for absolute propositional knowledge would be logical knowledge such as 'If p and q, then p.'

Contrary to absolute propositional knowledge, perspectival propositional knowledge can only be known from a particular point of view. An example for perspectival propositional knowledge is my knowing what the date is today or what the time is now. Statements of both kinds of propositional knowledge are truth-apt.

Practical knowledge (knowledge-how), however, is not truth-apt, that is, states of practical knowledge are neither true nor false. Moore distinguishes expressible practical knowledge from ineffable practical knowledge. Examples for effable practical knowledge are 'knowing how to make an omelette' and 'knowing what coffee smells like,' that is, capabilities on the one hand, and sensory perceptions on the other.

Ineffable practical knowledge, he claims, is the kind of knowledge enabling us to acquire and process those three other kinds of knowledge. The reason why ineffable knowledge is ineffable is that it "has nothing to answer to,"[37] that is, it is without content, whereas the three other kinds of knowledge all have their specific content. For something to be effable, there must be some kind of truth-evaluable content to be made effable, that is, to be expressed in language. The way Moore sees it, ineffable knowledge is needed to process the content of other states of knowledge. It thus enables us "to make sense of what [we] glean in [our] transactions with the world and with other people."[38]

Having thus argued that the concept of knowledge is principally compatible with the concept of ineffability (given that it does not require us to posit something like ineffable truths), Moore then proceeds to motivate the concept of ineffable knowledge in a positive fashion by arguing that one of the most fundamental philosophical puzzles can be resolved by means of it.

The puzzle, which I will henceforth refer to as the 'Paradox of the Idealistic Appeal' (PIA), arises as follows.[39]

Let's say that detached thought about the world means forming what Moore would call 'absolute representations' of the world. A representation is absolute "iff it is from no point of view.... Equivalently, a representation is absolute iff it can be integrated by simple addition with any other possible representation."[40]

Moore defines a point of view as a "location in the broadest possible sense."[41] All the features that define the location of the subject count toward the characterization of the point of view:

> Hence points of view include points in space, points in time, frames of reference, historical and cultural contexts, different roles in personal relationships, points of involvement of other kinds, and the sensory apparatuses of different species.[42]

A point of view is thus a vantage point from which to "look" at the world, as it were, which takes into account certain features of reality and leaves out others.

Having clarified these terms, Moore then goes on to argue for the possibility of detached thought about the world, that is, for the possibility of forming absolute representations, as follows:

> Consider any possible true representation p from any point of view π. One of the members of C [a single conception of reality] must be derived from the account of how p is made true by reality. This account, since it serves for pitting p against any other possible true representation, including any possible true representation from a point of view incompatible with π, cannot itself be from π. So given that all the members of C are from the same points of view, none of them can be from π. But π was chosen arbitrarily. So none of the members of C can be from any point of view. Absolute representations are possible.[43]

For Moore, a prime example for an absolute representation, that is, a representation that is not from any point of view, is a non-indexical sentence such as $e = mc^2$.

Some may consider an argument to the effect that detached thought about the world is possible quite unnecessary, given that science, especially physics, seems to demonstrate impressively what the argument intends to establish. However, not everyone shares these intuitions about science, and thus, it is important to show that there is an independent argument for the possibility of detached thought about the world.

So it seems that, on the assumption that the representations we form of the world are representations of a mind-independent reality, we have good reason to believe that thought about the world that is not dependent on a specific perspective or point of view is possible; and indeed, science seems to fit the bill.

On the other hand, there is also a strong sense in which thought about the world is "soaked" (Moore) in perspective: doesn't forming a representation of the world depend on there being a mind in the first place? And if so, isn't it possible that the world we form representations of depends for its existence on our forming representations of it? This intuition underlies many formulations of idealism. The Paradox of the Idealistic Appeal can thus be summarized as follows:

PIA

1. Given that detached thought about the world is possible, we have good reasons to believe that the world exists independently of us.[44]
2. However, the way in which we experience the world gives us reasons to believe that the world exists dependently on us/our minds.
3. (1) and (2) are mutually exclusive; they cannot both be true.
4. Thus, we either need to find a way to decide which reasons have more weight, or we need to find a way to reconcile these two claims.

The way Moore positively motivates his account of ineffable knowledge is by arguing that it can solve PIA by reconciling (1) and (2), that is, by enabling us to accommodate our idealist intuitions coherently in an overall picture of reality. His argument runs as follows.[45]

Roughly, idealism can be defined as the view that the form (or metaphysics) of the world of which we produce representations depends (at least partly) on our representations.[46] Idealism can be understood as the the view that "things in space and time are only appearances or phenomena, i.e., items that exist only as the contents of actual or possible representations."[47] In short, idealism is the view that there exists some sort of necessary dependence relation between reality and mind.[48]

There are at least two general ways in which idealism can be understood. According to what could be referred to as 'empirical idealism', the dependence relation between mind and reality is *immanent*, that is, it has an ontological connotation of some sort. There are, of course, numerous ways in which it could be spelled out what exactly it means for a dependence relation to be immanent. For example, one way in which the dependence relation could be pinned down ontologically is by claiming that there are facts that accommodate the perspectivity contained in the dependence relation. And this, in turn, could be done by assuming the existence of something like perspectival facts. As I have argued in Chapter 4, views of this kind are untenable.

According to what is usually referred to as 'transcendental idealism', the dependence relation between mind and reality is *transcendent*, that is, it is not part of the "furniture of the world," meaning it has no ontological consequences. If the dependence relation between mind and reality is not located in our ontology, it must be located in our thought about the world. The most prominent way of spelling out what exactly transcendental idealism could come down to has, of course, been provided by Kant (he actually invented the term), who argues in the First Critique that the experienced perspectivity of the objects of our perception can be explained by the way in which the human cognitive apparatus functions. At the beginning of the 'Transcendental Aesthetic' in the *Critique of Pure Reason*, Kant states:

> In whatever way and through whatever means a cognition may relate to objects, that through which it relates immediately to them, and at which all thought as a means is directed as an end, is intuition. This, however, takes place only insofar as the object is given to us; but this in turn, is possible only if it affects the mind in a certain way. The capacity (receptivity) to acquire representations through the way in which we are affected by objects is called sensibility. Objects are therefore given to us by means of sensibility, and it alone affords us intuitions; but they are **thought** through the understanding, and from it arise concepts. But all thought, whether straightaway (*directe*) or through a detour (*indirecte*), must ultimately be related to intuitions, thus, in our case, to sensibility, since there is no other way in which objects can be given to us.[49]

This passage illuminates the view that lies at the heart of Kant's transcendental idealism: since we can only relate to objects via *intuition*, the objects in the external world (the "thing-in-itself") can only be objects of our *thought* but not objects of our *knowledge*. The thing-in-itself can be *thought of* as that which is causing us, that is, our minds, to have appearances. Yet it cannot be *known to* play that role because we cannot relate to it in an unmediated fashion:

> Space itself, however, together with time, and, with both, all appearances, are **not things**, but rather nothing but representations, and they cannot exist at all outside our mind; and even the inner and sensible intuition of our mind (as an object of consciousness), the determination of which through the succession of different states is represented in time, is not the real self as it exists in itself, or the transcendental subject, but only an appearance of this to us unknown being, which was given to sensibility. ... Accordingly, the objects of experience are **never** given **in themselves**, but only in experience, and they do not exist at all outside it.[50]

Hence, we cannot know the mind-independent world "as it is." Consequently,

> what we are talking about is merely an appearance in space and time, neither of which is a determination of things in themselves, but only of our sensibility; hence what is in them (appearances) are not something in itself, but mere representations, which if they are not given to us (in perception) are encountered nowhere at all.[51]

Kant does not mean to say that the thing-in-itself, that is, the noumenal world, does not exist. Things-in-themselves exist and exercise "a degree of influence on sense."[52] What Kant argues for is a combination of 'empirical realism', which preserves the reality of ordinary things given to us in experience, with 'transcendental idealism', according to which the properties of objects given to us in experience (like their causal powers and their spatial and temporal location) are determined by our minds. They are so determined because two forms of pure intuition, space and time, structure our sensations into the experience of things in space[53] and in time.[54] Space and time are not features of the world as it is but they are a priori necessary conditions for any human experience whatsoever. Moreover, human understanding imposes 'categories' like causality and dependence, unity and plurality, upon the manifold of sensible intuitions (i.e., upon the received sensory content that has been structured by space and time).[55] Thus, the objects of ordinary experience are *empirically real* but *transcendentally ideal*: they are not to be identified with anything that lies beyond, and thus transcends, the bounds of possible experience.

Transcendental idealism is a way to reconcile the two mutually exclusive claims of PIA by distinguishing between levels: at a transcendent level, the claim that our representations are representations of a mind-independent reality is rejected; at a non-transcendent level it is affirmed. Take the following claim for example:

A: The existence of the physical universe depends on the existence of our representations of it.

The transcendental idealist would determine the truth-value of this sentence as follows:

B: A is transcendently true but non-transcendently (immanently) false.

The idea of transcendental idealism is thus to claim that (A) is true of "our mind-dependent phenomenal world" but false of "the mind-independent physical world." The problem with this idea, however, is that it is self-refuting. This is because (B) constitutes a representation of precisely the kind that transcendental idealism says we *cannot* produce:

> It is no good treating this claim as transcendently true but immanently false. The transcendent interpretation does not exist. If it did, it would not be transcendent. If we really cannot produce a representation to the effect that the physical universe depends on the existence of our representations without saying something false, then the physical universe does not depend on the existence of our representations. At a more general level, we cannot represent limits to what we can represent. For if we cannot represent anything beyond those limits, then we cannot represent our not being able to represent anything beyond those limits.[56]

(B) is neither true nor false of the physical world; it is thus a nonsensical claim and cannot serve to reconcile the two mutually exclusive claims of PIA. It is also impossible to argue something like 'transcendental idealism is true of the way in which human beings conceive of the world but it is not true of the world itself' because that would imply relativism about truth, which I have rejected earlier.

Alternatively, someone might try to argue that whether or not transcendental idealism is true depends on the theory of truth we employ. However, the truth-value of a proposition should never depend on the underlying theory of truth. Both on a correspondence and on a coherence view of truth, for example, only one of the following two claims can be true: 'The objects of the world depend for their existence on my conceiving them' or 'It is not the case that the objects of the world depend for their existence on my conceiving them'. Claiming that transcendental idealism is a truth that cannot be stated is also not a way out, for that would be equivalent to claiming that transcendental idealism is an ineffable truth, which I have argued to be incoherent (see Chapter 4). We can see from all this that B has no explanatory power because, given that it is nonsensical, it doesn't make a positive claim and therefore, doesn't explain anything about the physical world.

However, despite the fact that transcendental idealism is neither plainly true nor ineffably true, many would admit that the transcendental idealist's claim is, for some reason, still very appealing. Something just seems right about the claim that what our representations answer to is in some way dependent on those very representations.

Moore explains this appeal in terms of the Wittgensteinian concept of 'being shown' that p. Having ineffable knowledge (or being in a state of ineffable understanding) is thus identical to being shown that p without being ontologically committed to p. He summarizes his account as follows:

While we cannot coherently state that transcendental idealism is true, we are shown that it is, where 'A is shown that x' is defined as '(i) A has ineffable knowledge, and (ii) when an attempt is made to put that knowledge into words, the result is: x'. Provided that we can make sense of (i) and (ii), this proposal has the threefold merit of: avoiding self-stultification; being compatible with the incoherence of transcendental idealism; and providing an account of transcendental idealism's appeal.[57]

In support of (i), Moore argues that, if all cases of knowledge can be said to be "dispositional states which can serve to explain purposive behaviour,"[58] then nothing in that description precludes the possibility of there being ineffable knowledge. In support of (ii), he argues that, even though any 'x' serving as what could be called a 'pseudo-expression' of an ineffable insight[59] must be considered nonsense, there is nevertheless a sense in which we can expect convergence on the way in which such pseudo-expressions are picked. The reason why we can expect convergence is that human beings share two characteristics: we are all finite beings, and we all aspire to transcend our finitude. And because this is so, we have "a shared sense of when a piece of nonsense is 'apt' to replace 'x' in the schema, where 'aptness' is a quasi-aesthetic attribute, such as might occur in poetics."[60]

Consequently, some pieces of nonsense will be more apt, and some less, for that attempt. For example, the nonsensical statement 'The existence of the physical universe depends on the existence of our representations of it' is more apt to express my ineffable insight about the way in which I receive the world than the nonsensical statement 'xyz'.[61]

Even though the example of transcendental idealism together with PIA, is a most vivid way of introducing the notion of ineffable knowledge, Moore does not think that the concept of ineffable knowledge applies only to cases like PIA. Rather, ineffable knowledge features in all kinds of different contexts. Having ineffable knowledge can also mean achieving

> an inexpressible insight into how one implements, combines, and exploits whatever one knows, an insight into how one works with, and reasons with, whatever one receives. The knowledge one thereby exercises is a kind of understanding. It is knowledge how to process knowledge. It is constituted by various receptive capacities, in particular conceptual capacities.[62]

I think what Moore is getting at in this passage is precisely what I have called 'logical knowledge' in the previous section, that is, the ineffable knowledge enabling us to think logically and thereby to process the vast amount of propositional knowledge we receive and form it into a coherent and unified structure.

Moore's second example for ineffable knowledge is

my knowing how to exercise the concept of greenness: my knowing what it is for something to be green. This does not consist in my knowing that anything is the case. It is rather a matter of my having the wherewithal to know that various things are the case. For instance, it enables me to know that the leaf I am looking at is green. But it does not itself consist in my knowing that anything is the case because it does not answer to how the world is.[63]

What Moore mentions here is a case of phenomenal knowledge, which I have mentioned already in Chapter 1 and which will be discussed further in Chapter 7.

Finally, Moore's prime example of ineffable knowledge is knowing how to use language, that is, a case of knowledge-how (as discussed in the first part of this chapter).[64]

Moore has thus provided a sophisticated argument for the existence of ineffable knowledge motivated by a number of examples. I will now address an objection against Moore's account brought forth by Timothy Williamson and outline some ways in which Moore could defend himself against them. Then I will explain my own worries about Moore's account.

Williamson's objection is an objection from externalism. Moore names as one of the main examples for ineffable knowledge the knowledge enabling one to understand one's own idiolect:

> My understanding of English is a prime example. I would certainly count that as ineffable, even though it includes large tracts of effable knowledge such as my knowledge that the past tense of a regular English verb is formed by adding 'ed'—or, for that matter, my knowledge that the word 'rabbit' denotes rabbits, and my knowledge that the word 'green' denotes green things. Understanding, of the sort that I have in mind, has nothing to answer to. Of course, I may think that I know what a particular word in English means and be wrong: I may think that the word 'rabbit' denotes hares as well as rabbits. If that is the case, then what I understand is strictly speaking not English. But I do still *have* my understanding.[65]

Williamson raises the following worry about this:

> Moore's prime example of ineffable knowledge is one's understanding of one's own idiolect. He claims that it has nothing to answer to: 'rabbit' denotes hares in my idiolect if I think it does. Work by Burge and others undermines this conception of an idiolect. One is fallible even about one's own idiolect and one's own concepts.[66]

Williamson is referring here to Tyler Burge's seminal paper 'Individualism and the Mental,'[67] which constitutes a cornerstone of the internalism/externalism debate. In that paper, the following two scenarios are sketched.

6.5.1 Scenario One

A person with a pain in his thigh, call him Larry, goes to the doctor and tells him that he has arthritis in his thigh. This is a false belief because, by definition, one cannot have arthritis in one's thigh but only in one's joints. We are then asked to imagine the exact same situation in the next possible world, that is,

> We are to conceive of a situation in which the patient proceeds from birth through the same course of physical events that he actually does, right to and including the time at which he first reports his fear to his doctor. Precisely the same things (nonintentionally described) happen to him.[68]

The only difference between the two possible worlds is the conventional meaning of the term 'arthritis': in the counterfactual world 'arthritis' designates the (original) disease arthritis *as well as* other rheumatoid ailments, including pains in the thigh.

Larry's two mental states in the actual and in the counterfactual world differ in content although his physical and nonintentional mental histories remain entirely the same. The only difference between the two worlds is the conventional usage of the term 'arthritis':

> However we describe the patient's attitudes in the counterfactual situation, it will not be with a term or phrase extensionally equivalent with 'arthritis'. So the patient's counterfactual-attitudes contents differ from his actual ones.[69]

Burge then draws the following conclusion: "The difference in [Larry's] mental contents is attributable to differences in his social environment."[70] He elaborates his point by mentioning several variations of the thought experiment, each relying on different variants of error like misunderstanding or misconception, partial understanding, etc., and argues that his argument applies to all cases in which it is possible to attribute to someone a mental state or event whose content involves a notion that the subject falsely or incompletely understands. The thought experiment can also be run reversely.

6.5.2 Scenario Two

We are asked to imagine a person who has full and correct understanding of the term 'arthritis' in the actual world and tells the doctor (correctly) that he has arthritis. In the counterfactual world, however, 'arthritis' applies to rheumatic ailments of all sorts. So the patient's beliefs in the two worlds (and hence his mental states) differ because of the different usage of the term 'arthritis'. Burge states:

The reversal of the thought experiment brings home the important point that *even those propositional attitudes not infected by incomplete understanding* depend for their content on social factors that are independent of the individual, asocially and non-intentionally described. For if the social environment had been appropriately different, the contents of those attitudes would have been different.[71]

Burge's argument suggests that, in addition to being determined by understanding, inference patterns, and other features, the contents of a person's attitudes depend on communal practice. As Scenario Two intends to establish, this supposedly holds even when a person fully understands the content of her mental attitude.

Burge thus argues for a form of externalism about mental contents. According to this view, whatever a person thinks or says is *determined* by aspects of the world external to the subject's mind. This is a stronger claim than merely stating that mental states are *caused* by external factors. It is the claim that a person S's given mental state ms could not have existed as it does had S not been embedded in the very external environment that determines the content of ms. The relations between S and its external environment thus make up the identity of ms.

I think there are several ways in which Moore could counter Williamson's worry that his prime examples of ineffable knowledge aren't valid examples at all. The first one is by emphasizing his point that

[the conceptual capacities which constitute ineffable knowledge] have nothing to answer to. What matters is what can be done with them. One's insight does not therefore consists of receiving anything. It derives from a certain mode of reception, a mode of making sense.[72]

This passage emphasizes that Moore's claim that the understanding of one's own idiolect constitutes an example of ineffable knowledge does not depend on our language use being infallible. Moore could admit that we are sometimes mistaken about the contents of our mental states without having to give up his claim that the understanding of one's own idiolect constitutes an example of ineffable knowledge.

I see two other ways for Moore to defend himself against Williamson's worry. Recall that Burge's account is only meant to apply to 'oblique occurrences' of expressions. If an expression occurs obliquely, it functions in a content-clause (i.e., in a 'that'-clause referring to mental states or events which provide the content of someone's intentional state, for example, belief) in such a way that it cannot be substituted with an extensionally equivalent expression without that substitution changing the truth-value of the sentence. A classic illustration for this is the water—H_2O-example:

if Bertrand thinks that water is not fit to drink, it does not follow that he thinks that H_2O is not fit to drink, even though water and H_2O can be considered extensionally equivalent. Burge claims that in these two cases, the mental states (and thus the thoughts) are distinct even though the expressions have the same extensions. The opposite of an oblique occurrence of a term is a non-oblique occurrence of a term: Burge claims that there would be no difference in the content of Bertrand's thought 'the water in the glass over there is impure' if water was replaced with H_2O. The reason is that the expression 'water,' in this context, is not a determining component of Bertrand's thought content. Burge summarizes:

> The crucial point... is the assumption that obliquely occurring expressions in content-clauses are a primary means of identifying a person's intentional mental states or events. . . . For any distinct contents, there will be imaginable contexts of attribution in which, even in the loosest, most informal ways of speaking, those contents would be said to describe different mental states or events... Most of the cases we discuss will involve extensional differences between obliquely occurring counterpart expressions in that-clauses. In such cases, it is particularly natural and normal to take different contents as identifying different mental states or events.[73]

Assuming that Burge's externalist account is correct, the first defense is that Moore could simply add a qualification to his examples of ineffable knowledge, thus restricting it to nonoblique occurrences of expressions. As Burge himself claims, it is impossible that a person be mistaken about her nonobliquely occurring expressions. Williamson's worry that the prime examples of Moore's account of ineffable knowledge aren't examples at all would not apply in this case.

Another way of defending Moore's account is to challenge Burge's argument. This could be done as follows.[74]

Consider Scenario (1). Larry thinks he has arthritis in his thigh, not knowing that arthritis denotes a disease which only occurs in people's joints. Larry, who expresses his belief with the sentence 'I have arthritis in my thigh', thus arguably believes two things: the first-order belief that (A) he has arthritis in his thigh, and the second-order belief that (B) the sentence 'I have arthritis in my thigh' is the right way to express his belief. In order to account for the mistake attributed to the patient in Burge's example, one of the following three options must hold: either, Larry's belief (A) is false, or Larry's belief (B) is false, or both (A) and (B) are false. The fact that (B) is false is clear from the setup of Burge's thought experiment—Larry has, by stipulation, a false belief about which sentence expresses his belief correctly. What about belief (A)? How do we correctly describe Larry's belief (A)? There are two options. Either, we attribute to him the concept 'tharthritis,' which applies both to arthritis and to the disease he has in his thigh. In that case, he would (truly) believe that he has tharthritis in his thigh. Or, we attribute to Larry the public concept 'arthritis.' In that case, he would (falsely) believe that he has arthritis in his thigh.

As a way to decide which belief-attribution is correct, Crane suggests that we look at the patient's dispositions:

> a problem with Burge's book is presented by the fact that a psychologist would not be able to distinguish between the non-verbal behaviour ... of two Burgean twins in certain experimental situations...This would seem to be so in our case too: up to the time described by the thought experiment, [the patient] has (*ex hypothesi*) all the same dispositions to (non-verbal) behaviour in the actual and the counterfactual situations. This suggests that we should attribute the concept *tharthritis* to him.[75]

In other words, Crane holds that we have no reason to assume that Larry employs different concepts in the actual and in the counterfactual situations because his dispositions to act in certain ways remain exactly the same. Arguably, the patient has the same concept in both scenarios, namely 'tharthritis', whereas he lacks the concept 'arthritis' in both scenarios. Thus, in both scenarios, Larry's belief is that he has tharthritis in his thigh. The crucial difference between the scenarios is not a difference in the content of the patient's beliefs, but a difference in the correctness of her utterance: 'I have arthritis is my thigh' expresses his belief correctly only in one of the two scenarios, namely in the scenario where 'arthritis' denotes a disease in joints and thighs. Crane has thus provided a powerful argument against the intuition that different belief ascriptions can be true of physically identical subjects. I conclude that, even though objections from externalism need to be taken seriously by anyone who wants to defend Moorean ineffable knowledge, they don't constitute a decisive objection against its existence.

However, I would like to raise three additional objections to Moore's account. Recall that Moore argues that all kinds of knowledge are states enabling their subjects to act on their beliefs, desires, etc. What characterizes ineffable knowledge and distinguishes it from ordinary, expressible knowledge is that it does not consist in receiving input from the world and forming representations based on that input. Rather, ineffable knowledge derives from a specific *mode* of reception. According to Moore, prime examples of ineffable knowledge are certain states of understanding: knowing how to exercise the concept 'green'; knowing what it is for something to be green; knowing how to process (effable) knowledge; knowledge how to use language. Ineffable knowledge can thus

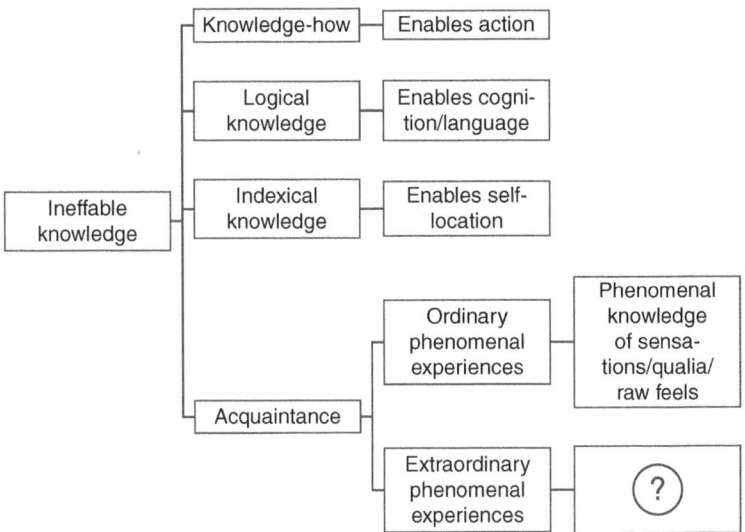

Figure 6.1 Varieties of ineffable knowledge

be understood as knowledge how to acquire and process knowledge. It is not itself a representation of how things are, which is why it is ineffable. However, Moore's account fails to address three central questions:

1. *Nonsense-convergence*: Why is it that, very often, we agree on nonsensical expressions constituting our attempts to express the ineffable (think about the way in which we formulate idealism, for example)? Does it matter that it is nonsense, as long as you and I and maybe others find it meaningful?
2. *Verification*: If ineffable knowledge is a kind of knowledge-how, what would be an appropriate principle of verification of knowledge-possession? For example, my knowledge how to ride a bike enables me to ride a bike. Thus, an external observer can verify that I possess knowledge how to ride a bike by asking me to ride it. Is there an analogous way to verify that a person possesses ineffable knowledge of the kind Moore suggests?
3. *Unifying principle*: Moore fails to develop a unifying principle of ineffable knowledge. He motivates ineffable knowledge by means of a very specific example, namely, transcendental idealism, and then goes on to enumerate a few more examples of ineffable knowledge, for example, knowledge how to exercise the concept 'green', knowledge how to use language, etc. Yet these examples

seem quite disconnected; it is unclear what it is that they have in common that makes them all cases of ineffable knowledge in the way introduced through the example of transcendental idealism.

In the following chapter, I will continue my discussion by introducing two further kinds of of ineffable knowledge, indexical and phenomenal knowledge. I then proceed to develop my own account of ineffability as experienced in the specific contexts of aesthetics, religion, and philosophy. This account also manages to answer the three central questions about ineffable knowledge Moore's account fails to answer.

CHAPTER 7

INEFFABLE KNOWLEDGE II

7.1 Subjective Ineffable Knowledge

In the previous chapter, we first examined two familiar kinds of ineffable knowledge, knowledge-how and logical knowledge, and we noted that these two kinds of knowledge, together with propositional knowledge, enable human action and human cognition respectively. What characterizes these two kinds of ineffable knowledge is that they relate a subject to the world surrounding it: knowledge-how enables us to act in and interact with the world; logical knowledge enables us to process the vast amounts of propositional knowledge we gather every day, and to assemble it into one unified picture of reality.

We then took a close look at A. W. Moore's account of ineffable knowledge. We found that Moore's account provides some very compelling examples of instances of ineffable knowledge relating, not only to some kind of ability to deal with the world (as in the cases of knowledge-how and logical knowledge), but to an ability to accommodate irreducible subjectivity in the world.

In this chapter, we will now turn to a systematic examination of the kinds of ineffable knowledge that concern the irreducibly subjective aspects of human life, that is, the kind of knowledge that enables us to locate ourselves in the world and to ascribe properties to ourselves (indexical knowledge), and the kind of knowledge generated by our sensual interaction with the world (phenomenal knowledge).

I will first introduce indexical and phenomenal knowledge and explain the sense in which they are ineffable. I will then proceed to argue that they do not exhaust the whole range of ineffable knowledge out there: what is still missing is the kind of knowledge that enables us to phenomenally recognize ourselves as Selves. Consequently, in the last section of this chapter, I develop an account of this kind of knowledge, which I refer to as 'Self-acquaintance', and which completes the varieties of ineffable knowledge out there. I will demonstrate how Self-acquaintance explains our paradigmatic cases of philosophically intriguing ineffability, as found in aesthetic, religious, and philosophical contexts, and I will argue that the metaphysics of ineffability should thus be explained in terms of this particular kind of ineffable knowledge.

7.2 Indexical Knowledge

Indexical knowledge is the kind of knowledge involved in the ascription of indexical or demonstrative concepts such as 'I', 'this', 'that', 'here', 'there', etc. What is special about indexical expressions is that they can have varying referents even though the linguistic expressions themselves remain the same. This is the reason why many philosophers believe that indexical expressions have two kinds of meaning: a linguistic meaning, or character, and a content.[1] The former characterizes the linguistic function of the expression, for example, the self-referentiality of the term 'I', whereas the latter characterizes the actual content expressed in each context. Take, for example, the two sentences uttered by Peter and Paul:

1. Peter: "I am hungry."
2. Paul: "I am hungry."

Their linguistic meaning is the same: both sentences ascribe the property of being hungry to the person uttering the sentence. Their content, however, is different because the first sentence says that Peter is hungry whereas the second says that Paul is hungry. The difference in content becomes even more salient in a scenario where only Peter really is hungry but Paul isn't. In such a case, only the first utterance would express a truth, whereas the second sentence would express a falsehood.

In order to determine the content of a sentence containing indexical expressions, we therefore need a context: who is the speaker, at what time, in which location and possible world is the sentence uttered, etc. Without such a context, we can understand the linguistic meaning of an indexical utterance but we cannot determine its content. In order to determine its content, we would have to know what the indexical expressions refer to. Given that the reference of indexical expressions is entirely context-dependent, we can say that indexical expressions without context are empty terms.

Indexical knowledge is the knowledge enabling us to use indexical terms correctly. Moreover, indexical knowledge is ineffable.

We are all familiar with John Perry's supermarket example:

> I once followed a trail of sugar on a supermarket floor, pushing my cart down the aisle on one side of a tall counter and back the aisle on the other, seeking the shopper with the torn sack to tell him he was making a mess. With each trip around the counter, the trail became thicker. But I seemed unable to catch up. Finally it dawned on me. I was the shopper I was trying to catch.
>
> I believed at the outset that the shopper with a torn sack was making a mess. And I was right. But I didn't believe that I was making a mess. That seems to be something I came to believe.[2]

Perry's example demonstrates the existence of a particular kind of knowledge characterized by the fact that it is not deducible from complete knowledge of the physical facts. Even the most detailed objective description of the supermarket scenario won't include the information that the person who is making the mess is, in fact, *me*. This suggests that, in addition to all the 'objective' facts out there, including all the facts about the particular person 'John Perry' or 'Silvia Jonas', there is a special kind of knowledge about one's Self *as such,* that is, about what it means to be a subject *from the subjective point of view.* Given that this special kind of knowledge cannot be deduced from any of the available facts constituting the physical world, this knowledge is ineffable. No possible description of the supermarket scenario will convey the crucial piece of knowledge to John Perry that *he* is the person making a mess. It is only when he realizes that the person making the mess is identical with himself that Perry stops his hunt for the person making a mess.

Another enlightening example for this is Rudolf Lingens:

> An amnesiac, Rudolf Lingens, is lost in the Stanford library. He reads a number of things in the library, including a biography of himself, and a detailed account of the library in which he is lost. He believes any Fregean [descriptive] thought you think might help him. He still won't know who he is, and where he is, no matter how much knowledge he piles up, until that moment when he is ready to say, "*This* place is aisle five, floor six of Main Library, Stanford. *I* am Rudolf Lingens."[3]

Again, the example shows that even the most complete, detailed, objective descriptions of a situation or a person do not allow Lingens the essential inference that *he* is that person and that he is *there*. David Lewis, who picks up on this example in order to argue for irreducibly *de se* beliefs, puts it like this:

> Book learning will help Lingens locate himself in logical space. But none of this, by itself, can guarantee that he knows where in the world he is. He needs to locate himself not only in logical space but also in ordinary space.[4]

According to Lewis, what Lingens is missing is a piece of nonpropositional knowledge.[5] He explains this knowledge in terms of the concept of a 'self-ascription' of properties: once Lingens understands that *he* is Lingens, he ascribes the property of being Lingens to himself. This self-ascription cannot be reduced to a proposition such as 'Lingens believes that Lingens is Lingens'—he could equally hold such a belief in a world where he believed Lingens was, say, his neighbor. Rather, the belief he forms after ascribing the property of being Lingens to himself is 'I am Lingens!'. Hence, it is not the properties involved in these self-ascriptions that are ineffable, but the self-ascription itself.

William Seager has proposed a very similar way of thinking about indexical knowledge, that is, as generated by "a self-representational sub-system within the overall cognitive economy... whose function is to transform incoming information into indexical knowledge."[6] What is important to note is that this self-representation does not carry any information *about* the Self. It is

> primitive and information-free. Its distinctive role is to embody indexical knowledge, not by explicitly encoding the information but rather by the way it integrates perception and action with the information already within the system.[7]

We can imagine this as a process whereby the self-representation in question functions inferentially like a name: *SELF* is making a mess, not someone else. Also in Lingens' case, self-recognition happens exactly at the point when this self-representation kicks in: his information that *some man* in aisle five, floor six of Main Library, Stanford, is lost, turns into the information that *he* is lost when self-representation replaces 'some man' with *SELF* (or 'I').

Verbal expressions of such self-ascriptions (Lewis) or self-representations (Seager) always involve indexicals such as 'I' or 'here'. The problem with indexical terms is, however, that they lack a definite meaning: when Lingens says 'I am in the library' and Silvia says 'I am in the library', the term 'I' refers to two completely different objects. The sentence 'I am in the library' is true of anybody uttering it in a library. The same holds for other indexical expressions such as the demonstratives 'here', 'there', 'this', 'that', etc.

As we have seen earlier, the knowledge needed to use indexical expressions correctly, that is, to correctly self-ascribe an identity, a location, etc., cannot be expressed propositionally. In this sense, indexical knowledge is ineffable.

7.3 Phenomenal Knowledge

A further kind of subjective ineffable knowledge is phenomenal knowledge. The most famous example motivating phenomenal knowledge is Frank Jackson's Mary, which we already discussed in Chapter 4.

Suppose that Mary, having been confined to a black-and-white room all her life, has been reading numerous physics and biology books and now knows everything there is to know *propositionally* about color perception, that is, facts about light waves and wavelengths, retina receptors, neural processing, etc. So there is a way in which we can truly say that Mary knows all the facts about color perception. Let's now imagine that Mary is released from her room and perceives the color red for the first time in her life. Even though she already knew all the facts about color perception before she got out of the room, most of us feel that she learns something additional when actually seeing red herself for the first time: she learns what it is like *phenomenally* to see red.[8] In other words, Mary gains phenomenal knowledge.

Jackson used his example, which has come to be known as the Knowledge Argument, to argue against physicalism, that is, against the view that everything there is to know about the world can be captured in terms of physics. The limited space of this chapter won't allow me to enter the huge debate about physicalism in great depth here, but I do want to give a few indications as to how I think the kinds of knowledge involved in the Mary example are best interpreted.

As I argued in Chapter 4, perspectival facts and their corresponding perspectival propositions are incoherent notions because they ultimately lead to a non-unified picture of reality. I therefore agree with the physicalist insofar as I believe that all facts and corresponding propositions we postulate must either be physical facts or facts that are nonphysical themselves but coherent with the physical facts (such as facts about the nature of numbers or other abstract objects, for example). However, I also agree with Jackson insofar as I believe that Mary gains an entirely new piece of knowledge the moment she sees the color red for the first time. Hence, what I believe is that Mary gains phenomenal knowledge, and that knowledge is nonfactual, nonpropositional knowledge.

We now need to find a way to spell out what this could mean. One way is to think of phenomenal knowledge as knowledge involving demonstrative concepts, that is, indexical knowledge, an idea defended by Perry.[9] Let's call the knowledge Mary extracts from her physics books about what it is to see red P_R and the phenomenal knowledge she gains by actually seeing red $this_R$. Before seeing red, Mary knows that seeing red is P_R. Once she actually sees red, Mary understands that $this_R$ is seeing red and infers that $this_R$ is the phenomenal aspect of P_R. The process of understanding the phenomenal aspect of color perception is thus supposed to work exactly as in the case of the indexical self-ascriptions discussed earlier.

The advantage of aligning phenomenal knowledge with indexical knowledge in this way is that it allows us to explain Mary's epistemic gap between the physical and the phenomenal domains without postulating a nonphysical ontology. Given my arguments in the preceding chapters, it should be clear by now that I think this is the right way to go if we want to avoid incoherence. Despite this advantage, however, I think that there are good reasons to believe that indexical knowledge and phenomenal knowledge are two different kinds of knowledge. This is not to say that Mary doesn't also gain indexical knowledge upon leaving her room ('*This is what seeing red is like!*'), but it is not her new indexical knowledge that plays the central role in the debate about the knowledge argument.

Consider the following two analogous cases.[10] Imagine that Sharon was about to show Peter her favorite animal. When she shows him an armadillo, there are three thoughts Peter might form:

1. Sharon's favorite animal is $this_A$. (purely demonstrative)
2. $This_A$ is an armadillo. (demonstrative-qualitative identity statement)
3. Sharon's favorite animal is an armadillo. (purely qualitative)

Analogously, think about the possible thoughts Mary could form upon seeing red for the first time (let R be the qualitative concept of the phenomenal experience she is now having):

1. Seeing red is $this_R$. (purely demonstrative)
2. $This_R$ is R. (demonstrative-qualitative identity statement)
3. Seeing red is R. (purely qualitative)

In both cases, the crucial thought is the second one, that is, the thought that involves attributing a certain qualitative nature to an object that is picked out demonstratively. It is this thought that expresses the newly gained knowledge, that is, the knowledge that allows further inference to a purely qualitative statement such as 'Sharon's favorite animal is an armadillo.' or 'Seeing red is R'. The first thought, on the other hand, being purely demonstrative, does not contain any substantive knowledge. I take this to be a decisive refutation of the idea that phenomenal knowledge is nothing but demonstrative (indexical) knowledge. It is true that Mary's new knowledge might involve demonstrative thoughts, but the substantive piece of additional knowledge she gains when seeing red for the first time is not demonstrative but qualitative.

Another way to see this emerges when we try to think about the epistemic gaps between the physical and the indexical domains on the one hand, and between the physical and the phenomenal domains on the other.[11] Let's first take an indexical case, for example, the famously omniscient, yet ignorant gods.[12] Imagine two gods, omniscient with respect to all propositional knowledge, one sitting on top of the highest mountain, throwing down manna, the other sitting on top of the coldest mountain, throwing down thunderbolts. Each of the two gods knows everything there is to know about the world they inhabit, including that there are two gods, one of them sitting on top of the highest mountain throwing down manna, the other sitting on the coldest mountain, throwing down thunderbolts. In this sense, that is, with regard to the entire class of propositional knowledge about this world, both gods are omniscient. But if this is all they know, then both gods lack knowledge: neither of them knows which one of the two gods he is. Hence, both gods are missing a crucial piece of indexical knowledge that cannot be inferred from the propositional knowledge they possess. From their perspective, there is an epistemic gap between their factual and their indexical knowledge.

However, imagining this scenario *from an outsider's perspective*, the epistemic gap vanishes. We know that god A is the one throwing the thunderbolts and god B is the one throwing manna. An outsider knows everything about the gods and more than the gods themselves. So the gods' ignorance is *essentially indexical*; it disappears as soon as we zoom out of the subjective god-perspective into a purely objective perspective. This is to say that we can lack indexical knowledge about which person is *me*, what time it is *now*, what *this* is etc., from a subjective perspective. However, such knowledge is never lacking from an objective perspective.

Not so for phenomenal knowledge. Mary's ignorance as to what seeing red will be like for her, or what seeing red is like for others, does not disappear from the point of view of an external observer. Just like Mary doesn't know what seeing red will be like for her, also the observer doesn't know what seeing red will be like for her, and this not only holds for Mary's phenomenal experiences but for the phenomenal experiences of all beings that are not the observer himself. The phenomenal lives of other beings are private and *essentially inaccessible* from an outsider's perspective. This holds even if an observer is omniscient with regard to the entire class of propositional knowledge. Thus, no matter how far into objective space we zoom out of the Mary scenario, the epistemic gap between the physical and the phenomenal domains does not close.

The indexical and the phenomenal case are thus disanalogous with regard to the involved epistemic gaps: an indexical epistemic gap vanishes from the objective point of view, whereas a phenomenal epistemic gap doesn't. This is another reason to reject the view that phenomenal knowledge is nothing but a particular kind of indexical knowledge.

So if not in terms of indexical knowledge, how else are we supposed to understand phenomenal knowledge? I suggest that phenomenal knowledge is best understood in terms of the concept of 'acquaintance'.

Both Leibniz and Russell[13] argue that there is a way in which we can become directly acquainted with, and thereby aware of, the world outside of us. Leibniz holds that "Our direct awareness of our own existence and of our thoughts provides us with the primary truths *a posteriori*, the primary truths of fact."[14] He argues that these primary truths are immediate "because there is no mediation between the understanding and its objects."[15] In a similar fashion, Russell states that "We shall say that we have *acquaintance* with anything of which we are directly aware, without the intermediary of any process of inference or any knowledge of truths."[16]

Ernest Sosa identifies an ambiguity present in both passages. He points out that it is unclear whether 'awareness' refers to something that could be called 'intellectual awareness' or 'noticing', or to something that could be called 'experiential awareness'. According to him, the difference between those two concepts is that one can be *experientially* aware of something without being *intellectually* aware of it, whereas the reverse does not hold. His argument is that a subject S can be experientially aware ('e-aware') of, say, a chilly breeze CB simply by virtue of experiencing it (i.e., by virtue of undergoing the experience), whereas being intellectually aware ('n-aware') of CB would require S to form some kind of belief or judgment about CB, such as 'There is a chilly breeze'. If the concept 'being acquainted' is supposed to serve the purpose of providing an a priori justification for perceptual belief, then in order to avoid argumentative circularity, we ought to interpret it in the sense of being 'experientially aware'. This is because 'being acquainted with F', interpreted as 'being intellectually aware of F' already implies the formation of a propositional attitude P about F, so that 'being acquainted with F' cannot serve as a foundation based on which P can be formed. Being acquainted with something thus refers to

> mental phenomena epistemically more primitive than any 'noticings' or beliefs, to conscious states 'given in' or 'present to' consciousness. In our terminology, what foundationalists are thus led to is e-awareness: that is, to states constitutive of the subject's total mental life-slice, including both those noticed and also those which escape her notice.[17]

Knowledge by acquaintance explains the difference between the knowledge we gain through, say, somebody telling us that frogs are green (a description of frogs, resulting in propositional knowledge), and through seeing that frogs are green, slimy, etc. (getting acquainted with frogs, resulting in phenomenal knowledge). It also explains why McDowellian 'kidnapping strategies' using demonstrative concepts won't help express phenomenal knowledge: it simply cannot be passed on linguistically but requires personal, direct, phenomenal acquaintance.[18]

Three things need to be mentioned at this point. The first one is that I do not assume that acquaintance gives us a priori justified belief or infallible knowledge. The possibility of error about what we are acquainted with (e.g., in cases of hallucinations, illusions, or dreams) makes it quite improbable that acquaintance can give us infallible knowledge. I think that acquaintance gives us phenomenal knowledge, which is by definition not a kind of knowledge that can be rendered propositionally. Hence, knowledge by acquaintance constitutes a different epistemic category than propositional knowledge. In this sense, I follow Russell's characterization:

> Knowledge of things, when it is of the kind we call knowledge by acquaintance, is essentially simpler than any knowledge of truths, and logically independent of knowledge of truths, though it would be rash to assume that human beings ever, in fact, have acquaintance with things without at the same time knowing some truth about them.[19]

I am convinced that acquaintance plays an important role in the way we generate propositional knowledge, but I am not committed to any particular view about how exactly it contributes to the formation of true beliefs (I do think, however, that acquaintance is only one out of several components featuring in the formation of true belief). The question how exactly acquaintance serves to provide foundations for our belief formation processes, that is, the question how we can get propositional knowledge out of whatever it is we receive by acquaintance, is too intricate to discuss in any detail here.[20] But such a discussion is also not necessary for my purposes because I am not concerned with finding foundations for propositional knowledge here.

Second I want to say a few words about the acquaintance relation. As most acquaintance theorists, I take the acquaintance relation to be a primitive relation undefinable in more basic terms.[21] And as most acquaintance theorists, I don't see this as problematic, given that some unanalyzable factors have to be assumed in every analysis. This does not mean that one assumes to know everything there is to know about the nature and epistemic role of whatever it is one assumes as primitive: there is still enough room for profound questions and puzzlement even if one assumes something as primitive.

Moreover, I take it that most of us are sufficiently familiar with the acquaintance relation from our phenomenal lives. Being acquainted with something means knowing it "in the most direct way that it is possible for a person to be aware of that thing." For example, we are acquainted with the phenomenal qualities of whatever surrounds us constantly. Acquaintance is "the most direct way to apprehend a quality."[22] This familiarity with the acquaintance relation might be a bit of a compensation for the lack of analysis.

The third point I want to mention is the question of possible relata: *who* can be acquainted with *what* kind of entity? Again, I am not committed to a fully determinate class of things one can be acquainted with. What one admits as possible relata depends crucially on one's other ontological commitments. For example, a bundle theorist, who believes that the nature of objects is exhausted by the properties they instantiate, will most likely not believe that we can be acquainted with particulars, but only with universals.

One thing I am committed to, however, is that the acquaintance relation holds primarily between conscious beings on the one hand, and entities that are *not truth-apt* on the other. For example, depending on one's overall ontological commitments, I think that possible candidates to be acquainted with are: individuals; sense data; determinate properties (e.g., *that* particular shade of green); universals (e.g., greenness); abstract objects (e.g., numbers); facts; and, crucially, one's Self. I do not think that we are ever acquainted with truths (e.g., true propositions) but only with potential truth-makers.

The advantage of explaining phenomenal knowledge in terms of the concept of acquaintance is that it does not force us to posit a new class of objects or facts that would be difficult to square with our existing ontology and might even lead us into incoherence.

7.4 Self-Acquaintance

In the first section of this chapter, we discussed the concept of indexical knowledge and we saw that it is best understood in terms of a self-ascription, or self-representation, of properties. The insight required in order to proceed from a belief like 'Someone is making a mess' to 'I am making a mess' requires ascribing the property of mess-making to oneself.

We then noted that this self-ascription requires the postulation of a primitive entity that I will give the capitalized name 'Self'. The difference between Self and the uncapitalized term 'self' is that I use Self solely for the purpose of designating the central reference point of all our indexical self-ascriptions, whereas the ordinary term 'self' is used in a variety of less clearly defined ways. We call a person 'self-centered' if her chief concern is her own well-being; someone who believes in her own capabilities is 'self-confident'; an autodidact is a 'self-educated' person, etc. Capitalized Self, on the other hand, is supposed to denote the specific entity featuring as the focal point of indexical knowledge (with no commitment regarding what kind of entity the Self is exactly; see later). Consequently, when I say that gaining indexical knowledge involves a self-ascription of properties, what I mean is that it involves a Self-ascription of properties (for simplicity's sake, I will stick to the noncapitalized spelling in the cases of 'self-ascription' or 'self-representation' of properties, assuming from now on that it is clear that I am referring to the Self in these contexts).

In the second section of this chapter, we discussed the concept of phenomenal knowledge, which, as I argued, is best understood in terms of the concept of acquaintance.

I now submit the following: just like it is possible to get acquainted with the world surrounding us, that is, its objects and their properties, it is possible to get acquainted with one's Self, and this Self-acquaintance is what explains our paradigmatic cases of ineffability. I further submit that in moments of Self-acquaintance we gain ineffable phenomenal knowledge of our Selves. The fact that this knowledge is phenomenal knowledge explains why it is ineffable; the fact that the object of this knowledge is our Self explains why Self-acquaintance feels both extraordinarily insightful and extraordinarily meaningful. I am thus putting forth the following five claims:

1. The reference point of indexical self-ascriptions of properties is a primitive entity, which I call 'Self'. (Existence Claim)
2. It is possible to stand in an acquaintance relation with (i.e., to gain phenomenal knowledge of) one's Self. (Acquaintance Claim)
3. Self-acquaintance is phenomenal knowledge and, as such, ineffable. (Ineffability Claim)
4. The importance we attach to moments of Self-acquaintance is due to the object we get acquainted with. (Importance Claim)
5. The metaphysics of ineffability is to be explained in terms of Self-acquaintance. (Metaphysics Claim)

I will explain each point in turn.

7.4.1 *The Existence Claim*

Let's begin with my claim that the reference point of indexical self-ascriptions of properties, that is, the Self, is a primitive entity. Why do we need to postulate this entity and how are we supposed to understand it ontologically? That is to say: does it have a physical character and is it located somewhere "inside of us"?

As we have seen above, when Perry realizes that *he* is the person making a mess in the supermarket, and when Lingens understands that *he* is the person lost in the Stanford library, the knowledge they gain cannot be expressed propositionally. Perry and Lingens are aware of everything that can be said propositionally about their respective scenarios even before they gain indexical knowledge and understand that *they themselves* are the persons in question.

I have argued with Lewis and Seager that indexical knowledge is best understood as a self-ascription, or self-representation, of properties. Perry is looking for the person making a mess in the supermarket. When he understands that he is that person, his understanding consists in *self-ascribing* the property 'making a mess in the supermarket.'

The claim I want to defend here is that there is a primitive entity which is the entity to which properties are ascribed in self-ascriptions. In other words, my claim is nothing but an explicit formulation of what is already implicitly contained in the concept of a self-ascription. Whoever believes that there is such a thing as self-ascription of properties (I take it that pretty much everyone believes in this) is thereby committed to the belief that there is such a thing as the Self. Hence, not much argument is needed in order to establish the existence of the Self.

What is needed, however, is an elucidation of the ontological implications of assuming the existence of such an entity. Most philosophers are wary of postulating entities whose character and location are difficult or even impossible to determine, and it looks very much like the Self is precisely one of those cases.

Most of us speak of our Selves with the greatest of ease. When we refer to ourselves as 'self-conscious', 'self-confident,' or 'self-righteous', we even mention our Self explicitly, and we ascribe a particular property to it. On the other hand, if we asked someone where she thought her Self was located or what the physical nature of her Self was, we would most certainly get only vague answers such as "The Self is located inside of me" or "The Self is my brain/heart/soul." In other words, location and nature of the Self are far more difficult to determine than its mere existence.

However, only the *existence* of the Self is crucial to my argument. To be sure, a better understanding of its location, if it has one, and of its nature would be desirable because it would give more substance to my additional claim that we can get acquainted with our Selves, which is to say that we can gain phenomenal knowledge of our Selves. However, my argument does not require a decisive answer to questions about location and nature of the Self.

I do think that the Self is best understood as a primitive entity, simply because I don't think any possible analysis in terms of, perhaps, some kind of physical entity plus its individual properties plus its consciousness ever add up to something equivalent to our intuitive understanding of the Self. Perhaps the Self could be argued to supervene on those things, but they don't exhaust its nature. However, if someone disagreed with me on this point, my overall argument would not be affected. In fact, I believe it to be an advantage of my argument that it does not require a commitment to a particular notion of the Self.

7.4.2 *The Acquaintance Claim*

My second claim with regard to the Self is that we can gain phenomenal knowledge of it by standing in an acquaintance relation to it. I will begin by saying a few words about why there is nothing wrong with assuming such a possibility.

We have noted earlier that we gain phenomenal knowledge by getting acquainted with the world around us, that is, by getting acquainted with the objects composing our surroundings, their properties, and their relations. We gain phenomenal knowledge of this kind continuously, at every moment we move through the world: when we smell our coffee in the morning, when we see the red traffic light on the way to work, when we feel the smooth texture of a silk scarf, etc. Nothing about the enormous amount of phenomenal knowledge we collect every day seems particularly mysterious to us.

Now, some may feel that the idea that we can get acquainted with our Selves in the same way we get acquainted every day with our surroundings is problematic because there is a sense in which the Self differs importantly from all objects we normally get acquainted with. In order to address this issue, we need to understand better what, if anything, this difference consists in. I will consider a few ways in which this objection could be understood and show why none of these ways provides a good reason to dismiss the possibility of getting acquainted with one's Self.

The first possibility is this: perhaps the difference we feel there is between the Self and other things we can get acquainted with is that the Self is not a spatial object. Seeing and touching a red car acquaints us with the car's color, its firmness, its curves, etc. Nothing analogous is possible for the Self.

This point is quickly dismissed. After all, we do not only get acquainted with spatial things. We can imagine getting acquainted with redness alone, that is, with redness that is not instantiated by any spatial object, for example, when we are at the beach, the sun is shining, our eyes are closed and all we see behind closed eyes is an orange kind of red that results from the sunlight shining through our eyelids. In such a case, our acquaintance with redness or orangeness is not dependent on a spatial object instantiating these colors. A lack of spatiality is thus not a good reason to reject the possibility of getting acquainted with one's Self.

Perhaps the objection really is that in ordinary cases of acquaintance, we know what the causal source of the phenomenal experience is: if I get acquainted with an orange kind of red while lying with eyes closed at the beach, I know that this is because the sun is shining through the blood vessels of my eyelids. Nothing analogous can be said about moments of Self-acquaintance.

Also this argument can be rejected. It is not at all true that it is always clear what exactly is causally responsible for a given phenomenal experience. For example, we can imagine standing in a clearing in the middle of a forest at five in the afternoon and getting acquainted with the feeling of eeriness. While we are perfectly clear about the phenomenal nature of this experience (i.e., it is a feeling of *eeriness*), we are not at all sure what factor is causally responsible for the experience: is it the light? the sounds? the forest? the loneliness? all of it together? Lacking knowledge about the causal source of a phenomenal experience is not enough to reject the possibility of such an experience.

Perhaps the objection is that we can get acquainted only with things "outside of us," whereas the Self is conceived as something "inside of us." But also this way of spelling out the objection does not hold. After all, we do get acquainted with things inside of us constantly: stomach aches or butterflies, muscle stiffness, happiness, nervousness, or hunger are arguably all "inside of us."

Perhaps the objection is that we understand the nature of ordinary objects we get acquainted with, but we don't understand the nature of the Self. So how can we get acquainted with something if we don't even know what exactly it is?

But this objection is surely mistaken. We get to know things, also things we are not familiar with, through acquaintance, so it can't be an objection that we do not fully understand the Self. Acquaintance comes before understanding, not the other way round.

I think the best way of spelling out the worry about what is involved in getting acquainted with ordinary objects and properties on the one hand, and what would be involved in getting acquainted with an extraordinary object like the Self is that, for each ordinary phenomenal experience, it is clear which one of our senses is doing the job. It is sight that acquaints us with redness, touch that acquaints us with roughness, hearing that acquaints us with shrillness, smell that acquaints us with putridness, and taste that acquaints us with sweetness. Yet we don't know which of these five senses is the one that can acquaint us with the Self. After all, we can neither see, smell, touch, hear, or taste the Self—so which sense could possibly acquaint us with it? So it must be an entirely different, hitherto unknown sense. But how should we understand such a sense?

I have two answers to this objection. The first one is quite simple: even if each instance of acquaintance is accompanied by a phenomenal experience, this does not mean that acquaintance implies sense perception. So my claim that it is possible to get acquainted with the Self does not imply that Self-acquaintance is a function of our five senses.

My second answer is that even if Self-acquaintance requires postulating an additional sense over and above the usual five, this is not as problematic as it may at first seem. Examples for nonsensory perceptions have already been discussed in the philosophical literature. Keith Yandell,[23] for example, argues that there are cases where we perceive things nonsensorily, that is, when we suddenly know that somebody is present without having any other accompanying sensations, or when we suddenly realize that we are being stared at without knowing where the staring person is. Also mathematics has sometimes been taken to be a case in point: Russell, for example, has argued for something like knowledge by acquaintance of numbers.[24]

In scientific literature too, cases of nonsensual perception have been described. One of the most famous examples is Oliver Sacks' description of a couple of brain-damaged twins conventionally referred to as "idiot savants." Clinical tests displayed a complete inability of the two twins to understand and perform the most elementary arithmetic operations of addition and subtraction, multiplication, and division. However, when it was observed that they 'conversed' in six-digit numbers and the numbers were noted and examined, it turned out that all the numbers were prime numbers. Moreover, when Sacks 'joined' their conversation by throwing in eight-digit prime numbers, the twins seemed very pleased and responded in further prime numbers. The game continued until they had reached 20-digit numbers. Given their complete inability to perform basic mathematical operations, Sacks draws the conclusion that the twins "do not seem to 'operate' with numbers, non-iconically, like a calculator; they 'see' them, directly, as a vast natural scene."[25]

If, as I argue, acquaintance necessarily implies a phenomenal experience but not necessarily a sense perception, then the objection from sense perception against my proposal does not hold.

I have considered several objections to my claim that we can get acquainted with our Self and have shown why these objections do not hold. One question remains to be answered here, which is: how is my proposed Self-acquaintance different from ordinary self-awareness, that is, what distinguishes the rare moments of getting phenomenally acquainted with one's Self from the omnipresent awareness we have of ourselves *qua* conscious beings at all times?

The short answer to this question is: the difference between ordinary self-awareness and extraordinary Self-acquaintance is precisely the factor of *acquaintance*, that is, the presence of an immediate, direct phenomenal experience of one's Self, as opposed to the mediated, indirect way in which we are aware of ourselves in ordinary contexts. When we speak of self-awareness in ordinary contexts, what we mean is that we are aware of, for example, our thoughts and emotions, our beliefs and desires, our sense perceptions, our motivations, our opinions about things. That is to say, we are aware of ourselves *as* the thinkers of particular thoughts, the havers of certain sense perceptions, the bearers of certain properties, etc. In this sense, our self-awareness is mediated through other things such as thoughts and perceptions, whereas in moments of Self-acquaintance, we become directly phenomenally acquainted with the Self.

What about reflexive thought, that is, what about thought that is specifically about our Self? After all, while I am writing this, I am thinking about that mysterious entity, which I call the Self, and I try to make sense of it. Why should it not be possible for me to get to know everything there is to know about the Self by reflecting on it, as I do now?

The answer to this point is exactly the same answer as the one to the question why it is impossible to know what vanilla tastes like without ever having tasted vanilla: we can only know the phenomenal aspect of something by being acquainted with it, not by reflecting on it, or talking about it. No amount of hard thinking and no list of detailed descriptions of the taste of vanilla will make me come to know what vanilla tastes like. In the same way, even though it is certainly possible to refer to oneself, to self-ascribe properties, and to reflect on one's Self without ever being acquainted with it, no amount of hard thinking and reflection will give me direct, phenomenal knowledge of the Self.

I have so far argued for two claims: that there exists a mysterious entity I call the Self, and that it is possible to get acquainted with this entity. I will now proceed to explain my third claim, which is that Self-acquaintance qua phenomenal knowledge is ineffable.

7.4.3 *The Ineffability Claim*

As we already noted in Chapter 1, when we differentiated philosophically interesting from philosophically irrelevant cases of ineffability, sense perceptions (or what some people call 'qualia', 'raw feels', etc.) are ineffable, and their ineffability is entirely unmysterious. I compared the ineffability of the taste of saffron to the ineffability of a stone: expecting either one of them to be expressible would constitute a category mistake, simply because stones and sense perceptions are just not the kinds of things that can ever be expressed. We can describe stones, and we can also describe the taste of saffron, but we cannot *express* them. Only things that are propositional in form, or can be brought into propositional form, are candidates for expression. Recall our definition of ineffability:

Ineffability A nonlinguistic item y is ineffable if and only if it is metaphysically impossible that there be a linguistic item x whose content nontrivially entails the content of y and whose content is, in principle, communicable to other finite beings by users of a finite language.

Phenomenal knowledge is ineffable because it cannot be transmitted by words. No linguistic item can ever transport the phenomenal character of tasting vanilla, or of what it is like to see red. The same holds for the phenomenology of Self-acquaintance: no words can ever express what it is like to get acquainted with one's Self. This is because, in Moore's terminology, knowledge of this kind "has nothing to answer to."[26]

Once we understand the kinship between ordinary sense perceptions and Self-acquaintance, we understand that there is nothing mysterious about the associated ineffability claim. But this does not mean that the ineffability of moments of Self-acquaintance is, after all, a completely mundane business. What distinguishes ordinary phenomenal experiences from Self-acquaintance are the different degrees of attention involved: moments of Self-acquaintance feel important, mysterious, meaningful; ordinary sense perceptions do not.

So really what we need to explain now is this importance we attach to moments of Self-acquaintance. That is, we need to answer the question where in the mundane picture of acquaintance and phenomenal knowledge we can locate the feeling of extraordinariness that, as I have argued at length in Chapter 1, attaches to moments of meaningful ineffability.

7.4.4 *The Importance Claim*

The fourth claim I propose is that the importance we attach to moments of Self-acquaintance is due to the object we get acquainted with, that is, the Self. So the question we need to clarify is: What is so important about our Selves that it bestows such an extraordinary aura of meaningfulness, of heavyweight ineffable insight, onto the moments when we get acquainted with it?

Let me begin with a simple answer: the Self is interesting to us, always. Nothing has more relevance to our lives, to our well-being, to the way we make sense of our lives and to the way we navigate through it, than our Selves. The Self is the ultimate reference point for every human being. This fact alone is enough to explain why moments where we get acquainted with it feel extraordinary, important, and meaningful.

We can elaborate on this point and make it more precise: the Self is the main reference point for all of our experiences with the world. As the "haver," or recipient, of all our experiences, it is omnipresent in every single experience we have. On the other hand, it is hardly ever the *sole* object of our thought (we usually think of our Selves *in relation to something else*, for example, in relation to our well-being, our desires, our future plans, etc.). And it is even less often the sole object of our phenomenal experience.

So the Self is, on the one hand, the thing that concerns us most directly at all times, but on the other hand, it is also (most of the time) hidden from us. In addition to all these reasons for the importance we attach to the Self, there is the sheer rareness of the moments in which we get acquainted with it. Rare things are always more interesting, and sometimes even more mysterious, than the things we encounter every day.

7.4.5 *The Metaphysics Claim*

The final claim I made was that the metaphysics of ineffability is to be explained in terms of Self-acquaintance. To support this claim, three questions need to be answered.

The first one is: How can we know that it is *Self-acquaintance* that is happening in moments of meaningful ineffability, and not something else? Even if we were convinced by the first four claims (i.e., that such an entity must exist; that it is possible to stand in an acquaintance relation to it; that an experience of Self-acquaintance would be ineffable; and that the nature of the experience would explain the importance we attach to it), that would still not be enough to convince us that it is, in fact, Self-acquaintance that explains moments of meaningful ineffability.

The answer is that my entire examination led up to this conclusion. In the past chapters, I consecutively ruled out possible candidates for an explanation of ineffability. We saw that neither postulating ineffable objects, nor ineffable propositions, nor ineffable contents gave us a satisfactory explanation for ineffability. With these candidates, we either ended up in incoherence (such as in the case of ineffable objects and propositions), or (as in the case of ineffable content) we saw that the alleged ineffability evaporated on a closer look. We then turned our attention to cases of ineffable knowledge and realized that this was the most promising route to go because knowledge has the twofold advantage of being both sufficiently neutral ontologically to avoid running into incoherence, and it is suitable to explain the feeling of insightfulness attached to moments of meaningful ineffability.

Discussing four different types of ineffable knowledge, we saw that each one of them fulfils a particular role for us: knowledge-how enables us to act and interact with the world; logical knowledge enables us to structure our propositional knowledge into a coherent picture of the world; indexical knowledge helps us locate ourselves in the world by enabling us to self-ascribe properties; and phenomenal knowledge is what literally puts us in touch with the sensuous aspects of the world.

The final step from here onward, that is, the step from "ordinary" instances of ineffable knowledge to extraordinary ones, is now only a small one. The central yet hidden role of the Self already became apparent in our discussion of indexical knowledge, and the epistemic force of direct contact with (aspects of) the world clearly emerged from the discussion of phenomenal knowledge. We now only have to put these two together to arrive at the notion of Self-acquaintance: if we already know that there is such a thing as the Self, and if we already know that we can get acquainted with all kinds of things, then the possibility of Self-acquaintance suddenly seems very natural.

Moreover, we now understand what we should be looking for: a kind of ineffable knowledge that explains the meaningful and insightful phenomenology of experiences of ineffability, and more than that: a way of making sense of those experiences that does not require postulating the existence of any obscure entities but rather explains everything that needs to be explained in terms of what is already there, that is, in terms of what is already taken for granted. Self-acquaintance fits the bill: it is a kind of ineffable knowledge, it is not an obscure entity, and wherever we are, the Self is present as well.

The second question that needs to be addressed is: Why don't we normally recognize what is happening during moments of Self-acquaintance? In other words, why don't we describe moments where we experience meaningful ineffability as *moments of Self-acquaintance*?

I think there are two reasons for this. The first one is simply that such moments don't occur often enough to familiarize us with the experience and thus, to allow recognition. In this sense Self-acquaintance works just as any other kind of phenomenal experience: we need to encounter it often enough to be able to recognize future instances of a certain experience as an instance of *that* type of experience. When Mary walks out of her black-and-white room, for example, she wouldn't know that her experience of redness was an experience of *redness* unless she was told so. If she then experienced red several times over the course of some period of time, and she learned that such experiences are usually referred to as *redness* experiences, she would eventually be able to recognize red as an instance of the class of redness experiences. However, this recognitional capacity can only develop over time.

A second reason for the fact that we normally don't associate ineffable experiences with the specific concept of Self-acquaintance is, first of all, that Self-acquaintance is a specialist term probably only philosophers are familiar with. In the same way, without being a doctor, a person is very unlikely to recognize her backache as the symptom of a specific kind of bacterial infection. Second, in moments of Self-acquaintance, our recognition is immediately blurred by a process of interpretation and association that sets in as soon as we are having such experiences. In this way, the purely phenomenal aspect gets mixed up with all kinds of ways of trying to conceptualize it, which in turn depend on how we are predisposed in general to give voice to unfamiliar experiences. Let's imagine, for example, a person who is very religious and who is having the ineffable experience of being acquainted with her Self. Due to her religious predisposition, she is much more likely to describe the extraordinary quality of the experience in religious terms. A person who is not religious, on the other hand, is much more likely to frame her experience in nonreligious terms.

However, the language people use in order to try and express ineffable experiences suggests that a sense of Self is often present, if not explicitly then implicitly. An example for a description of the ineffable with an explicit sense of Self is Wittgenstein, who speaks about our strong sense of the priority of Self over the world.[27] An example for a description of the ineffable with an implicit sense of Self is the world as a whole (the 'Absolute'): the Absolute as that which accommodates, defines, but also surpasses the Self and as such, elicits a strong sense of awe and wonder.

Hence, the historical examples we discussed in Chapter 1 show that the recognition of Self in moments of ineffable experiences is present at least on some level. However, it is our understanding of the Self that determines the way in which we will conceive of and try to express an experience of it: do we intuitively see the Self as a monadic entity hermetically sealed up against the rest of the world, or is it conceived of as an inherently relational entity that cannot be understood in isolation from the rest of the world? Is it to be understood as in some sense *prior* to what lies outside of itself (the view favored by idealists) or is it a posterior product of the way the world has evolved (a view perhaps more in line with physicalism and evolutionary theory)?

More generally, whatever convictions shape our thought in daily life (factors dependent on our background culture, education, religion, our personality, and general preferences) will also shape our attempts to express ineffable experiences, just as the general focus of societal and scientific inquiry (object- or subject-oriented?) will shape our conception. A vivid illustration of this fact is the way in which the focus of our historical examples of ineffability changes over time, from a mainly outwardly oriented view on the ineffable aspects of the world as a whole (Laozi, Gorgias, Plotinus) toward an entirely subject-oriented view on the ineffable aspects of subjectivity (Schopenhauer, Nietzsche, Wittgenstein).

The discussion of the different ways in which people can be predisposed to interpret extraordinary experiences leads us directly to another important question, which is: What is the connection between Self-acquaintance on the one hand, and on the other, the contexts in which it usually occurs, that is, aesthetic, religious, and philosophical contexts? Is something about those contexts particularly conducive to occurrences of ineffable experiences?

I think this question can be answered most straightforwardly for the case of philosophical contexts. Philosophy has always been concerned with locating the Self in an overall picture of reality, that is, with accommodating the subjective within the objective. Some philosophers manage to evoke the problem in such vivid terms that it can trigger Self-acquaintance, that is, it can trigger those ineffable experiences that led to the philosophical insights in the first place. For me, this is most true of Wittgenstein, Nietzsche, and Adorno.

It is less clear what is happening in aesthetic and religious contexts, and I can answer the question why I think those contexts are particularly prone to causing ineffable experiences only in the most general terms (the detailed work I must leave to specialists in philosophical aesthetics and the philosophy of religion). My best guess is that aesthetic and religious settings, for example, a classical concert or a religious service, are characterized to a much higher degree by sense perceptions than ordinary settings. That is to say, there is a strong focus on phenomenal aspects in aesthetic and religious settings (the colors and composition of paintings, the key and rhythm of a piece of music, the presence of an artist in a performance, the liturgy in a religious service, the embedding of religious symbols in religious rituals, etc.). Due to this emphasis of phenomenal aspects, we may attain a mode of reception more attuned or more sensitive to extraordinary phenomenal experiences than in ordinary settings, and this mode may stimulate or facilitate Self-acquaintance.

In addition to this, religious, aesthetic, and also philosophical contexts are often characterized by a close, investigative engagement with the subject (we can think here of the beholder of an artwork, a faithful believer, or a philosopher trying to work out his place in the world). The situatedness of us as individuals in the world around us constitutes one of the central focal points in those contexts, which may account for the fact that we are more prone to experience states of ineffable knowledge in those contexts than in other, more ordinary ones.

One advantage of my account of Self-acquaintance is that it manages to explain why ineffable experiences don't happen predictably. Not all people have an ineffable experience during a religious service, nor in the face of a particular piece of art. Ineffable experiences cannot be voluntarily induced. This suggests that they are not a matter of a specific aesthetic or religious content present in the respective context. If they were, we would expect the ineffable experience to be inducible and repeatable: same content, same experience. But, as a matter of fact, ineffable experiences happen unpredictably.

If we think about the ineffability experienced in aesthetic and religious contexts as a matter of Self-acquaintance, we understand that it is not the respective aesthetic or religious content that is responsible for the experience: it is an independent phenomenal experience acquainting us with our Selves that causes the experience of ineffability. This explains why a repetition of content will not necessarily trigger a repeated experience of ineffability.

Let's now take stock of what I argued in this chapter. After a discussion of indexical knowledge, in the course of which I argued for the existence of an entity I call 'Self', and a discussion of phenomenal knowledge, in the course of which I argued that phenomenal experiences are best explained in terms of the concept of acquaintance, I applied that very concept to the Self and argued that experiences of ineffability are to be explained in terms of this Self-acquaintance.

My central claim is thus that ineffability is caused by a shift in our perception. Through this shift, the focal point of all our phenomenal experiences, that is, the Self, becomes itself the object of acquaintance. The metaphysics of ineffability can thus be described as a combination of a distinct mode of experience (acquaintance) with a particular object (the Self).

We can now see how my account manages to solve the three problems I have identified for Moore's account. These are:

1. The problem of *nonsense-convergence*: why do we usually agree on nonsensical expressions constituting our attempts to express the ineffable?

2. What is an appropriate principle of *verification* for being in a state of Self-acquaintance?
3. What is the *overarching principle* of ineffable knowledge that connects the different instances of ineffable knowledge?

Answer (1): It is by virtue of the fact that the object of ineffable states of knowledge is our Self that we are inclined to use the same, or at least very similar, words for our attempts to express our ineffable knowledge. It is reasonable to assume that the Self that constitutes the object of Self-acquaintance for one individual resembles the Self that constitutes the object of Self-acquaintance for other individuals sufficiently to assume that the phenomenology of an ineffable insight is similar or even the same in different subjects. The similarity of the experience is then a possible explanation for the fact that different subjects attempt in similar ways to express what is inherently inexpressible. Moreover, their struggle to put their ineffable experience into language inclines them toward preexisting religious, aesthetic, or philosophical language.

Answer (2): The answer to the second worry is simply that there is no principle of verification for a state of Self-acquaintance. But this shouldn't worry us. The fact that there is no such principle makes perfect sense. Given that the object of Self-acquaintance is the Self of the respective subject in question, it is by definition impossible for an external observer to verify the ineffable insight. This is because an external observer has no access to another subject's Self. However, there is nothing mysterious about this inaccessibility, in the same way that there is nothing mysterious about the fact that we can't verify whether someone is *really* seeing red, or whether he is actually seeing green. There is nothing troubling about the fact that it can't be externally verified whether a subject is *really* getting acquainted with her Self.

Answer (3): The question of an overarching principle that makes all cases of philosophically relevant experiences of ineffability cases of ineffable *knowledge* has, of course, been answered already: the overarching principle that subsumes all cases of ineffable experiences under the general category of ineffable knowledge is that they are special cases of phenomenal knowledge, that is, special cases of knowledge by acquaintance. What makes them special is not the way in which the knowledge is generated (i.e., through an immediate, direct acquaintance) but the combination of that special mode of reception with the special object of the Self.

To conclude my exposition of Self-acquaintance, I would like to address the following three possible worries. The first worry is that my account of Self-acquaintance might be vulnerable to an objection similar to the one I raise against Nagel, that is, the worry that my account might result in an incoherent picture of reality, given that it postulates the existence of a special kind of highly subjective knowledge. My answer to this worry is that Self-acquaintance does not consist in experiencing *something different* like Nagel's perspectival facts that would be hard to square with our existing ontology. Rather, in moments of Self-acquaintance, we experience something familiar, that is, the Self, in a *different way*. Hence, nothing in my account requires the postulation of weird entities that could possibly lead us into ontological incoherence.

William James puts this point very nicely for the case of mystical experiences:

> Yet, I repeat once more, the existence of mystical states absolutely overthrows the pretension of non-mystical states to be the sole and ultimate dictators of what we may believe. As a rule, mystical states merely add a supersensuous meaning to the ordinary outward data of consciousness. They are excitements like the emotions of love or ambition, gifts to our spirit by means of which facts already objectively before us fall into a new expressiveness and make a new connection with our active life. They do not contradict these facts as such, or deny anything that our senses have immediately seized. It is the rationalistic critic rather who plays the part of denier in the controversy, and his denials have no strength, for there never can be a state of facts to which new meaning may not truthfully be added, provided the mind ascend to a more enveloping point of view.[28]

A second possible worry about my account is that moments of Self-acquaintance, being instances of phenomenal experiences, might after all be expressible through demonstrative concepts. Recall our discussion of nonconceptual content in Chapter 5 and the underlying question whether or not our recognitional capacities outstrip our conceptual capacities (which would be a basis for arguing that some contents are too fine-grained to be conceptual). I denied this question, arguing with McDowell that we can align our recognitional capacities with our conceptual capacities through the use of demonstrative concepts and higher-order sortals: '*that* shade of color', '*that* sound of V7-ness', etc. In this way, we can refer to and uniquely identify any shade of color we want, which means that we can point it out to someone else and eventually, following a process of familiarization, form a linguistic expression that will be understood by every competent language user as referring to *that* shade of color. Can we express Self-acquaintance in the same way?

In order to answer this question, we must be very clear about what we mean by 'expression'. Of course we can refer to our Selves demonstratively, pointing at ourselves and uttering 'that Self'. However, it is the phenomenal knowledge generated by moments of Self-acquaintance that is ineffable. No demonstrative in the world will enable me to 'communicate' the feeling of getting acquainted with my Self to anyone else, just like no concept in the world will enable me to communicate to someone else how rain feels on my skin. I can, of course, try to give a *description* of such experiences, but the phenomenal aspect of such experiences is essentially private and incommunicable. Hence, the knowledge generated through Self-acquaintance is essentially ineffable and the application of demonstrative concepts cannot change that.

The third question I anticipate is how my account of ineffability is relevant for the historical figures I quoted at the beginning of my book, for example, for someone like Plotinus, Schopenhauer, or Adorno. I wish I could provide an extensive answer now, going through all the historical examples again, and trying to provide a reading of those sources in terms of Self-acquaintance, but I cannot possibly fulfil this task here. Not only because it would expand the size of my book to a nonmanageable size, but also because trying to apply contemporary concepts and theories to historical sources requires a careful examination that ensures the adequacy and substitutability of historical and contemporary concepts—a task requiring the expertise of philosophers specializing in the history of philosophy. I have indicated earlier how I think talk of the Absolute and talk of idealism can be related to the Self. Perhaps someone with a specific interest in the work of one of those historical figures and in the ineffability claims involved therein may find my account helpful to develop a better understanding of those specific references to ineffability.

I would like to conclude this chapter with the best attempt of expressing the essentially ineffable experience of Self-acquaintance I could find: Prince Myshkin's descriptions of the mystical states preceding his epileptic fits:

> The sensation of life and *self-awareness* increased almost tenfold at those moments, which had a duration like that of lightning. The mind, the heart were flooded with an extraordinary light; all his unrest, all his doubts, all his anxieties were as if pacified at once, were resolved into a kind of higher calm, full of a serene, harmonious joy and hope, full of reason and the final cause. But these moments, these flashes were still merely the presentiment of that final second (never more than a second), with which the fit itself began. That second was, of course, unendurable....These nebulous expressions seemed to him very clear, though too weak. But that it was really 'beauty and prayer', that it really was 'the highest synthesis of life', of that he could be in no doubt... These moments were simply *an extraordinary intensification of self-awareness* and at the same time of *a self-perception in the highest degree direct*.[29]

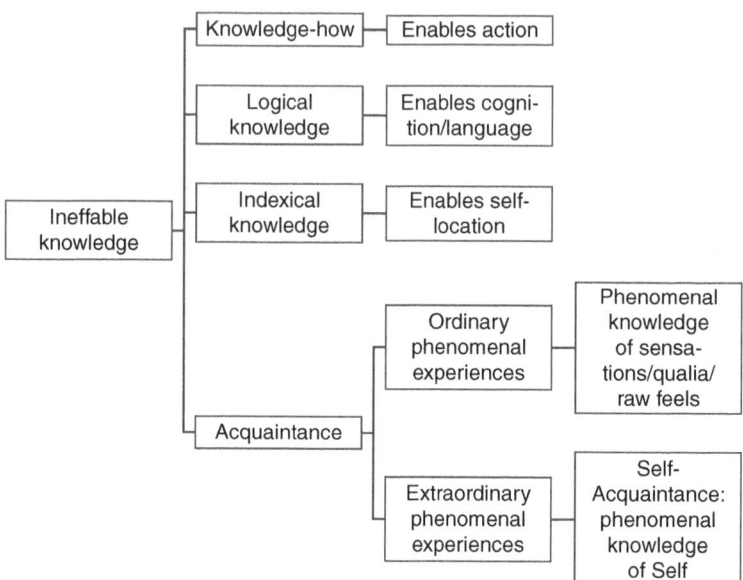

Figure 7.1 Varieties of ineffable knowledge

The prince's description of his ineffable experiences and the role the Self plays in them is, of course, infinitely superior to my dry philosophical exposition. I hope, however, that my examination of the metaphysics of ineffability may be helpful at least to some in increasing their understanding and thus, their appreciation of all sorts of talk of ineffability.

CHAPTER 8

CONCLUSION

Can art, religion, or philosophy afford ineffable insights—and if so, what are they? My book answers this question positively: yes, art, religion, and philosophy can afford ineffable insights. These insights are moments in which we get acquainted with our Self.

I began my argument by raising the question as to why we attach importance to what we are unable to put into words. I speculated that this might be the case because we feel that there is *something* of importance lying behind the linguistic barrier. My goal was to examine to what extent this intuition is justified, particularly whether we have reason to think that there are metaphysically substantial entities of some sort that resist expression.

My arguments in Chapters 3 to 5 showed that neither ineffable properties and objects, nor ineffable propositions, nor ineffable content are suitable candidates for an explanation of the metaphysical underpinnings of ineffability. In Chapters 6 and 7, I argued that ordinary ineffability is best explained in terms of four kinds of ineffable knowledge: knowledge-how, basic logical knowledge, indexical knowledge, phenomenal knowledge. The meaningful ineffability we sometimes experience in aesthetic, religious, and philosophical contexts is a special case of ineffable knowledge, which I labeled 'Self-acquaintance.'

To conclude this book, I would like to say a few words about the possible philosophical applications of my theory of ineffability, specifically with regard to the often-referred-to contexts of aesthetics and religion. In what sense is it helpful to know that the ineffability we experience in aesthetic and religious contexts is an experience of Self-acquaintance?

Self-acquaintance is of course not an exhaustive explanation of what is going on in meaningfully ineffable moments. When I experience ineffability in the face of a work of art, for example, while sitting in front of Marina Abramovic during her performance *The Artist is Present*, many external factors contribute to the unique character of that particular experience: Marina's facial expression, the location, the atmosphere, the sounds, smells, colors around me. Likewise, there are also many internal factors that will influence how I will interpret the experience afterwards: my education, my cultural background, my religion will bring particular concepts to my mind in which to frame the experience. To the extent that such internal and external factors differ from person to person and from context to context, the quality of our ineffable experiences and the way in which we describe them will differ as well. The concept of Self-acquaintance alone cannot do justice to the uniqueness of every individual ineffable experience. But it can serve as a common metaphysical ground.

This is even more true for the context of religion. When I have an ineffable religious experience, for example, during prayer, the concept of Self-acquaintance does not accommodate every possible way in which such an experience can be interpreted. A theist will probably insist that the experience is caused by God and perhaps also that it is God I am experiencing, not the Self. An atheist, on the other hand, might dismiss someone's ineffable religious experience as nothing but an imagination.

However, Self-acquaintance can perhaps serve as something like a 'minimal metaphysics' for religious ineffability that both a theist and an atheist can agree on. 'Self' is a term that is sufficiently neutral to be acceptable both for a theist and for an atheist as a starting point for an explanation of the metaphysics of ineffability. Depending on one's religious convictions, the term 'Self' can then be suitably expanded. On a theistic reading, for example, Self-acquaintance might be understood specifically as acquaintance with God: according to Genesis 1.27, God created the Self in His image, so by becoming acquainted with our Selves, we are becoming acquainted with God. According to an atheist reading of ineffable religious experiences, on the other hand, Self-acquaintance might perhaps be best interpreted as an acquaintance with a Self that is longing for mysticism and other-worldly explanations of life and the world.

I am thus far from claiming that the concept of Self-acquaintance explains everything that needs explanation about experiences of ineffability. I do believe, however, that it provides a common ground for any account of the metaphysics of ineffability.

NOTES

Introduction

1. Danto 1973: 46.
2. Davidson 1974: 5.
3. Kennick 1967: 181.
4. Russell 1935: 143f.
5. I elaborate on the distinction between expression and description in Chapter 2.
6. Sense perceptions are relevant to my project, though, because they generate phenomenal knowledge, which is a kind of ineffable knowledge. I elaborate on this in Chapter 7.
7. I give a more precise definition of "experiences" in Chapter 2.
8. Actually, it would be more precise to speak of a family of relate doctrines here, rather than of "the" doctrine of idealism; cf. Rosen 1994.
9. Cf. Moore 1997 and Rosen 1994 for elaborate arguments to this effect.
10. Cf. Walker 1995; Moore 1997.
11. Cf. Carr 1999: 10.
12. Rosen 1994: 279.
13. Rosen 1994: 279.
14. Sheffer 1909: 129.
15. Laozi 2007: Ch. 1.
16. Laozi 2007: Ch. 41.
17. Laozi 2007: Ch. 32.
18. Cheng 2003: 203.
19. Lau 1963: 117.
20. Lau 1963: 104.
21. Sextus Empiricus 1949: 7.65. References to this argument can also be found in Pseudo-Aristotle's *On Melissus, Xenophanes, and Gorgias*.
22. Plotinus 1918a: Book V, Ch. 3, Passage 13.
23. Plotinus 1918b: Book VI, Ch. 9, Passage 10.

24. Maimonides 1956 [1190]: 204.
25. Kant 2003 [1763]: p. 159 (footnote).
26. Kant 2008 [1755]: 146.
27. Kant 1998 [1787]: B650.
28. Kierkegaard 1985 [1844]: IV 204 (p. 37).
29. Cf. Gurrey 1990: 203.
30. Schelling 1980 [1795]: §3.
31. Schelling 1980 [1795] §3.
32. Schelling 1989 [1859]: 231.
33. Schopenhauer 1966 [1859]: §31 (p. 173).
34. Nietzsche 2003 [1873]: 875–890.
35. Nietzsche 2003 [1873]: 880.
36. Heidegger 1962 [1927]: 62.
37. Wheeler 2014.
38. Scharfstein 1993: 122.
39. Heidegger 1982 [1959]: 59.
40. Heidegger 1935: 204.
41. Heidegger 1935: 206.
42. Heidegger 1935.
43. Bennett-Hunter 2014: p. 30.
44. For example Knepper 2009.
45. For example, Anscombe 1971; Hacker 2000; McGinn 1999.
46. For example, Diamond 1995; Kremer 2001.
47. McGinn 1999: 494.
48. What I call 'proper assertions' is sometimes referred to as the Tractatus' 'frame'. The Preface, §§3.32–3.326, 4–4.003, 4.111–4.112, and 6.53–6.54 are usually considered to count toward the proper assertions. §6.54 reads: "My propositions serve as elucidations in the following way: anyone who understands me eventually recognizes them as nonsensical, when he has used them—as steps—to climb up beyond them. (He must, so to speak, throw away the ladder after he has climbed it up.)."
49. This example is due to Chomsky 2002.
50. McGinn 1999: 493.
51. Wittgenstein 2003 [1922]: §§2.171; 4.12–4.121.
52. Wittgenstein 2003 [1922]: §6.1201.
53. Wittgenstein 2003 [1922]: §5.62; cf. Hacker 2000.
54. Adorno 1993: 102.
55. Adorno 1993: 102.
56. I argue extensively for this claim in Jonas 2013.
57. Dostoyevsky 2004. [1869]: Part 2 Ch. 5.

58. I discuss the expressive powers of metaphorical language in Chapter 5.
59. Two exceptions are Scharfstein (1993) and Kukla (2005). However, neither of the two works intends to provide a systematic examination of the metaphysics of ineffability. Scharfstein's emphasis lies on the history of the concept of ineffability; Kukla's examination constitutes a classification of different kinds of ineffability according to "strength" (a taxonomy similar to the one I give in Chapter 2).
60. Scruton 2010.
61. Scruton 2010.
62. James 2002 [1902]: 428.
63. It may seem strange to some of my readers to call God an object, in which case I suggest the term 'being' or 'supreme being'. It is worth emphasizing that objects need not be concrete; they can be abstract, which might make it easier for some to speak of God as an object.
64. Secondary kinds of truth-bearers include sentences, assertions, statements, utterances, etc.

Terminology

1. I will not discuss any issues related to the intentionality of mental states; neither will I comment on the difficulties of stating what 'aboutness' amounts to.
2. I say "part of the content" because Wendy surely receives many more pieces of content in that situation, for example, the color of Peter's clothes, how his crying sounds, etc.
3. It is worth pointing out that this definition of content is consistent with compositional, causal, and model-theoretic theories of content. Thanks to Jack Woods for helpful discussions on this point.
4. Moore 1997: 280.
5. For related discussions cf. Dorter 1990; DeSousa 2002.
6. Cf. Korsmeyer 1985 for discussion.
7. Some have argued that mental states *are* mental events (e.g., Lewis 1987; Kim 1973); more commonly, however, mental events have been analyzed in terms of change, which excludes at least those mental states that don't exhibit change. My definition of experiences is neutral with regard to the question whether there is a difference between mental events and mental states. Likewise, it is consistent with both possible answers to the question whether mental events need to have phenomenal qualities or not.

8. Space restrictions prevent me from engaging thoroughly with the huge body of literature discussed under the label 'qualia.' It will be sufficient for my purposes, however, to point out the following: either qualia are an independent (rather than merely supervenient) metaphysical category, or they are not. If qualia are a metaphysical category of their own, then my argument in Chapter 4 applies to them by applying to those truths for which they are supposed to be the truth-makers. If, on the other hand, qualia can be reduced to some neurophysiological phenomena, then they are irrelevant for my discussion anyway.
9. What I call 'bodily sensations' are sometimes referred to as 'raw feels,' a term introduced by Thomas Reid (Reid 2003 [1764]), or 'qualia,' a term introduced by Charles S. Peirce (Peirce 1958 [1866]: §223) and Clarence Irving Lewis (Lewis 1929: p. 121).
10. Cf. Armstrong 1968; Dennett 1991.
11. Reid 2003 [1764].
12. Peirce 1958 [1866]; Lewis, C.I.: 1929: p. 121.
13. Jackson 1977.
14. Chisholm 1957.
15. Travis 2004.
16. I discuss his theory in detail in Chapter 4.
17. Whatever one may understand by the term 'metaphysically substantial concept' exactly, it roughly refers to a concept whose extension is somehow mirrored in the structure or composition of reality.
18. Horwich 1998: 10.
19. Horwich 1998: 19.
20. Horwich 1998: 17.
21. According to Horwich, principles relating truth, reference, and satisfaction ought to be *derivable* from any set of axioms defining truth, rather than being axioms *themselves*.
22. Horwich considers all instances of the Equivalence Schema epistemically basic and a priori; thus, it is unproblematic for him to conclude that truth is not susceptible to reductive explanation (Horwich 1998: 145).
23. Horwich 1998: 11.
24. It is somewhat ironic that the only theory of truth that, *prima facie*, doesn't have to grapple with ineffability—because it is an entirely *formal* account of truth—has ineffability cropping up in its formulation. Thanks to Angela Matthies for pointing this out to me.
25. Horwich 1998: 20.

26. Besides the fact that some truths can't be formulated with the tools the theory provides, it is also unclear how to understand the truth of the Equivalence Schema in a noncircular way.
27. Horwich 1998: 4.
28. Horwich 1998: 3f.
29. Horwich 1998: x.
30. Horwich 1998: 6.
31. Horwich 1998: 101.
32. Horwich 1998: 101.
33. Horwich 1998: 101.
34. Horwich 1998: 102.
35. Horwich 1998: 102.
36. Horwich 1998: 19 footnote 3.
37. An intuitive thought that makes the validity of deflationist theories of truth doubtful concerns animal behavior. More precisely, there are animals that seem to possess something very similar to the truth-concept without having the capacity to think of truth in terms of an Equivalence Schema. Ravens, for example, are notorious liars. They deliberately make their fellow ravens believe that they are hiding their food in certain places by actually performing actions that look like hiding food. However, as soon as they feel unobserved, they take the food some place else. I find it very plausible to call this kind of behavior a willful misrepresentation of facts. I also find it very plausible to hold that a willful misrepresentation of facts requires the misrepresenter to possess the concept of truthful representation, so that ravens, for example, arguably possess something like a concept of truth and falsehood. Even though this is not a well-developed argument, I am fairly certain that it can be developed into an argument against the claim that truth is a concept possessed exclusively by beings with language. In addition to the deflationist's inability to deal with ineffability, this point about lying animals inclines me to think that deflationary accounts of truth cannot possibly tell us everything there is to know about truth.
38. It is worth mentioning that traditional, non-deflationary accounts of truth, that is, those that belong to either one of the four big classes of Correspondence Theories, Coherence Theories, Pragmatist Theories, and Unanalysability Theories, do not challenge the correctness of the Equivalence Schema. Rather, their intuition is that it does not contain everything there is to say about the essential nature of truth, and that a satisfactory account of truth must contain additional content.

39. I take facts to be a subclass of all possible states of affairs, namely those states of affairs that obtain in the actual world.
40. For an explicit argument against the view that all truth-bearers are propositions see, for example, Thomson 1969.
41. Kennick 1967: 181.
42. Cf. Priest 2000 and 2002.
43. Alston 1989: 29.
44. Soskice 1985: 44.
45. Cf. Hesse 1963.
46. I consciously refrain from talking about artistic expression here because the question of what can and what cannot be achieved by means of artistic expression will be dealt with in Chapter 5.
47. An obvious exception to this rule are sign languages, which, although consisting of gestures only, must of course be considered proper languages and therefore, fall under the class of linguistic expression.
48. Again, I explicitly exclude artistic expression from this claim.
49. Oxford English Dictionary Online, Entry on 'to express.'
50. Oxford English Dictionary Online, Entry on 'to convey.'
51. Oxford English Dictionary Online, Entry on 'to express.'
52. Moore 2003a: 173.
53. Moore 2003a: 173, footnote 13.
54. I elaborate both on Lewis' argument and on Moore's refutation in Chapter 4.
55. Leave aside the question of what exactly propositions are, that is, whether they are sets of possible worlds, sets of maximal descriptions of worlds, ordered n-tuples, etc.
56. Note, however, that as a consequence of this restriction, Moore's definition of 'x expresses y' does not apply to propositional attitudes not aimed at truth, such as desires, fears, hopes, etc. This constitutes a significant limitation of the verb 'to express,' and I am not sure that this limitation corresponds to the way we ordinarily think about expression. For example, if Peter says 'I hope it is not going to rain tomorrow!,' then that sentence arguably does constitute an instance of expression, namely the expression of Peter's hope that it won't rain tomorrow, even though neither Peter's assertion nor the hope he expresses through his assertion are truth-apt. Moreover, given that Moore restricts his definition to truth-apt entities such as sentences, he thereby rules out single terms. This is once again rather unusual, given that also single terms are usually taken to be expressive. For example, the term 'wooden' expresses the property of being wooden. The fact that Moore's definition is confined in this way may be enough for some philosophers to reject it as an adequate definition

of expression. To be fair, Moore does at least mention that the standards of expressibility he adopts are purely stipulative. However, he also expresses his conviction that his way of defining expressibility corresponds to "the most interesting questions about inexpressibility, from a philosophical point of view" (p. 172).

57. Carroll, Lewis 1994 [1872]: 98ff.
58. Moore 2003b: 162.
59. There is of course no question of right or wrong when it comes to definitions. However, some definitions cover our intuitions better than others, and I hope that the standards I adopt manage to cover our intuitions as closely as possible.
60. As will become clear in the course of my book, the distinction between finite and infinite beings will turn out to be irrelevant as well. This is because I will argue that ineffability is a matter of ineffable knowledge, and ineffable knowledge could neither be expressed by finite nor by infinite beings (see Chapter 6). Nevertheless, I think it is important to discuss all these possible distinctions at this point, in order to address as many of the intuitions the reader might have about expressibility as possible.
61. Compare the definition of 'to share' at Oxford English Dictionary Online, Entry on 'to share.'
62. Davidson 1974: 5.
63. Davidson 1974: 5.
64. Davidson 1974: 16.
65. Waismann discusses Frege's definition of the concept 'number' by means of a definition of equinumerosity. Frege argues that two sets are equal in number if they can be paired up in a one-to-one relation. Waismann points out that this attempt to establish that two sets are numerically equivalent is circular.
66. Waismann 1951: 109.
67. If I say: "Tiffy is too weak to lift the stone but Samson can lift it," it is clear from the context that "can" refers to Samson's physical ability and not to some other circumstance (e.g., that Samson can lift the stone because he happens to be at Tiffy's today).
68. There are far more than three kinds of possibility (e.g., epistemic possibility, conceptual possibility, *de dicto* possibility, *de re* possibility, human possibility, technical possibility, etc.). However, the three kinds I picked will suffice to make my point. For elaborate discussions on this topic see Gendler/Hawthorne 2002.
69. Gendler/Hawthorne 2002: 4f.

70. Note that this definition of ineffability immediately rules out the trivial cases in which the alleged ineffability is a result of nescience, physical constraints, or category mistakes.

Ineffable Properties and Objects

1. Cf. Inwood 1992: 27.
2. James 2002 [1902]: 419.
3. Schopenhauer 1966 [1859]: §52; my italics.
4. For more examples refer back to the introduction.
5. Cheng 2003: 203.
6. Plotinus 1918: Book V, Ch. 3, Passage 13.
7. Or at the very foundation, whichever metaphor one prefers.
8. Scharfstein 1993: 149.
9. Scharfstein 1993: 152f.
10. Kant 1998 [1787]: B33.
11. Kant 1998 [1787]: B208.
12. Kant 1998 [1787]: B106.
13. Kant 1998 [1787]: B37ff and B46ff.
14. See Kant's antinomies, specifically the first (of spatiotemporality), second (of atomism), and fourth (of a necessary being) (Kant 1998 [1787]: B454–488).
15. Hegel 1977 [1807]: 11.
16. Inwood 1992: 28.
17. Hegel 1971 [1830]: 113-119 (§79-82).
18. I will say a bit more about these terms later. For now, our intuitive grasp of these notions will be enough.
19. See, for example, Peirce 1958 [1866]: CP 2.341.
20. Kaplan 1975.
21. An equivalent way of defining haecceities is this: "F is a haecceity = df. $(\exists x)$(F is the property of being identical with x)," whose implicit logical structure is such that "necessarily, for any property y, y is a hexadecimal if and only if there exists an x such that Ryx, where R is the dyadic relation, . . . being the property of being identical with." (Rosenkrantz 1993: 3).
22. Leibniz excludes relational properties. Max Black's scenario takes relational properties into account as well.
23. Kant uses the example of two indistinguishable drops of water to argue against the principle of the Identity of Indiscernibles; Kant 1998 [1787]: A 263f = B 319f.
24. Russell 1927: 116.
25. Black 1952: 156.

26. Adams 1979: 10.
27. In cases of three or more spheres, the arrangement must be circular to meet the description.
28. Cf. Stern 2009: 353ff for a related discussion in the context of Hegelian sense-certainty.
29. Hacking 1975: 255f.
30. Sider 2006. Other advocates of bare particulars include Armstrong 1997 and Moreland 1998.
31. "One often hears a complaint about 'bare particulars.' This complaint has bugged me for years. I know it bugs others too, but no one seems to have vented in print, so that is what I propose to do." Sider 2006: 387.
32. Sider 2006: 387.
33. Sider 2006: 389.
34. Sider 2006: 392.
35. Except in cases of exact identicals. I will discuss this problem later.
36. At this point it is interesting to note that haecceities, if they existed, could help both the substratum and the bundle theorist to support their argument. The substratum theorist could try to defend his claim that particulars are more than the conjunction of the universals they instantiate by adding haecceities to the picture: each particular would then have one unique nonqualitative property over and above its universals. The bundle theorist could make an analogous move and claim that each bundle of universals making up a particular contains one property, that is, the haecceity, which accounts for the bundle's unique identity. However, haecceities don't exist, as we have seen above, so this move won't help either side.

Ineffable Propositions

1. For completeness' sake, a third reason for a proposition's ineffability must be mentioned: if there were ineffable properties or objects, and such properties or objects were involved in propositions, then those propositions would most likely not be expressible. However, I demonstrated the impossibility of inexpressible objects and properties is Chapter 3. Consequently, ineffable propositions of this kind are also impossible and will therefore not be considered in this chapter.
2. Hawthorne/Oppy 1997: 186.
3. Thomas Hofweber defends his internalist account of properties against arguments from discovery-fugitive propositions; see Hofweber 2006: 171.
4. Hawthorne/Oppy 1997: 186.

5. Russell 1935: 143f. The claim that performing infinitely many tasks in a finite time is a merely medical impossibility has given rise to some controversy; cf. Moore 1989.
6. Bolander 2014: 4.
7. That is, paradoxical self-referential sentences. Of course not all self-referential sentences entail a paradox. 'This sentence has five words,' for example, is self-referential but not in the least bit paradoxical.
8. Cf. Shaw 2013: 95 ft. 25 for a similar point. Cf. Schnieder 2010 for a discussion of the specific property *being a predicate that does not apply to itself* in connection with Grelling's paradox.
9. Cf. Beall 2009; Priest 2006, 2002.
10. Cf. Martin 1967; Kripke 1975; Field 2008.
11. Cf. Zermelo 1904.
12. Boolos 1971: 221. In formalized language: $\forall x \exists y \phi(x, y) \rightarrow \exists f \forall x \phi(x, fx)$, which can also be rendered as 'For all sets x there exists a choice function which picks out exactly one member of each of the members of x'.
13. The Axiom of Separation states that 'Given any formula ϕ and set A, there exists a set B whose members are exactly those members of A which satisfy ϕ'). In formalized language: $\forall w_1, \ldots, w_n \forall A \exists B \forall x (x \in B \leftrightarrow [x \in A \land \phi(x, w_1, \ldots, w_n, A)])$.
14. For a more elaborate treatment of this example, cf. Posy 2005: 324.
15. Nelson 1986; 2011:81ff; Voevodsky 2010.
16. There are, of course, general worries that have been raised with regards to the view that propositions are sets of possible worlds. For example, it is unclear how one would distinguish between distinct necessary truths such as '2+2 = 4' and 'Either snow is white, or snow is not white'. These are clearly two different propositions; however, given that they are both necessarily true, they are both identical with the same set of possible worlds (namely the set containing all possible worlds) and therefore indistinguishable. Another worry arising as a consequence of the first one is that, if one believed one necessary truth, and given that the content of one's belief would thus be the set of all possible worlds, one would arguably believe all necessary truths (for further discussion cf., for example, Stalnaker 1984 and 1999). I will ignore those worries here. If one of them turned out to be a decisive objection against the view that propositions are sets of possible worlds, so much the worse for Lewisian excess propositions.
17. Cf. Chapter 2 for a more elaborate discussion.
18. Kaplan 1995.
19. Lewis 1986: 104f.

NOTES

20. Someone might argue that we could imagine a machine that produces expressions of those propositions which cannot ever constitute the content of a being's thought. However, on my account, the machine would not be producing genuine expressions since they could not possibly be understood by anyone else. See the discussion of the possible extensions of 'can' above.
21. Lewis 1986: 106.
22. Lewis 1986: 106.
23. Lewis 1986: 106.
24. Cf. Lewis 1986: 27ff.
25. Cf. Savage 1972.
26. Lewis 1986: 108.
27. Something similar can be argued with respect to other propositional attitudes such as desires.
28. Nagel 1974.
29. Nagel 1986: 163.
30. Page references are to his (1974).
31. Nagel 1974: 441.
32. Jackson 1982: 127.
33. Jackson 1986: 291.
34. It is important to note that the conclusion does not hold in exactly one case: if the person expressing the truth is the person occupying perspective P. This suggests that such a truth is ineffable to everyone except the subject occupying the respective perspective. However, according to my definition of ineffability and expressibility given in Chapter 2, potential communicability to others is a necessary condition for expressibility. Hence, perspectival-fugitive propositions must be considered ineffable.
35. Horwich 1998: 10.
36. Moore 2003b: 163.
37. Cf. Moore 1997: 283.
38. Recall that I have ruled out deflationary theories of truth for this examination precisely because they preclude the existence of nontrivially ineffable truths.
39. Lakoff/Johnson 1980: 485.
40. Lakoff/Johnson 1980: 469f; their emphases.
41. Moore 1997: 73.
42. Moore 2003b.
43. A point of view is "a location in the broadest possible sense"; they "include points in space, points in time, frames of reference, historical and cultural contexts, different roles in personal relationships, points

of involvement of other kinds, and the sensory apparatuses of different species" (Moore 1997: 6).
44. Moore 1997: 42.
45. Moore 1997: 6.
46. If someone were ready to deny that representations are made true by a single, unified reality, then my argument would not stand (although I am not aware of anyone holding such a view). A consequence of such a view is that meaningful disagreement about the truth or untruth of representations is impossible—again, an undesirable result.
47. Plato 1961 [428–348 BCE]: 170e–171c (p. 876f).

Ineffable Content

1. See Chapter 2, for an elaborate discussion.
2. Bermúdez 2007: 66.
3. Refer to Chapter 1 for an elaborate discussion of philosophically relevant and irrelevant cases of ineffability.
4. Peacocke 2001a: 243.
5. I elaborate on this later.
6. Peacocke 2001a: 243.
7. Bermúdez 1998: 50.
8. Stalnaker 1999: 351f.
9. See Bermúdez 2007 for a brief overview of the different positions of the debate. I am ignoring arguments that respond to an ambiguity pointed out by Richard Heck (2000), namely that the conceptual/nonconceptual distinction can either be seen as a distinction between two different types of content ('content-view') or between two different types of content-bearing state ('state-view'). Cf. Bermúdez 2007: 68.
10. Konkle 2009.
11. Crane 1988: 142.
12. This point is due to Mellor 1988: 147ff.
13. Dretske 1981: Ch. 6.
14. Dretske 1983: 61.
15. Dretske 1983: 61.
16. This point is due to Armstrong 1983: 65.
17. Evans 1982: 229.
18. Peacocke 1992: 67ff. Peacocke argues for two kinds of nonconceptual content, 'scenario content' and 'proto-propositional content.' Both are arguments for the claim that the fineness of grain of our perceptual experiences outstrips our conceptual resources.

19. Luntley 2003.
20. McDowell 1994: 56f.
21. Note that nothing in this argument precludes the further assumption that our capacities for discrimination are sometimes enhanced through the acquisition of new concepts (cf. Bermúdez 2007: 62 on discrimination enhancement through training).
22. McDowell 1994: 57. McDowell's strategy is obviously not confined to colors but can be employed for all kinds of fine-grained perceptual content.
23. Of course, what cannot be expressed, not even by means of demonstratives, is *what it is like* to perceive a particular color shade, that is, the inherently subjective aspect involved in all phenomenal experiences. In order to understand what perceiving 'that shade' is like, we have to perceive it ourselves. This is just the kind of trivial ineffability of sense perceptions I mentioned in Chapter 1. I will discuss the concept of ineffable phenomenal knowledge further in Chapter 7.
24. Peacocke 2001b: 610.
25. In his (2001a), Peacocke argues that recognitional capacities must be distinguished from demonstrative capacities because the former rely on memory capacities in a way in which demonstrative capacities do not. This point does not affect the success of the demonstrative strategy against arguments from fineness-of-grain, however.
26. Peacocke 2001b: 614.
27. See the discussion of 'global' strategies of lifting the conceptual constraint.
28. Carroll, Noel 2006: 78.
29. Wittgenstein [2009] 1953: § 610. See also: "People nowadays think that scientists exist to instruct them, poets, musicians, etc. to give them pleasure. The idea that these have something to teach them—that does not occur to them." (Culture and Value, 1980, p. 36).
30. Dewey 1934: 74.
31. Langer 1957: 91.
32. Danto 1973: 45.
33. Polanyi/ Prosch 1975.
34. De Clercq 2000: 87.
35. De Clercq 2000: 87.
36. De Clercq 2000: 94.
37. De Clercq 2000: 96.
38. Luntley 2003.
39. Luntley 2003: 406/407.

40. Luntley 2003: 412.
41. Luntley 2003: 415. Luntley does not elaborate on what is involved in the transition from being a novice to learning the concept of a dominant 7th.
42. Luntley 2003: 415.
43. Luntley 2003: 424.
44. Kennick 1961: 316.
45. Kennick 1961: 320.
46. Kennick 1961: 318.
47. This view is also held by Malcolm Budd (1996: 84f).
48. Davies 1994: 161.
49. Davies 1994: 161.
50. Raffman 1988, 1993.
51. Raffman 1988: 688.
52. Raffman 1988: 695.
53. Russell 1935: 143f.
54. James 2002 [1902]: 380f.
55. Gurrey 1990: 199.
56. Gurrey 1990: 199.
57. Lakoff/Johnson 1980: 485.
58. Lakoff/Johnson 1980: 454. We also discussed their example in Chapter 4.
59. Lakoff/Johnson 1980: 469f.
60. Black 1962: 46.
61. Black 1962: 46.
62. Soskice 1985: 131.
63. Soskice 1985: 141.
64. Alston 1989: 18f.
65. I understand a 'statement' as an affirmative expression of a proposition (the proposition being or providing the content of the statement).
66. Alston 1989: 27f.
67. Alston 1989: 29.

Ineffable Knowledge I

1. Ryle 1949: 29.
2. Ryle 1949: 30.
3. By an 'intelligent' action, I will understand an 'intentional' action. Unintentional "actions" like developing a rash or breaking one's leg while skiing are arguably not even proper actions, or at any rate, are not intentional actions. Stanley/Williamson apply the same reading.

4. Cf. Stanley/Williamson 2001: 430.
5. David Wiggins makes this point; 2009: 273.
6. Williamson 1997: 44.
7. Stanley/Williamson 2001: 429.
8. Stanley/Williamson 2001: 433f.
9. Stanley/Williamson 2001: 429.
10. Rosefeldt 2004: 378.
11. Wiggins 2009: 271.
12. Carroll 1895.
13. Frege 1884: 4.
14. Frege 1884: IIIf (my emphasis).
15. Frege 1893/1903: 12.
16. Frege's system is essentially second-order logic, as we would now understand it (for an elaborate exposition of Frege's Basic Laws, see Heck 2012). He bases his system on six Basic Laws, which are, in modern terms:

    1. $\vdash a \to (b \to a)$, $\vdash a \to a$ (Implication, Self-Identity)
    2. $\vdash \forall x(Fx) \to Fa$ (BL IIa), $\vdash \forall F(M_x Fx) \to M_x Gx$ (BL IIb) (Universal Instantiation)
    3. $\vdash a = b \to \forall F(F_b \to F_a)$ (Indiscernability of Identicals)
    4. $\vdash \neg(a \neq b) \to a = b$ (Law of Excluded Middle)
    5. $\vdash \forall F \forall G(extF = extG \leftrightarrow \forall x(Fx \leftrightarrow Gx))$ (Interchangeability of Equal Functions)
    6. $\vdash a = \backslash ext\varepsilon(a = \varepsilon)$ (Singleton)

    Additionally, there are two rules of inference: modus ponens and a rule of substitution equivalent to what we now call a 'second-order comprehension principle' (cf. Frege 1893/1903: 61).
17. Frege 1879: 15.
18. Frege 1879: 6.
19. Frege 1884: 5.
20. Frege 1884: 4.
21. Frege 1879: 5; I inserted the German words in order to remind the reader that with 'objects,' Frege does not only mean objects like a table or a chair but also logical objects like numbers. The German word *Dinge* is much more comprehensive than the English word *objects*.
22. Ricketts 1985: 6.
23. Kitcher 1979: 241.
24. Frege 1884: VII.
25. Frege 1884: X.
26. Frege 1884: 4.

27. Burge 1998: 335.
28. Cf. Frege 1884: 3.
29. This expression first appeared in Wilfrid Sellars's article 'Being and Being Known' (1960).
30. Moore 1993: 301.
31. This holds although the word 'ineffable' in fact denotes the property of what lies beyond the limits of expression. With regard to the philosophy of language, it would be interesting to examine possible extensions of the concept 'ineffable'. This cannot be done within the limited framework of this book, however.
32. Frege 1897: 128.
33. Moore 1993: 289.
34. Moore 1993: 295f.
35. Moore 1997: 181.
36. Moore 1997: 192.
37. Moore 1997: 184.
38. Moore 1997: 185.
39. When I say that it is one of the most fundamental philosophical puzzles, I don't mean to suggest that it is part of the canon of classical paradoxes like the Liar or the Set of all Sets not members of themselves; rather, what I am alluding to is the fact that the puzzlement about how to reconcile subjective and objective perspectives on the world is as old as philosophy itself.
40. Moore 1997: 280.
41. Moore 1997: 6.
42. Moore 1997: 6. As mentioned earlier, it remains unclear whether Moore's examples of locations, such as "real" spacetime locations on the one hand and "metaphorical" locations such as roles in personal relationships on the other, have anything substantial in common.
43. Moore 1997: 73ff.
44. 'Independently of us' ought to be spelled out in a suitable way (e.g., independent of our minds, of our thought about the world, of us conceiving the world, etc). However, for the purpose of my argument, it will suffice to assume that the idea has enough intuitive force to be intelligible without an elaborate argument.
45. Cf. Moore 1997: chapters 7–9.
46. This formulation differs markedly from Bishop Berkeley's original formulation of idealism: *esse est percipi*—to be is to be perceived (from his Treatise concerning the Principles of Human Knowledge (1710).
47. Van Cleve 2009: 349.
48. "The basis of modern idealism is Kant's doctrine of the Transcendental Ego of Apperception. By this formidable term Kant merely

meant the fact that the consciousness 'I think them' must (potentially or actually) accompany all our objects. Former skeptics had said as much, but the 'I' in question had remained for them identified with the personal individual. Kant abstracted and depersonalized it, and made it the most universal of all his categories, although for Kant himself the Transcendental Ego had no theological implications" (James 2002 [1902]: 448f).

49. Kant 1998 [1787]: B33.
50. Kant 1998 [1787]: B520f/A492f.
51. Kant 1998 [1787]: B522/A494.
52. Kant 1998 [1787]: B208.
53. Kant 1998 [1787]: B37ff.
54. Kant 1998 [1787]: B46ff.
55. Kant 1998 [1787]: B106.
56. Moore 1997: 117.
57. Moore 1997: xii.
58. Moore 1997: 173; defining knowledge in this way anticipates and avoids the worry that, if knowledge were defined as a factive state of mind, one can only know facts, and facts are always potentially expressible.
59. I refer to instances of 'ineffable knowledge' and instances of 'ineffable insights' synonymously.
60. Moore 1997: xiif.
61. In *Beyond the Limits of Thought* (2002), Graham Priest makes a similar point. He argues that semantic paradoxes occur when we try to express the limits of our thought, and argues that this is the case because the limits of thought are actually inexpressible: in order to describe a limit, we would have to go beyond it. Yet if we could go beyond it, it would not be a limit. Therefore, both what lies beyond the limits of conceptual thought and the limits themselves are ineffable.
62. Moore 1997: 189 (my emphasis).
63. Moore 2003b: 165.
64. It is worth mentioning here a related line of argument that can be found both in the philosophy of science and in cognitive science. This is the argument for subdoxastic mental states. Personal level states are those mental states that characterize a subject's point of view phenomenally, that is, that account for a subject's phenomenal experience. Subpersonal, or subdoxastic states are those mental states that characterize a subject's processing (computation) of personal level experiences. Subdoxastic content is often argued to be nonconceptual (cf. Stich 1978; Davies 1989), and a classic example for this kind

of nonconceptual content is what is sometimes referred to as 'tacit knowledge of the rules of syntax' (Bermúdez/Cahen 2011: 11). The alleged fact that this kind of content is nonconceptual is explained by an assumption according to which a person's representations of syntactic rules are permanently inferentially isolated from the rest of that person's propositional attitudes and knowledge structures. Nonconceptual content is thus explained by means of the idea of cognitively impenetrable mechanisms (cf. Raftopoulos/Müller 2006).

65. Moore 1997: 184.
66. Williamson 1999: 44.
67. Burge 1979. Burge's work is inspired by Hilary Putnam's 'Twin Earth' argument (Putnam 1975) for semantic externalism.
68. Burge 1979: 600.
69. Burge 1979: 601.
70. Burge 1979: 601.
71. Burge 1979: 605.
72. Moore 1997: 189.
73. Burge 1979: 599.
74. This argument is due to Crane 1991.
75. Crane 1991: 19.

Ineffable Knowledge II

1. Cf., for example, Kaplan 1989.
2. Perry 1979: 3.
3. Perry 1977: 492.
4. Lewis 1979: 520.
5. Lewis 1979: 521.
6. Seager 2001: 253f.
7. Seager 2001: 254.
8. Jackson 1986: 291.
9. Perry 2001: 145–148.
10. The argument from analogy is due to Chalmers 2004: 185.
11. Chalmers 2004: 186f.
12. Lewis 1979.
13. For those proficient in either French or German, the reference to the respective distinctions between 'savoir' and 'connaître', as well as between 'wissen' and 'kennen' is quite helpful to distinguish knowledge by description from knowledge by acquaintance. Cf. Russell 1964 [1912]: 23.
14. Leibniz 1996 [1704]: Book IV, Ch. 9.

15. Leibniz 1996 [1704]: Book IV, Ch. 9.
16. Russell 1964 [1912]: p. 46.
17. Sosa 2003: 277.
18. This relates back to my initial classification of examples of ineffability in the introduction, where I stated that phenomenal knowledge is trivially ineffable because it can be acquired only by means of sense perceptions, never by means of language.
19. Russell 1964 [1912]: 72.
20. For some recent discussion, cf. Chalmers 2010, Fumerton 2005, Gertler 2012.
21. Cf., for example, Fumerton, who argues that the acquaintance relation "cannot be informatively subsumed under a genus, and ... cannot be analyzed into any less problematic concepts" (Fumerton 1995: 76).
22. Conee 1994: 144.
23. Yandell 1993: 25ff.
24. Russell 1911.
25. Sacks 1985: Ch. 23.
26. Moore 1997: 184.
27. Wittgenstein 2003 [1922]: §5.62.
28. James 2002 [1902]: 427f.
29. Dostoyevsky 2004. [1869]: Part 2 Ch. 5; my emphases.

BIBLIOGRAPHY

Adams, Robert Merrihew. 1979. "Primitive Thisness and Primitive Identity." *The Journal of Philosophy* Vol. 76, No. 1: 5–26.
Adorno, Theodor W. 1993. *Hegel: Three Studies*, trans. Shierry Weber Nicholsen. Cambridge, MA: MIT Press.
Alston, William. 1989. *Divine Nature and Human Language*. Ithaca: Cornell University Press.
Anscombe, G. E. M. 1971. *An Introduction to Wittgenstein's* Tractatus. South Bend: St Augustine's Press.
Armstrong, David Malet. 1968. *A Materialist Theory of Mind*. London: Routledge and Kegan Paul.
———1983. "Indeterminism, Proximal Stimuli, and Perception." *The Behavioural and Brain Sciences* Vol. 6: 64–65.
———1997. *A World of States of Affairs*. Cambridge: Cambridge University Press.
Beall, J. C. 2009. *Spandrels of Truth*. Oxford: Oxford University Press.
Bennett-Hunter, Guy. 2014. *Ineffability and Religious Experience*. London: Pickering and Chatto Publishers.
Bermúdez, José Luis. 1998. *The Paradox of Self-Consciousness*. Cambridge, MA: The MIT Press.
———2007. "What Is at Stake in the Debate about Non-Conceptual Content?" *Philosophical Perspectives* Vol. 21, No. 1: 55–72.
Bermúdez, José, and Cahen, Arnon. 2011. "Non-Conceptual Mental Content." *Stanford Encyclopedia of Philosophy*. Available at: http://plato.stanford.edu/entries/content-non-conceptual/.
Black, Max. 1952. "The Identity of Indiscernibles." *Mind. A Quarterly Review* Vol. 61, No. 242: 153–164.
———1962. "Metaphor." In Max Black. *Models and Metaphors. Studies in Language and Philosophy*. Ithaca: Cornell University Press.
Bolander, Thomas. 2014. "Self-reference." *Stanford Encyclopaedia of Philiosophy*. Available at: http://plato.stanford.edu/archives/spr2014/entries/self-reference/.
Boolos, George. 1971. "The Iterative Conception of Set." *The Journal of Philosophy* Vol. 68, No. 8, 215–231.
Budd, Malcolm. 1996. *Values of Art: Painting, Poetry, and Music*. London: Penguin Books.

Burge, Tyler. 1979. "Individualism and the Mental." *Midwest Studies in Philosophy* Vol. 4, 73–121.
———1998. "Frege on Knowing the Foundation." *Mind, New Series* Vol. 107, No. 426: 305–347.
Carr, David. 1999. *Subjectivity: The Self in the Transcendental Tradition*. Oxford: Oxford University Press.
Carroll, Lewis. 1895. "What the Tortoise said to Achilles." *Mind* Vol. 4, No. 14: 278–280.
———1994 [1872]. *Through the Looking Glass*. London: Penguin Books.
Carroll, Noel. 2006. "Aesthetic Experience: A Question of Content." In Matthew Kieran (ed.). *Contemporary Debates in Aesthetics and the Philosophy of Art*. Oxford: Blackwell Publishing, pp. 69–97.
Cheng, Chung-ying. 2003. "Dao (Tao): The Way." In Antonio S. Cua (ed.). *Encyclopedia of Chinese Philosophy*. London: Routledge, pp. 202–205.
Chalmers, David. 2004. "Imagination, Indexicality, and Intensions." *Philosophy and Phenomenological Research* Vol. 68, No. 1: 182–190.
———2010. *The Character of Consciousness*. Oxford: Oxford University Press.
Chisholm, Roderick. 1957. *Perceiving: A Philosophical Study*. Ithaca: Cornell University Press.
Chomsky, Noam. 2002. *Syntactic Structures*. Berlin: De Gruyter.
Conee, Earl. 1994. "Phenomenal Knowledge." *The Australasian Journal of Philosophy* Vol. 72: 136–150.
Crane, Tim. 1988. "The Waterfall Illusion." *Analysis* Vol. 48: 142–147.
———1991. "All the Difference in the World." *The Philosophical Quarterly* Vol. 41: 1–25.
Danto, Arthur. 1973. "Language and the Tao: Some Reflections on Ineffability." *Journal of Chinese Philosophy* Vol. 1: 45–55.
Davidson, Donald. 1974. "On the Very Idea of a Conceptual Scheme." *Proceedings and Addresses of the American Philosophical Association* Vol. 47: 5–20.
Davies, Martin. 1989. "Tacit Knowledge and Subdoxastic States." In A. George (ed.). *Reflections on Chomsky*. Oxford: Blackwell Publishing.
Davies, Stephen. 1994. *Musical Meaning and Expression*. London: Cornell University Press.
DeSousa, Ronald. 2002. "Emotional Truth." *Proceedings of the Aristotelian Society*, Supplementary Volumes, Vol. 76: 247–263.
DeClercq, Rafael. 2000. "Aesthetic Ineffability." *Journal of Consciousness Studies* Vol. 7, No. 8–9: 87–97.
Dennett, Daniel. 1991. *Consciousness Explained*. Boston: Little, Brown.
Dewey, John. 1934. *Art as Experience*. London : G. Allen and Unwin.
Diamond, Cora. 1995. "Throwing Away the Ladder: How to Read the Tractatus." In *The Realistic Spirit*. Cambridge, MA: MIT Press, pp. 179–204.
Dorter, Kenneth. 1990. "Conceptual Truth and Aesthetic Truth." *The Journal of Aesthetics and Art Criticism* Vol. 48, No. 1: 37–51.
Dostoyevsky, Fyodor. 2004. [1869]. *The Idiot*, trans. David McDuff. London: Penguin.

Dretske, Fred. 1981. *Knowledge and the Flow of Information*. Cambridge, MA: MIT Press.

———1983. "Précis of 'Knowledge and the Flow of Information.'" *The Behavioural and Brain Sciences* Vol. 6: 55–63.

Evans, Gareth. 1982. *The Varieties of Reference*. Oxford: Oxford University Press.

Field, Hartry. 2008. *Saving Truth from Paradox*. Oxford: Oxford University Press.

Frege, Gottlob. 1879. "Begriffsschrift, a Formula Language, Modelled upon that of Arithmetic, for Pure Thought." In J. Heijenoort. 1967. *From Frege to Gödel. A Source Book in Mathematical Logic, 1879–1931*. Cambridge, MA: Harvard University Press.

———1884. *The Foundations of Arithmetic. A Logico-Mathematical Enquiry into the Concept of Number*, trans. J. L. Austin (1950). Oxford: Basil Blackwell.

———1893/1903. *The Basic Laws of Arithmetic*, trans. M. Furth (1964). Berkeley: University of California Press.

Fumerton, Richard. 1995. *Metaepistemology and Skepticism*. Lanham, MD: Rowman and Littlefield.

———2005. "Speckled Hens and Objects of Acquaintance." *Philosophical Perspectives* Vol. 19: 121–138.

Gendler, Tamar Szabó, and Hawhorne, John (eds.). 2002. *Conceivability and Possibility*. Oxford: Oxford University Press.

Gertler, Brie. 2012. "Renewed Acquaintance." In Declan Smithies and Daniel Stoljar (eds.). *Introspection and Consciousness*. Oxford: Oxford University Press, pp. 93–128.

Gurrey, C. S. 1990. "Faith and the Possibility of Private Meaning. A Sense of the Ineffable in Kierkegaard and Murdoch." *Religious Studies* Vol. 26: pp. 119–205.

Hacker, Peter M. S. 2000. "Was He Trying to Whistle it." In Alice Crary and Rupert Read (eds.). *The New Wittgenstein*. London: Routlegde, pp. 353–388.

Hacking, Ian. 1975. "The Identity of Indiscernibles." *The Journal of Philosophy* Vol. 72, No. 9: 249–256.

Hawthorne, John, and Graham Oppy. 1997. "Minimalism and Truth." *Noûs* Vol. 31, No. 2: 170–196.

Heck, Richard. 2000. "Non-Conceptual Content and the Space of Reasons." *The Philosophical Review* Vol. 109: 483–523.

———2012. *Reading Frege's Grundgesetze*. Oxford: Oxford University Press.

Hegel, Georg W. F. 1971 [1830]. *Hegel's Logic. Being Part One of the Encyclopaedia of the Philosophical Sciences (1830)*, trans. William Wallace. Oxford: Clarendon Press.

———1977 [1807]. *Phenomenology of Spirit*, trans. A. V. Miller. Oxford: Oxford University Press.

Heidegger, Martin. 1935. "The Origin of the Work of Art." In Richard Kearney and David Rasmussen. 2005. *Continental Aesthetics. Romanticism to Postmodernism. An Anthology*. Oxford: Blackwell Publishing, pp. 182–211.

———1962 [1927]. *Being and Time*, trans. J. Macquarrie and E. Robinson. New York: Harper and Row.

———1982 [1959]. *On the Way to Language*. New York: Harper and Row.

Hesse, Mary. 1963. *Models and Analogies in Science.* London: Sheed and Ward.
Hofweber, Thomas. 2006. "Inexpressible Properties and Propositions." In Dean Zimmermann (ed.) *Oxford Studies in Metaphysics* Vol. 2. Oxford: Oxford University Press, pp. 155–206.
Horwich, Paul. 1998. *Truth.* Oxford: Clarendon Press.
Inwood, Michael. 1992. *A Hegel Dictionary.* Oxford: Blackwell Publishers.
Jackson, Frank. 1977. *Perception: A Representative Theory.* Cambridge: Cambridge University Press.
———1982. "Epiphenomenal Qualia." *The Philosophical Quarterly* Vol. 32, No. 127: 127–136.
———1986. "What Mary didn't Know." *The Journal of Philosophy* Vol. 83, No. 5: 291–295.
James, William. 2002 [1902]. *The Varieties of Religious Experience. A Study in Human Nature.* Mineola: Dover Publications.
Jonas, Silvia. 2013. "Against Metaphysics Running Amok: Hegel, Adorno, and the Ineffable." In Lisa Herzog (ed.). *Hegel's Thought in Europe. Currents, Crosscurrents and Undercurrents.* Hampshire: Palgrave Macmillan, pp. 133–147.
Kant, Immanuel. 1998 [1787]. *Critique of Pure Reason,* trans. Paul Guyer and Allen Wood. Cambridge: Cambridge University Press.
———2003 [1763]. "The Only Possible Argument in Support of a Demonstration of the Existence of God." In David Walford (ed.). *Immanuel Kant, Theoretical Philosophy, 1755–1770.* Cambridge: Cambridge University Press.
———2008 [1755]. *Universal Natural History and Theory of the Heavens,* trans. Ian Johnston. Available at: http://records.viu.ca/~johnstoi/kant/kant2e.htm#contents.
Kaplan, David. 1975. "How to Russell a Frege-Church." *The Journal of Philosophy,* Vol. 72, No. 19: 716–729.
———1989. "Demonstratives." In Joseph Almog, John Perry, and Howard Wettstein (eds.). *Themes from Kaplan.* Oxford: Oxford University Press, pp. 481–563.
———1995. "A Problem in Possible World Semantics." In Walter Sinnott-Armstrong, Raffman Diana, and Nicholas Asher (eds.). *Modality, Morality and Belief: Essays in Honor of Ruth Barcan Marcus.* Cambridge: Cambridge University Press, pp. 41–52.
Kennick, William. 1961. "Art and the Ineffable." *The Journal of Philosophy* Vol. 58, No. 12: 309–320.
———1967. "The Ineffable." In Paul Edwards (ed.). *The Encyclopaedia of Philosophy.* New York: Macmillan, pp. 181–183.
Kierkegaard, Søren. 1985 [1844]. *Philosophical Fragments: Johannes Climacus,* trans. Howard V. Hong and Edna H. Hong. Princeton: Princeton University Press.
Kim, Jaegwon. 1973. "Causation, Nomic Subsumption, and the Concept of Event." *Journal of Philosophy* Vol. 70: 217–236.
Kitcher, Philip. 1979. "Frege's Epistemology." *The Philosophical Review* Vol. 88, No. 2: 235–262.

Knepper, Timothy. 2009. "Ineffability Investigations: What the later Wittgenstein Has to Offer to the Study of Ineffability." *International Journal for Philosophy of Religion* Vol. 65, No. 2: 65–76.
Konkle, Talia, et al. 2009. "Motion Aftereffects Transfer between Touch and Vision." *Current Biology* Vol. 19, No. 9: 745–750.
Korsmeyer, Carolyn. 1985. "Pictorial Assertion." *The Journal of Aesthetics and Art Criticism* Vol. 43, No. 3: 257–265.
Kremer, Michael. 2001. "The Purpose of Tractarian Nonsense." *Noûs* Vol. 35, No. 1: 39–73.
Kripke, Saul. 1975. "Outline of a Theory of Truth." *Journal of Philosophy* Vol. 72: 690–716.
Kukla, André. 2005. *Ineffability and Philosophy*. New York: Routledge.
Lakoff, George, and Mark Johnson 1980. *Metaphors We Live By*. Chicago: University of Chicago Press.
Langer, Suzanne. 1957. *Problems of Art*. New York: Holiday House.
Laozi. 2007 ca. 400 B. C. E. *Tao Te Ching*, trans. James Legge. Miami: BN Publishing.
Lau, D. C. 1963. *Lau Tzu. Tao Te Ching*, Middlesex: Penguin Books.
Leibniz, Gottfried Wilhelm. 1996 [1704]. *New Essays on Human Understanding*, ed. Peter Remnant and Jonathan Bennett. Cambridge: Cambridge University Press.
Lewis, Clarence Irving. 1929. *Mind and the World Order. Outline of a Theory of Knowledge*. New York: Charles Scribner's Sons.
Lewis, David. 1979. "Attitudes De Dicto and De Se." *The Philosophical Review* Vol. 88, No. 4: 513–543.
———1986. *On the Plurality of Worlds*. Oxford: Blackwell Publishing.
———1987. "Events." In his *Philosophical Papers* Vol. II. New York: Oxford University Press, pp. 241–69.
Luntley, Michael. 2003. "Non-Conceptual Content and the Sound of Music." In *Mind and Language* Vol. 18, No. 4: 402–426.
Maimonides, Moses. 1956 [1190]. *Guide of the Perplexed*, trans. Michael Friedländer. New York: Hebrew Publishing.
Martin, R. M. 1967. "Towards a Solution to the Liar Paradox." *Philosophical Review* Vol. 76: 279–311.
McDowell, John. 1994. *Mind and World*. Cambridge, MA: Harvard University Press.
McGinn, Marie. 1999. "Between Metaphysics and Nonsense. Elucidation in Wittgenstein's Tractatus." *The Philosophical Quarterly* Vol. 49, No. 197: 491–513.
Mellor, Hugh. 1988. "Crane's Waterfall Illusion." *Analysis* Vol. 48: 147–150.
Moore, A. W. 1993. "Ineffability and Reflection: An Outline of the Concept of Knowledge." *European Journal of Philosophy* Vol. 1, No. 3: 285–308.
———1997. *Points of View*. Oxford: Oxford University Press.
———2003a. "Ineffability and Nonsense." *Proceedings of the Aristotelian Society*, Supplementary Volumes, Vol. 77: 169–193.
———2003b. "Ineffability and Religion." *European Journal of Philosophy* Vol. 11, No. 2: 161–176.

Moreland, James P. 1998. "Theories of Individuation: A Reconsideration of Bare Particulars." *Pacific Philosophical Quarterly* Vol. 79: 251–263.

Nagel, Thomas. 1974. "What Is It Like to Be a Bat?" *The Philosophical Review* Vol. 83, No. 4: 435–450.

———1986. *The View from Nowhere*. Oxford: Oxford University Press.

Nelson, Edward. 1986. *Predicative Arithmetic*. New Jersey: Princeton University Press.

———2011. "Warning Sings of a Possible Collapse of Contemporary Mathematics." In Michael Heller and Hugh Woodin. *Infinity: New Research Frontiers*. New York: Cambridge University Press.

Nietzsche, Friedrich. 2003 [1873]. "Über Wahrheit und Lüge im außermoralischen Sinne." In Giorgio Colli and Mazzino Montinari (eds.). *Friedrich Nietzsche. Kritische Studienausgabe* Band I. München: De Gruyter.

Peacocke, Christopher. 1992. *A Study of Concepts*. Cambridge, MA: MIT Press.

———2001a. "Does Perception have a Non-Conceptual Content." *The Journal of Philosophy* Vol. 98, No. 5: 239–264.

———2001b. "Phenomenology and Non-Conceptual Content." *Philosophy and Phenomenological Research* Vol. 58: 381–388.

Peirce, Charles S. 1958 [1866]. *Collected Papers*. Cambridge, MA: Belknap Press of Harvard University Press.

Perry, John. 1977. "Frege on Demonstratives." *The Philosophical Review* Vol. 86, No. 4: 474–497.

———1979. "The Problem of the Essential Indexical." *Noûs* Vol. 13, No. 1: 3–21.

———2001. *Knowledge, Possibility, and Consciousness*. Cambridge, MA: The MIT Press.

Plato. 1961 [c. 428–348 BCE]. *The Collected Dialogues of Plato, including the Letters*, ed. Edith Hamilton and Huntington Cairns. New York: Random House.

Plotinus. 1918a [c. 204–270 CE]. *The Divine Mind, Being the Treatises of the Fifth Ennead*, trans. Stephen Mackenna and B. S. Page. Boston, MA: Charles T. Branford Company. Available at: http://oll.libertyfund.org/title/1271.

———1918b [c. 204–270 CE]. *On the One and Good, Being the Treatises of the Sixth Ennead*, trans. Stephen Mackenna and B. S. Page. Boston, MA: Charles T. Branford Company. Available at: http://oll.libertyfund.org/title/1271.

Polanyi, Michael, and Harry Prosch. 1975. *Meaning*. Chicago: University of Chicago Press.

Posy, Carl. 2005. "Intuitionism and Philosophy." In Stewart Shapiro (ed.). *The Oxford Handbook of Philosophy of Mathematics and Logic*. Oxford: Oxford University Press, pp. 318–355.

Priest, Graham. 2000. "Truth and Contradiction." *The Philosophical Quarterly* Vol. 50, No. 200: 305–319.

———2002. *Beyond the Limits of Thought*. Oxford: Oxford University Press.

———2006. *In Contradiction*. Oxford: Oxford University Press.

Putnam, Hilary. 1975. "The Meaning of 'Meaning'." *Philosophical Papers* Vol. II: Mind, Language, and Reality. Cambridge: Cambridge University Press.

Raffman, Diana. 1988. "Toward a Cognitive Theory of Musical Ineffability." *The Review of Metaphysics* Vol. 41, No. 4: 685–706.
Raftopoulos, Athanassios/Müller, Vincent. 2006. "The Phenomenal Content of Experience." *Mind and Language* Vol. 21, No. 2: 187–219.
Reid, Thomas. 2003 [1764]. *An Inquiry into the Human Mind, on the Principles of Common Sense*. Electronic reproduction. Farmington Hills, MI: Thomson Gale. Available at: http://galenet.galegroup.com/servlet/ECCO?c=1&stp=Author&ste=11&af=BN&ae=T110558&tiPG=1&dd=0&dc=flc&docNum=CW117422497&vrsn=1.0&srchtp=a&d4=0.33&n=10&SU=0LRF&locID=oxford.
Ricketts, Thomas. 1985. "Frege, The Tractatus, and the Logocentric Predicament." *Noûs* Vol. 19, No. 1: 3–15.
Rosefeldt, Tobias. 2004. "Is Knowing-how Simply a Case of Knowing-that?" *Philosophical Investigations* Vol. 27, No. 4: 370–379.
Rosen, Gideon. 1994. "Objectivity and Modern Idealism: What Is the Question?" In Michaelis Michael and John O'Leary-Hawthorne (eds.). *Philosophy in Mind*. Dordrecht: Kluwer Academic Publishers, pp. 277–319.
Rosenkrantz, Gary. 1993. *Haecceity. An Ontological Essay*. Dordrecht: Kluwer Academic Publishers.
Russell, Bertrand. 1902. "Letter to Frege." In J. Heijenoort. 1967. *From Frege to Gödel. A Source Book in Mathematical Logic, 1879–1931*. Cambridge, MA: Harvard University Press.
———1911. "Analytic Realism." In John Greer Slater and Frohmann Bernd (eds.). 1992. *Logical and Philosophical Papers* (1909–13). London: Routledge.
———1927. *The Analysis of Matter*. London: Kegan Paul.
———1935. "The Limits of Empiricism." *Proceedings of the Aristotelian Society* Vol. 36: 131–150.
———1964 [1912]. *The Problems of Philosophy*. Oxford: Oxford University Press.
Ryle, Gilbert. 1949. *The Concept of Mind*. Chicago: Chicago University Press.
Sacks, Oliver. 1985. *The Man Who Mistook his Wife for a Hat*. New York: Touchstone Books.
Savage, Richard. 1972. *Foundations of Statistics*. New York: Dover Publications.
Scharfstein, Ben-Ami. 1993. *Ineffability. The Failure of Words in Philosophy and Religion*. Albany, NY: SUNY Press.
Schelling, F. W. J. 1980 [1795]. "Of the I as the Principle of Philosophy or on the Unconditional in Human Knowledge." In *The Unconditional in Human Knowledge. Four Early Essays*, trans. Fritz Marti. Lewisburg: Bucknell University Press.
———1989 [1859]. *The Philosophy of Art*, trans. Douglas W. Stott. Minneapolis: University of Minnesota Press. In Richard Kearney and David Rasmussen 2005. *Continental Aesthetics. Romanticism to Postmodernism. An Anthology*. Oxford: Blackwell Publishing, pp. 127–138.
Schopenhauer, Arthur. 1966 [1859]. *The World as Will and Representation*, trans. E. F. J. Payne. Mineola, NY: Dover Publications.

Scruton, Roger. 2010. "Effing the Ineffable. How Do We Express what Cannot be Said?" In Big Questions Online. Available at: http://www.bigquestionsonline.com/columns/roger-scruton/effing-the-ineffable.

Seager, William. 2001. "The Constructed and the Secret Self." In Andrew Brook and Richard C. DeVidi (eds.). *Self-Reference and Self-Awareness*. Amsterdam: John Benjamins Publishing.

Sellars, Wilfrid. 1960. "Being and Being Known." *Proceedings of the American Catholic Philosophical Association*: pp. 28–49. Reprinted in his (1963): *Science, Perception and Reality*. London: Routledge and Kegan Paul.

Sextus Empiricus. 1949 [c. 160–210 BCE]. *Against Professors*. (Loeb Classical Library No. 382.) Cambridge, MA: Harvard University Press.

Shaw, James R. 2013. "Truth, Paradox, and Ineffable Propositions." *Philosophy and Phenomenological Research*, LLC: Vol. 86 No 1: pp. 64–104.

Sheffer, Henry M. 1909. "Ineffable Philosophies." *The Journal of Philosophy, Psychology and Scientific Methods* Vol. 6, No. 5: pp. 123–129.

Sider, Theodore. 2006. "Bare Particulars." *Philosophical Perspectives* Vol. 20: 387–397.

Sosa, Ernest. 2003. "Privileged Access." In Quentin Smith and Aleksandar Jokic (eds.). *Consciousness. New Philosophical Perspectives*. Oxford: Oxford University Press, pp. 273–294.

Soskice, Janet. 1985. *Metaphor and Religious Language*. Oxford: Clarendon Press.

Stalnaker, Robert. 1984. *Inquiry*. Cambridge, MA: MIT Press.

———1999. *Context and Content*. Oxford: Clarendon Press.

Stanley, Jason and Timothy Williamson. 2001. "Knowing How." *The Journal of Philosophy* Vol. 98, No. 8: 411–444.

Stern, Robert. 2009. "Individual Existence and the Philosophy of Difference." In his *Hegelian Metaphysics*. Oxford: Oxford University Press, pp. 345–370.

Stich, Stephen. 1978. "Beliefs and Subdoxastic States." *Philosophy of Science* Vol. 45: 499–518.

Thomson, James F. 1969. "Truth-Bearers and the Trouble about Propositions." *The Journal of Philosophy* Vol. 66, No. 21: 737–747.

Travis, Charles. 2004. "The Silence of the Senses." *Mind* Vol. 113, No. 449: 57–94.

Van Cleve, James. 2009. "Kant, Immanuel." In Jaegwon Kim, Ernest Sosa, and Gary Rosenkrantz (eds.). *A Companion to Metaphysics*. Oxford: Blackwell Publishing, pp. 349–353.

Voevodsky, Vladimir. "What if Current Foundations of Mathematics are Inconsistent?" Available at: https://video.ias.edu/voevodsky-80th

Waismann, Friedrich. 1951. *Introduction to Mathematical Thinking. The Formulation of Concepts in Modern Mathematics*. New York: Harper and Row.

Walker, Ralph C. S. 1995. "Verificationism, Anti-Realism and Idealism." *European Journal of Philosophy* Vol 3, No. 3: 257–272.

Wheeler, Michael. 2014. "Martin Heidegger." *Stanford Encyclopedia of Philosophy*. Available at: http://plato.stanford.edu/archives/fall2014/entries/heidegger/.

Wiggins, David. 2009. "Knowing How To and Knowing That." In Hans-Johann Glock and John Hyman (eds.). *Wittgenstein and Analytic Philosophy. Essays for P.M.S. Hacker.* Oxford: Oxford University Press, pp. 263–277.
Williamson, Timothy. 1999. "Review of A.W. Moore, Points of View." *Philosophical Books* Vol. 40, No. 1: 43–45.
Wittgenstein, Ludwig. 2003 [1922]. *Tractatus Logico-Philosophicus. Logisch-philosophische Abhandlung.* Frankfurt a.M.: Suhrkamp.
——2009 [1953]. *Philosophical Investigations*, trans. G. E. M. Anscombe, P. M. S. Hacker, and Joachim Schulte. Oxford: Blackwell Publishing.
Yandell, Keith. 1993. *The Epistemology of Religious Experience.* Cambridge: Cambridge University Press.
Zermelo, Ernst. 1904. "Proof that every Set can be Well-Ordered." In Jean van Heijenoort. 1967. *From Frege to Gödel. A Source Book in Mathematical Logic, 1879–1931.* Cambridge, MA: Harvard University Press, pp. 139–141.

INDEX

Abramovic, Marina, 111, 183
Absolute, 22, 52–60
  belief in an ineffable, 71
  defined, 51–3, 57–9
  haecceities and, 60, 67, 71
  Hegel on, 53, 57, 58
  Kant on, 55–7
  and the Self, 176
  terminology, 51–3, 55
  truth and, 20
  see also One; Will
absolute facts, 95
absolute ground of reality, 14
absolute "I," 14–15
absoluteness, 52–60
accuracy conditions of experiences, 33
acquaintance, 164–6
  knowledge by, 202n13
  see also Self-acquaintance
acquaintance relation, 165
Adams, Robert, 63
Adorno, Theodor W., 19–20, 23, 51, 177, 181
  on the nonidentical, 20
aesthetic content
  as independent category of content, 112
  ineffability of, 6–7, 118
  as nonrepresentational, 117
  see also aesthetic experience: contents of
aesthetic experience
  and the Absolute, 53
  contents of, 111–20 (*see also* aesthetic content)
aesthetic ineffability, 120
  see also aesthetic experience
aesthetics, 113
Alston, William, 39, 125–6
analog content, 106–7
  vs. digital content, 106
analytic philosophy, founders of, 19
animal perception, 110–11
anti-intellectualists, 130
  see also knowledge-how
arithmetic, 136, 137, 181
  see also mathematical propositions; numbers
art, 113, 118, 128
  vs. language, 17
  see also aesthetic experience
attention, perceptual. *See* awareness
Augustine of Hippo, Saint, 121
awareness
  experiential vs. intellectual, 164
  twofold structure of, 113–15
axiom of choice (AC), 79–81
  defined, 79
axiom of separation, 79
axioms, Peano. *See* Peano arithmetic

bare particulars, 67–70
Beckett, Samuel, 20
Beethoven, Ludwig van, 114
"being shown," 148
Bennett-Hunter, Guy, 17

INDEX

bivalence, principle of, 78
Black, Max, 62–7, 70, 122–3
blind spot of the knowledge of the knowing subject, 15
bodily sensations, 188n9
   vs. sense perceptions, 33
   vs. the truth aptitude of experiences, 33
   see also sense perceptions
bundle theory (of universals), 68–70
Burge, Tyler
   externalist account of, 152, 153
   idiolects and, 150
   "Individualism and the Mental," 150–4
   Moore and, 153
   on self-evidence in Frege's theory, 139
   thought experiment of, 153–4
   Tim Crane on, 154

"can," 46–8
Canetti, Elias, 20
Cantor's paradox, 77
Carroll, Lewis, 44, 135–6
category mistakes, ineffability due to, 6
Celan, Paul, 20
choice, axiom of. *See* axiom of choice
classes, Frege's theory of, 137
cognitively impenetrable mechanisms, 202n64
Cohen, Paul, 79
comparison metaphors, 122–3
concept possession, 110
concepts, 102, 139
   as means to refer to informational content vs. constituents of informational content, 104
conceptual constraint, 103
conceptual content, distinguishing mark of, 115
conceptual metaphors, 93–4, 122
conceptual/nonconceptual distinction, 103, 196n9
   see also nonconceptual content: vs. conceptual content
conceptual schemes, 46
concrete objects, 6, 56
   as ineffable by definition, 6
content assignments, principle of humanity for, 84
content-bearing state, types of, 196n9
content(s), 27–8, 42–4
   conceptual vs. nonconceptual, 196n9 (*see also* conceptual/nonconceptual distinction)
   definitions and meanings of, 27–9, 33, 43, 101, 187n3
   ineffable, 101–3, 128
   Lewis's theory of, 83
   the predicate "ineffable" applied to, 23
   vs. representations, 31–2
content-view (conceptual/nonconceptual distinction), 196n9
contingent truths, 43
continuum hypothesis, 80, 81
contradictory content, 104–6
   see also self-refutation
Crane, Tim, 105, 111, 154

Danto, Arthur, 113
Dao, 51
Daoism, 10–11
   see also Laozi
Davidson, Donald, 4, 46
Davies, Stephen, 118
De Clercq, Rafael, 113, 114–15, 117
de se beliefs, irreducibly, 159–60
deflationist theory of truth, 34–6, 38, 74–5, 90–2, 189n37
   defined, 34
demonstrative knowledge. *See* indexical knowledge
demonstrative vs. recognitional capacities, 197n25

description
  vs. expression, 38, 41, 48
  knowledge by, 202n13
Dewey, John, 112
dialetheism, 78
digitalization, 106
Divine. *See* Absolute; God
Dostoyevsky, Fyodor, 20
Dretske, Fred, 106–7, 111
Duns, John. *See* Scotus, Duns

Eckhart, Meister, 121
empirical idealism, 56, 145
empirical intuition, 139
Entailment Problem, 42–3
epistemic states, the predicate "ineffable" applied to, 23
equivalence axioms, 36–8
Equivalence Schema, 24, 34–7, 90, 188n22, 189nn37–8
Erhard, J. B., 15
Evans, Gareth, 107–8, 111, 119
excess propositions, 82–7
experiences, 32–4
  definition and nature of, 34, 187n7
  truth aptitude of, 33
experiential awareness, 164
expressibility, 45
  categorical, 41–9
  defined, 38, 47–8, 73, 82, 86–7, 191n56, 195n34
  ineffability and, 38–49
  linguistic vs. nonlinguistic, 40–1
  literal, 39–40
  meanings of, 39
expression, linguistic, 45, 82, 91
  definitions of, 38, 40–6, 48–9, 73, 82, 86–7, 190n56
  Moore on truth and, 91–5
  possibility of genuine, 16
Extension Problem, 42–5
  defined, 42
external observers, 179
externalism, 150

facts
  categories of, 95
  see also perspectival-fugitive propositions/facts
fineness-of-grain argument, 107–10, 118, 119
finite vs. infinite beings, 191n60
finitude-fugitive propositions, 76
flat-footed responses, 68, 69
Frege, Gottlob, 129
  on arithmetic, 136, 137
  Basic Laws of, 64, 136–7, 139–41, 199n16
  foundations of the logicism of, 141–2
  Kant and, 136
  on logical thought, 136–42, 199n16
  on numbers, 137, 191n65
  self-evidence and, 139, 141
functional roles, 83

God, 56, 67, 163
  and the Absolute, 53
  acquaintance with, 184
  apophatic approach to, 13
  as ineffable, 12–13, 22, 51, 82, 120
  knowledge of, 7, 13
  as an object, 187n63
  religious experience and, 7, 8, 82, 120, 184
  and the Self, 184
  (metaphorically) talking about, 121, 124–6
Gödel, Kurt, 79, 81–2
Goldbach's conjecture, 80, 81
Gorgias, 11, 23, 177
Grelling's paradox, 77
Gurrey, C. S., 121

Hacking, Ian, 67
haecceities, 60–7
  and the Absolute, 60, 67, 71
  vs. absoluteness, 59
  defined, 60, 65, 66, 192n21
  first- and second-order, 66

Hegel, Georg Wilhelm Friedrich
  on the Absolute, 53, 57, 58
  dialectical thinking and dialectical method, 57, 58
  and the ineffable, 19–20
  Theodor Adorno on, 19
Heidegger, Martin, 16, 17
Hesse, Mary, 39–40
Higgs boson, 75
Hölderlin, Friedrich, 15
Horwich, Paul, 34–8
humanity, principle of, 84

"I," 159, 160
  absolute, 14–15
  see also Self
idealism
  basis of modern, 200n48
  Berkeley's original formulation of, 200n46
  criticisms of, 8
  definitions and nature of, 145
  empirical, 56, 145
  vs. realism, 8–9, 56
  terminology, 8–9
  see also transcendental idealism
idealistic appeal. *See* paradox of the idealistic appeal
identity of indiscernibles, principle of the, 61–4, 192n23
Idiot, The (Dostoyevsky), 20
idiot savants, 171
impredicative definitions, 77
inaccessibility of propositions, 75–9, 81, 85, 90
  contingent, 75–6, 80–1
  strict, 75, 76, 78–9, 85, 90, 97
incompleteness theorem, 81, 82
indescribability vs. ineffability, 38
indexical knowledge, 158–61
  phenomenal knowledge as, 161–3
indexical terms, 160
"Individualism and the Mental" (Burge), 150–4

individuality, 8
  see also haecceities
individuation, 65–8, 70, 102
  see also haecceities
ineffability, 2
  is caused by a shift in perception, 178
  defining, 25, 41, 73, 192n70, 195n34, 200n31
  four ways of application of the predicate "ineffable," 22–4
  getting a grip on the topic of, 2–4
  history of, 10–22
  meanings of, 51
  philosophically irrelevant/trivial vs. relevant/interesting/meaningful/mysterious, 3–9, 21, 48, 49, 51, 61, 75–8, 102, 104, 119, 120, 172–5, 179, 183 (*see also* meaningfulness)
  philosophy and, 1–2
  reasons for a proposition's, 75
  reasons for an object's, 71f
  that which is ineffable in principle, 4, 5, 76, 119
  types of, 4–9
ineffable content, 23, 41, 101–4, 111, 112, 115, 128
  aesthetic experiences and, 127
  arguments for, 127
  metaphors and, 123, 126, 128
  motivating the existence of, 120
  varieties of, 127f
  see also content(s); nonconceptual content
ineffable experiences, 51
  characteristics of, 73
ineffable knowledge/nonrepresentational knowledge/ineffable insights, 1, 129, 142–56
  art and, 15
  categories of, 130 (*see also* objective ineffable knowledge; subjective ineffable knowledge)
  examples of, 149–50, 154

Moore on, 142–5, 148–50, 152–5
  (*see also* Moore: on knowledge)
 vs. ordinary expressible knowledge, 154
 and other types of knowledge, 143
 pseudo-expression of, 149
 terminology for, 201n59
 unifying/overarching principle of, 149, 155–6, 179
ineffable properties and objects, 51–2, 67
ineffable propositions, 23, 73–5, 81–4, 87
 arguments for, 86
 defining, 73, 77
 examples of, 80–2, 84
 identifying the weak points of theories of, 89–90
 in mathematics, 79–82
 reasons for a proposition's ineffability, 90, 193n1
 varieties of, 99f
 see also perspectival-fugitive propositions; semantic paradoxes
ineffable truths, concept of, 38, 90–2, 99–100
Infinite, 52
 see also Absolute
in-principle formulability of all truths, 34
in principle ineffability, 4, 5, 76, 119
Intellect, 11
intellectual awareness/noticing, 164
intelligent action, 131, 198n3
intension, concept without an, 141
interaction metaphors, 123
internalism/externalism debate, 150
intuition
 Kant and, 16, 55–6, 139, 146, 147
 Kantian spatial and temporal, 136
 types of, 139 (*see also* pure intuition; rational intuition)
 see also intuitions
intuition structure, forms of pure, 56
intuitionists, 80, 81

intuitions, 55, 70, 89, 95, 154, 191nn59–60
 aesthetic, 15
 idealism and idealist, 8, 9, 145, 146 (*see also* idealism)
 Kant and, 8, 13, 146
 metaphysical, 64, 95
 a priori, 19, 56
 regarding phenomenal knowledge, 89
 religious experiences and, 22, 87, 120
 about science, 144
 sensible, 55, 146, 147
 see also intuition; philosophical intuitions
Inwood, Michael, 57
irreducible aspect of knowledge-how ascriptions, 134
irreducible metaphors, 122–3, 125, 126, 128
irreducibly *de se* beliefs, 159–60
irreducibly metaphorical thought and language, 39, 121, 123, 125, 126
irreducibly nonpropositional language, 130
irreducibly personal meaning, 121
irreducibly subjective aspects of life, 89, 157

Jackson, Frank, 89, 90, 95, 161–3
James, William, 21–2, 53, 120, 180
Johnson, Mark, 123

Kafka, Franz, 20
Kant, Immanuel, 148
 on Absolute/world as a whole, 55–7
 Critique of Pure Reason, 13–14
 "Transcendental Aesthetic," 146–7
 on empirical realism, 56, 147
 Frege and, 139
 on God, 56
 identity of indiscernibles and, 192n23
 ineffability and, 13–14, 56

Kant, Immanuel—*Continued*
  intuition and, 16, 55–6, 136, 137, 139, 146, 147
  intuitions and, 8, 13, 146
  on knowledge, 139
  metaphysics and, 9, 56
  on nature, 13–14
  on objects of thought vs. objects of knowledge, 55–6, 146–7
  on transcendental ego of apperception, 200n48
  see also transcendental idealism
Kaplan, David, 60
Kaplan's paradox, 82–3, 85–6
Kennick, William, 4, 117–18
kidnapping strategy, 108, 115–17, 127, 165
Kierkegaard, Søren, 14, 23
Kitcher, Philip, 138–9
knowing subject, subjectivity of the, 15
knowledge
  concept of, 143
  defined, 201n58
  ineffability and, 142
  the predicate "ineffable" applied to, 23
  states of, 142
  types of, 143, 202n13
  see also under individual topics
knowledge argument, 89, 161
knowledge-how, 130–5
knowledge-how/knowledge-that debate, 130–2
knowledge-that, as propositional, 130
  see also propositional knowledge
knowledge-that and knowledge-how ascriptions, 131–5

Lakoff, George, 123
Langer, Suzanne, 112
language, 16–17
  irreducibly metaphorical thought and, 39, 121, 123, 125, 126
  irreducibly nonpropositional, 130
  religious, 121–2

Wittgenstein and, 17–19
  see also expression; linguistic meaning; metaphors
Laozi, 1, 51, 54, 177
  Daodejing, 10–11
Lebesgue measurable vs. nonmeasurable sets, 79
Leibniz, Gottfried Wilhelm, 60, 164
Leibniz's law. *See* identity of indiscernibles
Lewis, David, 85–6
  and the definition of expression, 82, 86–7
  on functional roles, 83
  functionalist access conditions and, 74
  indexical knowledge and, 168
  ineffable propositions and, 82–7
  on ineffable truths, 42
  on inexpressible propositions, 34, 84
  Kaplan's paradox and, 82–3, 85, 86
  principle of humanity for content assignments, 84
  on propositions, 74, 82, 83
  rational choice theory and, 83–4
  Rudolf Lingens and, 159–60
  self-ascriptions and, 160, 168
  theory of content of, 83
Lewisian excess propositions, 82, 86, 87
  see also Lewis, David
liar paradox, 77, 78
Lingens, Rudolf (fictional character), 159–60, 168
linguistic expression. *See* expression; language
linguistic ineffability, 92
linguistic item with content, 44
linguistic meaning, 158
literary figures who engage with the ineffable, 20
logic, 139
  see also under Frege, Gottlob
logical knowledge, 130
  basic, 135–42

logical laws, 141
logical possibility vs. metaphysical possibility, 47
Luntley, Michael, 115–17

Mahler, Gustav, 111, 119
Maimonides (Moses ben Maimon), 12–13, 22, 51
mathematical propositions unformulable, 79–82
see also arithmetic
McDowell, John, 108, 115, 117, 119, 127, 180
McGinn, Marie, 18
meaning, 6–7
  linguistic, 158
meaningfulness, feeling of, 3, 73, 74, 119, 120, 128, 167
  see also under ineffability
Mellor, Hugh, 142
mental content. *See* content(s)
mental events, experiences and mental states as, 32, 187n7
mental representations. *See* representations
"merely medical" constraints, 5, 119
  see also physical constraints
metaphorical statements
  literal expression of the propositional content of, 125–6
  types of truth claims in, 125–6
metaphors
  classes of, 122–3 (*see also* conceptual metaphors)
  computer-related, 124
  defined, 39, 121–3
  language and, 20, 93, 121–8
  literal expression of, 123–6
  nature of, 93
  open-ended, 125
  as referring to vs. defining objects, 124
  religious experience, religious language, and, 121, 123–8
  in science, 123–6
  truth and, 16
  William Alston on, 39, 125–6
metaphysical possibility vs. logical possibility, 47
metaphysical principles, 11–12
metaphysical vs. non-metaphysical readings, 17–18
metaphysically substantial concepts, 34
  defined, 188n17
metaphysically substantial haecceities, 63
mind-body problem, 88
mind-dependence and subject-dependence, 8–9
minimal metaphysics, 184
minimalism, 34–7
mode of reception, 152, 154, 177, 179
mode of representation, practical, 132–5
  see also practical mode of presentation
mode of thinking, 136, 140
modus ponens, 136
Moore, A. W., 173
  on absolute representations, 143–5
  criticisms of, 42–4, 92–6, 150, 152–6, 178–9
  expression, the Extension Problem, and, 42–5, 190n56
  on knowledge, 142–5, 148–50, 152–6, 178–9, 201n58
  on locations, 195n43, 200n42
  on point of view, 96, 144
  on the Specious View, 95
  on truth and linguistic expression, 91–5
motion aftereffect, 104, 105
M-similarity, 125
music, instrumental, 53–4
musical content, 119
musical experiences, nonconceptual content in, 115–16
Myshkin, Prince, 181–2

mystical states, 53, 120, 180, 181
  see also God; religious experience
mystics, language of, 121

Nagel, Thomas, 88, 90, 95, 96, 179–80
nature, the sublime in, 13
Nelson, Edward, 81
nescience, ineffability due to, 4–5
Nicholas of Cusa, 53
Nietzsche, Friedrich Wilhelm, 10, 16, 19, 23, 177
nonconceptual content, 101–3, 110–11, 127
  aesthetic content as, 112, 115–16
  central idea behind the notion of, 101–2
  Christopher Peacocke on, 109–11, 196n18
  vs. conceptual content, 103 (*see also* conceptual/nonconceptual distinction)
  confirmation condition for, 115
  debate about, 103
  and the definition of content, 28–9
  distinguishing mark of, 115
  Michael Luntley on, 115–17
  in perception, 103–11
  relative nonconceptuality and, 117
  as representational, 103
  subdoxastic content as, 201n64
  that is strictly inexpressible, 102
  types of, 196n18
  ways of motivating, 103–11
  see also content(s); ineffable content
nonconceptual experience, 102
  see also nonconceptual content
nonidentical, the, 19–20
non-inferential content of musical experience, 115–17
nonlinguistic items, 29–30, 42–4, 48–9, 73, 173
nonlinguistic vs. linguistic expressibility, 40–1
nonpropositional content, 28
  see also nonconceptual content

nonpropositional knowledge. *See* knowledge-how
nonpropositional representations, as having truth-values, 31
nonrepresentational knowledge. *See* ineffable knowledge/nonrepresentational knowledge/ineffable insights
nonsense-convergence, problem of, 155, 178
nonsensical statements, 17, 18, 148, 149
nonsensory perception, 171
numbers, 137, 191n65
  see also arithmetic

objective facts, 95
objective ineffable knowledge, 129–30
  see also knowledge-how
objects
  devoid of properties, 68
  nature of and use of the term, 187n63
  the predicate "ineffable" applied to, 22–3
  see also concrete objects
One, The, 11, 12, 22, 51, 55
  see also Absolute
Oneness, 11–12
open-endedness of a metaphor, 123

paradox of the idealistic appeal (PIA), 143, 145, 147–9
Parmenides, 11
Peacocke, Christopher
  on concepts, 102
  on conceptualization, 107, 109
  fineness-of-grain arguments and, 107, 109
  on nonconceptual content, 109–11, 196n18
  on recognitional vs. demonstrative capacities, 197n25
Peano arithmetic (PA), 81, 137

INDEX

Peirce, Charles Sanders, 60
perception
   ineffability as caused by a shift in, 178
   nature of, 107
perceptual awareness/perceptual attention. *See* awareness
perceptual content, nonconceptual. *See* nonconceptual content
Perry, John, 159, 161, 168
perspectival propositional knowledge vs. absolute propositional knowledge, 143
perspectival-fugitive propositions/facts, 87–90
   defined, 87–8, 90
   objections to the concept of, 88–90
   subitem linguistic, 90–5
   subitem metaphysical, 95–100
   vs. objective facts, 95
phenomenal experience, 162
phenomenal ineffability of aesthetic content, 117–20
phenomenal knowledge, 150, 161–6
   as demonstrative (indexical) knowledge, 161–3
phenomenological features of experience, 88
philosophical intuitions, 8, 87
   solipsistic, 19, 81–2
   see also idealism
philosophy, defined, 19
physical constraints
   ineffability due to, 5–6
   see also "merely medical" constraints
physicalism, 161
Plato, 98
Plotinus, 11–12, 22, 52, 54, 55, 177, 181
point of view, 32, 96, 143
   defined, 96, 144
Polanyi, Michael, 113, 114
possibilities
   descriptions of, 85–6
   types of, 47, 191n68

possible worlds
   haecceities and, 63–4
   propositions as sets of, 74, 82–7, 194n16
possible-worlds semantics, 103–4
practical knowledge, expressible vs. ineffable, 143
practical mode of presentation, 132–5
Priest, Graham, 78, 201n61
primordial speech, 16–17
proper assertions, 18, 186n48
properties, types of, 61
propositional attitudes, 30
propositional knowledge
   as absolute vs. perspectival, 143
   see also knowledge-that
propositions, 30
   defined, 74, 86, 103
   expressibility of, 74
   expressions and, 87 (*see also* expression)
   reasons for the ineffability of, 75
   as sets of possible worlds, 74, 82–7, 194n16
   true (*see* truth)
   as truth-bearers, 23, 36–8, 74
   truth-value of, 75–8, 147, 148, 152
   Wittgenstein on, 18
   see also ineffable propositions
proto-propositional content, 196n18
psychology vs. logic, 139
pure intuition, 139, 147
   structure and forms of, 56

qualia, 188n8
   see also sense perceptions
qualitative vs. relational properties, 61–3

Raffman, Diana, 118–19
Rambam. *See* Maimonides
rational choice theory, 83–4
rational intuition, 139, 141
   see also self-evidence

raw feels. *See* bodily sensations; sense perceptions
Real, the, 56
realism
  vs. idealism, 8–9, 56 (*see also* idealism)
  Kant's empirical, 56, 147
reality. *See* Absolute
Reals, 79
reception, mode of, 152, 154, 177, 179
recognitional vs. demonstrative capacities, 197n25
relational vs. qualitative properties, 61–3
relative existence, 97
relativism about truth, 148
religious contexts, ineffability found in, 7
religious experience, 51
  and the Absolute, 53
  characteristics of, 120
  contents of, 120–8
  see also under God; mystical states
religious language
  as irreducibly metaphorical, 121–2
  see also under metaphors
representation, mode of, 32
  practical, 132–5
representational nonconceptual content. *See* nonconceptual content
representations, mental, 29–32
  absolute, 143–5
  vs. content, 31
  definition and nature of, 29, 30, 32
  Moore on, 143–5
  truth-apt, 31–2
  types of, 30
Riemann hypothesis, 80, 81
Rosen, Gideon, 9
Russell, Bertrand, 76, 164
  on acquaintance, 164, 165, 171
  Frege's Basic Law V and, 136–7, 140
  on knowledge, 164, 165

  on nomic and causal relations, 62
  on numbers, 171
Russell's paradox, 77, 136–7, 140
Ryle, Gilbert, 130–2, 134

Sacks, Oliver, 171
"saying" vs. "showing," 17
scenario content, 196n18
Scharfstein, Ben-Ami, 54–5
Schelling, Friedrich Wilhelm Joseph, 10, 14–15
Schopenhauer, Arthur, 15–16, 23
  on aesthetic experience, 15–16
  on ineffable insights through art, 15–16
  on instrumental music, 53–4
science
  intuitions about, 144
  metaphors in, 123–6
Scotus, Duns, 60
Scruton, Roger, 21
Seager, William, 160, 168
Self, 168, 172, 179, 180, 184
  and the Absolute, 176
  defining, 167, 176
  intuitive understanding of, 169, 176
  speaking of our, 168
  see also "I"
Self-acquaintance, 166–7
  acquaintance claim regarding, 169–72
  concept of, 176, 184
  existence claim regarding, 167–9
  importance claim regarding, 173–4
  ineffability claim regarding, 172–3
  metaphysics claim regarding, 174–82
  vs. ordinary phenomenal experiences, 172, 173
  principle of verification for being in a state of, 179 (*see also* verification)
self-ascription, 168
  of properties, 160
self-awareness, ordinary
  vs. self-acquaintance, 172

self-evidence, 139–41
  defined, 139, 141
self-referential sentences, 77–8, 194n7
  see also semantic paradoxes
self-referentiality, 77, 100, 158
self-refutation, 98, 100, 148
  see also contradictory content
self-representation, 160
semantic paradoxes, 77–9, 201n61
  see also self-referential sentences
semantic primitives, 63
semantics, 29–30
  defined, 29
  see also possible-worlds semantics
sensation vs. belief, 103
sense perceptions, 6, 172
  as ineffable, 6, 172–3
  see also bodily sensations
sensibility, defined, 55, 146
separation, axiom of, 79
set theory, 79
Sextus Empiricus, 11
Sheffer, Henry, 10
Sider, Ted, 68–9
solipsistic philosophical intuitions, 19, 81–2
Sosa, Ernest, 164
Soskice, Janet, 124
Soul, 11
specification argument, 142
Specious View, 95
Stanley, Jason, 131–5
state-view (conceptual/nonconceptual distinction), 196n9
subdoxastic content and mental states, 201n64
subject of knowledge can never know itself, the, 15
subject-dependence and mind-dependence, 8–9
subjective character of experience, 88
subjective ineffable knowledge, 130, 157–8
  see also indexical knowledge; phenomenal knowledge

subjectivity, second-order. *See* second-order-subjectivity
sublimity of nature, 13
substitution metaphors, 122
substratum theory, 68–70
sufficient reason, principle of, 15
Supreme, The. *See* One
syntax, tacit knowledge of the rules of, 202n64

Tao Te Ching. *See* Laozi: *Daodejing*
Teresa of Ávila, 121
theory, concept of a, 93, 122
therapeutical reading, 18
thinking
  mode of, 136, 140
  see also thought
thisnesses. *See* haecceities
thought
  ineligible contents of, 87
  see also thinking
Through the Looking Glass (Carroll), 44
totality, 19
  Tractatus' frame (*see* proper assertions)
transcendental idealism, Kant's, 146–8
  criticisms of, 8, 148–9
  Kant's empirical realism and, 56, 147
  Moore on, 148–9
  paradox of the idealistic appeal (PIA) and, 147–9
  unifying principle of ineffable knowledge and, 149, 155–6
translatability of conceptual schemes, 46
translation, 46
truth
  concept of, 34, 36, 46, 74, 90–1, 189n37
  defining, 74, 141
  objective, 16
  subjectivist account of, 16
  see also truth-bearers
truth aptitude of experiences, 33
truth relativism, 98

truth theories, 34–8, 74, 148, 188n24
  identifying the weak points of, 89–90
  see also deflationist theory of truth
truth values, 31–2
truth-apt entities, 31, 42, 166, 190n56
truth-apt knowledge, 143
truth-bearers, 23, 34–8, 44, 74
  nonlinguistic, 42
  propositions as, 23, 36–8, 74
  secondary kinds of, 187n64
truth-evaluable, contents of experience as, 33
truth-makers vs. truth-bearers, 44
truth-value gaps, 78
T-schema. *See* equivalence schema

Unity, The. *See* One

values, truth. *See* truth values
verification
  for being in a state of Self-acquaintance, 179
  of knowledge-possession, 155
verification principle. *See* Self-acquaintance
Voevodsky, Vladimir, 81

Waismann, Friedrich, 46–7
Whole, 22, 51, 52
  see also Absolute; One

Wiggins, David, 134
Will, 15
  see also Absolute
Williamson, Timothy, 131–5, 150, 152, 153
Wittgenstein, Ludwig, 17–19, 111–12
  Hegel and, 19
  and the importance of the ineffable for every philosophical endeavor, 19
  ineffability and, 17, 22
  ineffable knowledge and, 19, 129, 148
  ineffable truths and, 19, 23
  language and, 17–19
  Marie McGinn on, 18
  metaphysical vs. non-metaphysical readings of, 17–18
  Moore and, 129, 148
  nonsensical remarks of, 17, 18
  on propositions, 18
  on saying vs. showing, 17
  Self-acquaintance and, 177
  sense of Self and, 176
  on solipsism, 19
  Theodor Adorno on, 19

Yandell, Keith, 171

Zermelo-Fraenkel set theory (ZF), 79

The manufacturer's authorised representative in the EU is Springer Nature Customer Service Centre GmbH, Europaplatz 3, 69115 Heidelberg, Germany. If you have any concerns regarding our products, please contact ProductSafety@springernature.com

Printed and bound by CPI Group (UK) Ltd, Croydon, CR0 4YY
23/03/2026
02076459-0016